# The End from the Beginning

## A Midrash on

## The First Three Verses

### Daniel Gruber

Elijah Publishing
PO Box 776
Hanover, NH 03755

ISBN-13: 978-1503391130

# TABLE OF CONTENTS

## THE THIRD VERSE

# INTRODUCTION

"Remember the first things of old; because I am God, and there is no other. I am God, and there is none like Me, declaring the end from the beginning, and from ancient times the things that are not yet done, saying, 'My purpose will be established, and I will do all My desire.'" (Isaiah 46:9-10)

This is a midrashic study of the beginning, with the understanding that in it God has declared the end. This is a look at the first three verses of the Scriptures, with the understanding that in them God has declared both His purpose and His desire.

"Exalted be the Name of the Holy One, blessed be He, because He tells the end from the beginning." (Midrash Exodus 15:27)

Samuel Butler, a 17th century English writer, observed that "Every man's work, whether it be literature or music or pictures or architecture or anything else, is always a portrait of himself."

Though Butler, who was not fond of religion or religious people, might have been skeptical of the project, he has provided a wonderful introduction for a study of the Bible. The Bible presents itself as being communication from God to humanity. On the surface, it is about humanity and our various conceits, successes, and failures; but at its core, it is a portrait of its Author.

Likewise, the world that God created, and especially the creature He made in His own likeness and image, is "a portrait of Himself." The world in general, and humanity in particular, are theomorphic. They have been formed to describe and reveal who God is.

The Rabbis say that God is *eyn sof*, beyond definition, and beyond knowing. There is surely no argument against that. An infinite God is beyond the grasp of finite humanity.

Yet at the same time, there is a problem with leaving it at that. Pharaoh said, "Who is the Lord, that I should obey His voice and send Israel away? I do not know the Lord and I also will not send Israel away." (Ex. 5:2) By his own admission, Pharaoh did not know the Lord, and by his own actions he declared that he had no desire to know Him.

Nevertheless, God wanted Pharaoh to know Him. God introduced Himself to Pharaoh through a process we know as the ten plagues. It was fatal for Pharaoh and his people.

Likewise, we are also told that "The sons of Eli were good for nothing; they did not know the Lord." (1Sam. 2:12) This implies, at the very least, that it is possible to know the Lord, and that knowing the Lord can make a person good for something. It can make a person good for the purposes for which he or she exists.

God said that there would be a time when, "all will know Me, from the least to the greatest..." (Jer. 31:34) And He explicitly promised Israel, "I will cause you to be engaged to Me in faithfulness, and you will know the Lord." (Hosea 2:22H)

That will be a significant advance from where we are now, but it hardly seems appropriate to speak of it as human progress. After all, Adam and Havah knew the Lord. So did Abraham, Isaac and Jacob. And Moses. And others.

When God promised the restoration of Israel, He said, "I will give them a heart to know Me, that I am the Lord. They will be My people, and I will be their God, because they will return to Me with all their heart." (Jer. 24:7)

God is beyond our comprehension, but that is not, however, the same as being unknowable. After all, He commands us to seek to know Him. "Because this is what the Lord says to the house of Israel: 'Seek Me and live.'" (Amos 5:4)

All of Scripture is written in the language of men. That is to say, it is one of God's means of communicating with men. But the language of men is something that God created. And He created humanity with the ability to use and understand language.

Language existed before humanity did. From the beginning and throughout the account of Creation, God speaks. Language is not something that God borrowed from humanity. Language, like Wisdom, existed with God even when nothing else did.

Human language is a representation of God's language, even as humanity is somehow a representation of God.

Shortly after God spoke Adam into existence, He gave Adam the task of naming the animals. "And whatever Adam called every living creature, that was its name." (Gen.2:19) Adam's speech did not have the same power as God's, but, on a lesser scale, it was a representation of God's speech.

There are some things that human words cannot express. Some very deep and meaningful things — both sorrow and joy — are beyond our ability to fully verbally communicate. "A heart knows the bitterness of its own soul, and a stranger does not share its joy." (Prov. 14:10)

God wants us to know Him, but how well can we know God's heart, His bitterness and His joy? I think we must always be inadequate for that task, but He gave the Scriptures to and through men so that we might know Him, so that we might encounter Him.

Do the Scriptures contain all that God is? To do that, they would have to be God. They are, instead, an accurate portrait of God, but with several dimensions missing. They are an invitation to come closer and meet Him as He is.

The languages God has given to humanity are one of the ways in which He, who has no inadequacies, has chosen to reveal Himself. Language itself is both innate to human nature and yet conceptually beyond understanding: audible sounds that symbolically convey meaning, and visible symbols of those sounds, both of which vary from language to language.

The very fact that the God of the Bible speaks to people tells us that hearing from Him can, and should, affect a person's behavior. It tells us that people can choose to respond to what they hear. If everything were already determined, there would be no reason for the Scriptures.

God knows everything that will be, but He presents us with the great possibility and requirement of choosing what we will be. "Today, if you will hear His voice..." (Ps. 95:7) "You will seek Me, and you will find, because you search for Me with all your heart." (Jer. 29:13) God wants "you" to seek Him and find Him.

It is there that "you" will find the purpose of "your" existence.

Searching by itself is insufficient, and studying by itself does not bring the knowledge of God. But, as it says in Talmud, "You are not required to finish the work, but neither are you free to refrain from it." (Tal. Abot 2:16)

Some of the things in this study, you already know; some of the things will be new and thought-provoking. Hopefully, those thoughts will lead to change in you. Doing this study has caused me to change.

The start of a quest for hopeful discovery is well worthwhile, especially when the quest is to know the Author and Judge of all that is. If you want to go on that quest, this study will be a step in the right direction. It will focus on three verses, the first three verses of the Bible, with three things in mind:

1) God knows and declares the end from the beginning.

2) Everything God says and does is connected to who He is and who we are supposed to be.

3) Understanding the beginning will help prepare us for the end.

The beginning is a very good place to start. The time between us and the beginning is continually increasing; the time between us and the end is continually decreasing. We do not know how long that remaining time is, but one day we will find out.

So, on to the beginning.

# THE FIRST VERSE

בראשית ברא אלהים את השמים ואת הארץ

In the beginning, God created the heavens and the earth.

# THE FIRST VERSE

## *B'resheet* / IN THE BEGINNING

The Scriptures begin, "In the beginning/*b'resheet*," prompting us to ask, "In the beginning of what?" The simple answer is, "The beginning of everything that has a beginning." And everything, except God, has a beginning.

The phrase indicates the origin of what we experience as Time, because "beginning" indicates a sequence or process, as in beginning-middle-end. It speaks of progression and change. There is, therefore, for every created thing, a beginning, a continuation, and an implied end.

The phrase also indicates the beginning of what we experience as Space, because Space is not eternally existent. It came into existence with what we experience as Time. In the currently prevailing view among astrophysicists, the universe did not exist until about 13.8 billion years ago.

Before that, in that prevailing view, there was only non-existence; the universe did not exist. Nor did the things of which it is made, and the forces by which they are ordered. What caused the universe to come into existence?

Some are uncomfortable with the universe having a beginning, so they propose a scenario where one universe disappears, but turns into another, which spontaneously arises. This scenario is a philosophical attempt to maintain the rejected view of an eternally self-existent universe. It is not based on any evidence, and it only postpones the question: If nothing we know is eternally self-existent, what was there before everything came into existence that caused it to come into existence?

The idea of nothing morphing into something is nonsensical. Nothing can't morph or do anything else. Some have fantasized that even as $0 = -1 + 1$, so "nothing" could fluctuate into existence and negative existence, whatever that might be. But zero is not nothing; it is something. It is a number on a number line, situated between negative and positive numbers.

Something that doesn't exist, on the other hand, can't change or fluctuate. It can't do anything, because it doesn't exist. This is not a question of probability; there is absolutely no possibility of nothing creating itself or anything else. Nothing can't do anything.

Additionally, our current science tells us that, though our universe did not always exist, Energy/Matter can neither be created nor destroyed. It can only change form. So the energy/matter that exists now could only have been created by something that exists independently of our universe.

The currently prevailing cosmology tells us that when the universe did come into existence, it was extremely dense and smaller than a subatomic particle. We don't know how it came into existence, and we don't know what the laws of physics might have been at the time, but they were different from the laws we know. The current laws of physics, not being eternally self-existent, were not applicable when the universe came into existence. They too were created at a certain point in time.

There are four fundamental forces known to modern physics: the strong nuclear force, the weak nuclear force, electromagnetism, and gravity. We know that none of these forces could have created the universe. The force which created the universe is unknown to modern physics. The four forces that modern physics knows were somehow produced from this one unknown force.

When we read, "In the beginning, God..." we understand that we are being told that God existed eternally before the beginning, before all things and beings. And He did not lack anything. All that He is, everything that is in God, is all that existed. Love, Mercy, Justice, Faithfulness, Truth, et. al., all existed; but none of them existed apart from God.

He chose to create the universe. There was no argument, no opposition, no vote. God did as He was pleased to do. For His own reasons, for His own purposes, He chose to create the heavens and earth. Everything that has come into existence exists only because of Him, because He had a purpose in creating it. As the Midrash says, "In every place, the Holy One, blessed be He, accomplishes His purpose, and He has not created one thing without purpose." (Mid. Num. 18.22)

We can ask, "Why does humanity exist?" "Why do I, or you, exist?" The Scriptural answer is, "For the fulfillment of His purpose." The task is to know and fulfill that purpose.

But God does not need something from us. He created us because love seeks to do good to others. He gives us the opportunity to know Him and be overwhelmed by His love. "What is a man, that You remember him? And the son of Adam, that you visit him?" (Ps. 8:5H)

God is infinite, i.e. without dimensions, and eternally existent. All created things, incuding Time, Space, and finite objects, exist because of Him and relative to Him. Their beginning, middle, and end are in His hands.

There is no place where God is not, and there is no time when God is not. For God, every place is here, and all of time is present before Him. As we sing in "Adon Olam": *Adon olam asher malak b'terem kol y'tzir nivra … v'akharey keekhlot hakol, l'vado yimlokh nora … b'li resheet, b'li taklit* — "The Lord of the universe who reigned before all was formed and created … and after all is finished, He alone will reign in majesty … without beginning, without end."

Inasmuch as God created the heavens, the earth, and everything in them, they all belong to Him. "The earth is the Lord's, and what fills it; the world, and those who inhabit it, because He has founded it upon the waters, and established it upon the floods." (Ps.24:1-2) In reality, God is the only one who has private property, i.e. the universe. Everyone else uses what belongs to God.

God exists outside of Time. He created Time — the linked sequence of momentary existence. Time, at least our time, relates to an existence that must be sustained and renewed. God created space and distance. We know that He exists independently of all that He created, for He existed before Creation. He is not limited to or by Creation. But, as we will see, He often chooses to limit Himself to enter into Time and Space.

The Scriptures begin with God, because He alone existed at the beginning. He created the beginning. Humanity is a very important part of the story, at least the story we know, but a secondary part. If the world is a stage, then God is the playwright, the director, the main character, the stage manager, and the primary audience. People are part of the supporting cast. We are all walk-ons.

Throughout human history, some people have assumed that they themselves were the whole show. They have sought to define existence in terms of themselves. They have imagined themselves to be the authors of their own identity and existence. Existentialists conclude that they alone must define their own existence. Hedonists conclude that all things exist solely to give them pleasure.

To all of these, the Scriptures say, "No, the conclusion you have reached is incorrect. You did not begin at the beginning, where the correct answer is to be found." A man does not create himself, nor his own purpose, identity, or justification. He is not able to. He can, however, choose to reject what God has for him, but he is not forced to.

God is the author. Consequently, a person needs to begin with God, not with himself. Even if a person begins with himself and adds in God at some later point, he still misses the very foundation of his own being, for he is ignoring the primary fact that he had no part in determining his own existence.

It does not denigrate humanity to conclude, 'God IS, therefore I am.' He who is without fault willed me into existence. From there, we can then ask, 'Now why am I here? Now that I know something about my beginning, I can try to find out why I'm here and what my end will be.'

# BEGINNINGS

God's use of particular words is always intentional. The purpose of a midrash is to search out that intent. It is, therefore, an attempt to understand the connections which God has made through His chosen use of particular words. This chapter is about one of those words.

Because all time is present before God, He is always aware of how He has expressed something and how He will express something. He tells us the end from the beginning. "Remember the former things of long ago, because I am God, and there is no other. I am God, and there is none like Me. I declare the end from the beginning, from ancient times what has not been done. I say: 'My purpose will stand, and I will do all that I please." (Is. 46:9-10) From the beginning, God has told us what the end will be. If we understand the beginning, then we can understand the end.

Every created thing has a beginning, but there are some specific things that are explicitly mentioned in the Scriptures as having a beginning. Because God explicitly mentions these specific things as having a beginning, we want to understand how they are connected to the outworking of His purpose in this age, i.e. what follows the beginning. We want to understand how they are connected to the conclusion of His purpose at the end of this age.

The specific things at which we will look are: 1. Wisdom, the beginning of God's ways; 2. Babylon, the beginning of the kingdom of Nimrod; 3. Amalek, the beginning of the nations; 4. Reuben, the beginning of Israel's strength; 5. The beginning of the firstfruits of the harvest; and 6. Lachish, the beginning of sin to Israel.

**1.** Wisdom is personified in the book of Proverbs, speaking and saying, "The Everpresent Lord possessed me as **the beginning of His ways**, before His wonders of old. I was appointed from eternity, from the beginning, before the world began." (Prov. 8:22-23)

15

The wisdom of God has always existed. It is an aspect of who God is. So when we look at "God" next, we will take a closer look at Wisdom.

Here we simply note that all God's ways begin with Wisdom. Therefore, for anyone who wants to walk in God's ways, His Wisdom is an absolute necessity.

We are told how to begin to find Wisdom. Job said, "And He [God] said to Adam, 'Know that the fear of the Lord, that is wisdom; and to turn away from evil is understanding.'" (Job 28:28)

Solomon said something similar: "The fear of the Lord is the beginning of wisdom; and the knowledge of what is holy is understanding." (Prov. 9:10) And he also said, "The beginning of Wisdom is: Possess Wisdom. Therefore with all that you possess, possess understanding." (Prov. 4:7)

Wisdom is the beginning of God's ways, and it will lead us into what He has prepared for the end.

**2.** God told Noa<u>h</u> and his descendants to spread abroad and fill the earth. **The beginning of Nimrod's kingdom**, called Babel (or Babylon), was humanity's disobedient response to that command. (Gen.10:10) It was in Babylon that people joined together in rebellion against God and said, "Come, let us build us a city, and a tower with its top in heaven. And let us make a name for ourselves; so that we are not scattered abroad upon the face of the whole earth." (Gen.11:4) Nimrod's kingdom is the archetype of all united rebellions against God.

The united rebellion of humanity against God was temporarily stopped when God destroyed their unity by separating them into different language groups, i.e. different nations. Individual nations have continued to rebel against God ever since, but it is only when the language barrier is overcome that all humanity can again be in a position to mount a united rebellion against God.

The beginning of Nimrod's kingdom was a united rebellion against God. The end of his kingdom will be another united rebellion against God. Later, we will look at that united rebellion as it is described in Psalm 2.

**3.** In his last prophecy, Balaam foretold the coming of Messiah and the consequent destruction of the nations who made themselves the enemies of Israel. Because God has established a special relationship with Israel, the enemies of God make Israel their enemy too. Balaam was hired to curse Israel, but God would not let him. God made him bless Israel instead.

"Then Balaam saw Amalek and uttered his oracle: '**A beginning of the nations** is Amalek, Amalek was the first of the nations; but his latter end is unto everlasting destruction.'" (Num. 24:20) God decreed utter destruction for Amalek because, shortly after God had redeemed Israel from slavery in Egypt, "Amalek came and fought with Israel in Rephidim." (Ex. 17:8)

"And the Lord said to Moses, 'Write this for a memorial in the book, and recite it in the ears of Joshua; for I will completely destroy the remembrance of Amalek from under heaven.' And Moses built an altar, and called its name 'The Lord is my banner,' for he said, 'Because the Lord has sworn that the Lord will have war with Amalek from generation to generation.'" (Ex. 17:14-16)

And Moses commanded the generation that would soon enter the land: "Remember what Amalek did to you by the way, when you came forth out of Egypt; how he met you by the way, and struck at your rear, all who were feeble and behind, when you were faint and weary; and he did not fear God. Therefore it is to be, when the Lord your God has given you rest from all your enemies around — in the land which the Lord your God gives you for an inheritance to possess — that you are to blot out the remembrance of Amalek from under heaven. You are not to forget it." (Dt. 25:17-19) Because Amalek had attacked the defenseless ones of Israel without provocation, the Lord decreed the destruction of Amalek.

King Saul was commanded to completely destroy Amalek. Instead, Saul spared Agag, the king of Amalek, and others. (cf. 1Sam. 15; 1Chr. 4:43, 18:11) If we didn't know what God had commanded Israel, we might think that Saul acted mercifully. Yet God explicitly commanded Saul to execute His judgment on Amalek because of their ambush of Israel in the wilderness. Saul was not being merciful; he was being openly defiant. As judgment, God took the kingdom away from him.

We do not know what the consequences of our actions will be, but God does. Haman, "the enemy of the Jews," was "the son of Hammedatha the Agagite". (cf. Est. 3) Haman was descended from Agag, the king of Amalek whom Saul spared. Haman sought to destroy all the Jews.

Amalek was the first of the nations which came to fight against Israel, especially the weary and the unprotected. From generation to generation, there have been more since that time. At the end of this age, all the nations will seek to do that. God has sworn that He will war against them.

Even as there will be an end to the kingdom of Nimrod and the rebellion of the nations against God, so there will be an end to Amalek and all the nations seeking to destroy Israel. The Lord promised Israel, "I am with you and will save you. Though I completely destroy all the nations where I scatter you, I will not completely destroy you. I will discipline you unto justice; I will not let you go unpunished.' (Jer. 30:11) The end of the war of the nations against Israel will come when all Israel chooses to pursue justice by turning to, and trusting in, the Lord, not in the strength and wisdom of men.

God named a certain man "Israel," and made a nation from him. That nation, and the land which God designated for them, He called by the same name. It is "A land which the Lord your God cares for; the eyes of the Lord your God are always upon it, from **the beginning** of the year to the end of the year." (Dt. 11:12)

**4.** Jacob, whom God called "Israel," called his own firstborn son "Reuben," and said Reuben was "**the beginning of my strength**." (Gen. 49:3, cf. Dt. 21:17) He was expressing a normal paternal view. Children will grow up to be their father's strength that endures.

King Solomon said: "As arrows in the hand of a mighty man, so are the children of one's youth. There is good for the man who has his quiver full of them. They will not be put to shame, but will subdue the enemies in the gate." (Ps. 127:4-5) He was echoing God's promise to Abraham: "Your descendant will possess the gate of his enemies." (Gen. 22:17)

The name "Reuben" means, "See, a son." God's explanation to Pharaoh for the coming destruction of Egypt was simple: "Israel is My firstborn son." (Ex. 4:22) Pharaoh had enslaved and sought to destroy God's firstborn son. Pharaoh did not comprehend who the Father of Israel is.

All children, and all people, belong to the Lord, but God's firstborn son has special significance for Him, as Reuben did for Jacob. As God's firstborn son, Israel is the beginning of God's strength in the earth. Israel is called to be a nation set apart to God, so that at the same time it can be the means and context for the redemption of the goyim/nations/Gentiles. .

One of God's primary purposes in choosing Abraham, Isaac, and Jacob was to use their descendants to bring the nations back to Himself. It was central to God's purpose that the patriarchs would have children, because no matter how faithful or righteous the patriarchs were, the purpose of their lives could not be fulfilled without physical descendants.

When God called Abraham, He promised him, "All the nations/Gentiles will be blessed **in** you." (Gen. 12:3) He repeated the promise to Isaac and to Jacob, saying, "**In** your seed, all the nations of the earth will be blessed." (Gen. 26:4, 28:14)

The blessing will go out to the Gentiles from Abraham and Israel, but the blessing will also bring Gentiles in. God says there are some He will count as Abraham's children though they are not physically descended from him. They will somehow be adopted. Just before God gave Abraham the covenant of circumcision, He said to him, "I have made you a father of many nations/Gentiles." (Gen. 17:5)

God told Jacob, "there will be a nation and a company of nations/Gentiles from you." (Gen. 35:11, cf. 48:4) And the Scriptures record their cry to God: "You are our Father, though Abraham is ignorant of us, and Israel does not acknowledge us. You, O Lord, are our Father, our Redeemer; Your Name is from everlasting." (Is. 63:16)

But at the time of God's initial promises to him, Abraham did not yet have the one son, Isaac, whom God had promised to him. The fulfillment of all of God's promises depended upon having that son. Through all of this, God communicated to Abraham, Isaac, Jacob, and their descendants the inestimable value of children, value with a purpose.

Reuben, by his later sexual behavior, personally disqualified himself to lead Israel. Simeon and Levi, who were Jacob's second and third sons, disqualified themselves by their cruelty. (cf. Gen. 49:3-7) That meant that Judah, and his descendants, would lead Israel. That meant that there would some day be a special son of Judah who would enable Israel to fulfill God's purpose. And as in the beginning, so in the end: "See, a son" will be Israel's strength.

**5.** God told Israel to bring "**the beginning of the firstfruits** of your land to the house of the Lord your God." (Ex. 23:19) Giving the firstfruits to God, the Lord of the Harvest, is a way of acknowledging His ownership of all things and our dependence upon Him. He is the one who sustains us.

It also points to God's special relationship with Israel, because, "Israel was holy to the Everpresent[1] Lord, **the firstfruits** of His harvest..." (Jer. 2:3) So when God tells Israel to bring to Him the firstfruits of our harvest, it is representative of bringing ourselves to Him, for we are the firstfruits of His harvest. We are to do what we were created to be.

When we are told that Israel is "**the firstfruits** [*resheet*] of His harvest," we are also being told that the harvest begins with Israel. God's harvest will then continue among the nations.

The farmer plants seed in the ground and reaps a harvest from it. God plants seed in the earth, in the lives of people, and intends to reap a harvest from that seed. He indicates clearly that He is not going to harvest a great quantity of religious activity, but rather hearts that act with compassion.

"Is not this rather the fast that I have chosen? to loose the chains of wickedness, to undo the bands of the yoke, and to let the oppressed go free, and to break every yoke? Is it not to share your bread with the hungry, and that you bring the poor, who are cast out, to your house? When you see the naked, that you cover him; and that you do not hide yourself from your own flesh?" (Is. 58:6-7) God is looking for a harvest of people who will work for the well-being of those in need.

What kind of seed does God plant? "'As for Me, this is My covenant with them,' says the Lord: 'My spirit that is upon you, and My words which I have put in your mouth, will not depart from your mouth, nor from the mouth of your seed, nor from the mouth of your seed's seed,' says the Lord, 'from now on and forever.'" (Is. 59:21) God plants His spirit and His word. We will encounter His spirit when we get to the second verse of the Bible; we will encounter His word in the third verse.

For now, it is sufficient to note that 1) He sends His word to the earth as a seed, and "it will accomplish that which I please, and it will prosper in the thing for which I sent it." (Is. 55:11) And 2) He tells us how His spirit and His words will be firmly planted in Israel. In the verse that precedes His promise about His spirit and His word, He promises that "'A redeemer will come to Zion, and to those in Jacob who turn from transgression,' says the Lord." (Is. 59:20) Not everyone in Jacob will turn, but some will. The same would, of course be true of any people.

**6.** God said, through Micah the prophet, "O you inhabitant of Lachish, harness the chariot to the steed. She was **the beginning of sin** to the daughter of Zion, because in you were found the transgressions of Israel." (Mic.1:13) At Lachish, Israel had chosen not to trust God. A failure to trust God is the beginning of all sin. It is the essential nature of all sin.

This is what happened: God had warned "Israel and Judah by all the prophets, and by all the seers, saying, 'Turn from your evil ways, and keep My commandments and My statutes, according to all the Torah which I commanded your fathers, and which I sent to you by My servants the prophets.' However they would not hear, but hardened their necks, like the neck of their fathers, who did not believe in the Lord their God." (2Kings 17:13-14)

Consequently, the king of Assyria attacked and defeated the northern kingdom of Israel, and sent the survivors into exile.

Then, in the days of Hezekiah, king of Judah, the next king of Assyria brought his army and encamped against Judah at Lachish.

Hezekiah knew what had happened to the northern kingdom of Israel; and he knew why it had happened. Instead of seeking the Lord to know what he should do, Hezekiah sought to appease the attacking king by sending him gold and silver from the Temple of the Lord. (2Kings 18:13-16) He took what had been given to glorify God, and stole it to appease men. He made the choice not to trust the Lord. Instead of calling Judah to repent and be faithful to God, he led them in unfaithfulness.

When the king of Assyria took the silver and gold, but then still demanded complete surrender, Hezekiah turned back again to the Lord. God responded and gave a miraculous deliverance. But the unfaithfulness of the people had not been undone.

"This is what the Everpresent Lord says: 'Cursed be the man who trusts in man, and makes flesh his arm, and whose heart departs from the Lord.'" (Jer. 17:5) People vacillate. Fear, pride, lust, pain, and other emotional forces undermine their resolve.

Whatever else may change, God does not. Through Micah the prophet, God characterized as "the beginning of sin" what Hezekiah led Israel to do. Through Micah the prophet, God also said, "He has told you, O man, what is good; and what does the Lord require of you, but to do justice, and to love mercy, and to walk humbly with your God?" (Mic. 6:8) That is what God requires. Neither His standard nor His purpose change.

God is patient, and He repeatedly calls people to turn back to Him, but, except for a ray of light, every beginning has an end. God is compassionate, but He lets people reap what they have sown. Hosea also prophesied in the days of Hezekiah, and he said, "They have sown the wind, and they will reap the whirlwind..." (Hos. 8:7)

Sin has a beginning, but it also has an end, whether that be through repentance and atonement or through judgment. When the end comes, whatever is not in accordance with God's purpose and character will be removed.

For all these beginnings, the beginning is not an end in itself. There is something more in view; something more that is to come. The reason for the beginning is what is to come. "In the beginning" communicates that there will be a meaningful progression towards the end.

## Footnote

1. The tetragrammaton, the four letter Hebrew Name of the God of Israel is often rendered in English as "LORD," following the choice of the LXX translators to use *kurios*. However, the thousands of times that the Name appears in the Scriptures indicate that it is related to God's eternal nature and His covenant relationship with Israel.

God told Moses, "I am who I am," or, equally correct, "I will be who I will be." (Ex. 3:14) The LXX has "I am THE BEING." French translators often use "l'Eternel" (the Eternal) to give the sense of God's presence in all of time. The Rabbis sometimes used *haMakom*, i.e. "the place," to give the sense of God's presence in every place. (e.g. Tal. Abot 5.4) In an attempt to give a sense of these different aspects of the Name, I have used "the Everpresent," or sometimes the traditional "Lord," in the appropriate places where the tetragrammaton appears.

## *Elohim* / GOD

In the word order of the Hebrew text, *elohim*, the One who creates, comes after *bara*, the action of creating. We, however, will look at the word *elohim* first, because that will help us understand what is involved in the act of creating.

What does *elohim* mean? the Ultimate? the Almighty? Omnipotent, omniscient, omnipresent? How should we express what defines God?

We are told in this first verse of the Scriptures that He is the Creator of all things. He thought up and called into existence everything that is. Maybe that's not the right way to express it. Is it right to speak of God thinking? He knows everything. How can He go from one thought to another? There isn't anything He doesn't know. There is nothing He must figure out.

Nevertheless, there are a variety of words and verses that ascribe thought or thinking to God. Perhaps the most majestic passage is Is. 55:8-9: "'For My thoughts are not your thoughts, nor are your ways My ways,' says the Lord. 'For as the heavens are higher than the earth, so are My ways higher than your ways and My thoughts than your thoughts.'"

God does have thoughts, but the difference and distance between His thoughts and ours is very great. His purposes, and His ways of accomplishing them, are not the same as ours. They are much higher.

I may have base thoughts — low, selfish, or mean. My thoughts may cloak dishonesty, envy, or pride. But God's thoughts are alway pure. They are as high as the heavens.

One of the ways in which God communicates His thoughts to humanity is through language. Even though people often say things without thinking, thought is a prerequisite for the existence of language. Language enables us to understand and communicate things that are intangible. With our minds, we can think about, and grasp, things that are not physical.

God wants us to know who He is, who we are, and why we are. We are to know that "the One who forms the mountains, and creates the wind, and declares to humanity what is His thought, who makes the morning darkness, and treads on the high places of the earth, the Everpresent Lord, the God of forces, is His Name." (Amos 4:13)

God wants us to know His thoughts, what is right and pleasing to Him. He tells us what He said to Himself during Creation: 'Let there be light." He tells us what He was thinking when Abraham stood before Him: "Shall I hide from Abraham what I am doing?" (Gen. 18:17) And then He told Abraham what He was about to do. He tells us that "Surely the Lord God will do nothing without revealing His secrets to His servants the prophets." (Amos 3:7)

Knowing God's thoughts is not intended to be academic knowledge for us, but the flow of life, for God gave us life, and He watches over what we do with it. He is not detached and reserved in response to our choices. He is passionately concerned. He is not an impersonal force, but a thinking, communicating, feeling being.

Does God have feelings? The Scriptures ascribe to Him joy (Zeph. 3:17) and love (Jer. 31:3), pain (Gen. 6:6) and anger (Ex. 32:11), compassion (Dt. 30:3) and contempt (Ps. 2:4). He sings, He weeps, He thunders, He comforts. There are things that please Him and things that enrage Him, things that grieve Him, and things in which He delights. He has feelings.

After Creation, God was pleased with all that He had made. When Adam rebelled, and his descendants filled the earth with violence and evil, God's feelings were different. "And God saw that the wickedness of humanity was great in the earth, and that every imagination of the thoughts of their heart was only evil continually. The Everpresent Lord was grieved that He had made humanity on the earth, and it pained His heart." (Gen. 6:6) When human hearts are filled with evil, God's heart is filled with pain.

There are a multiplicity of emotions and responses in a God who never changes, a God who is perfect in all His ways. He thinks and He feels. At a single moment, God has many different feelings, because billions of people are doing different things, some of them pleasing to God, some an abomination to Him.

He sees and hears all that happens on the earth. He is fully here, and He is fully there, wherever here and there are. He intimately knows and feels all that happens on the earth.

God was pained when we were slaves in Egypt, as He is when anyone is enslaved. How can people treat others this way? "And the Everpresent said, 'I have surely seen the affliction of My people who are in Egypt. And I have heard their cry because of their slave drivers, for I know their sorrows. So I have come down to deliver them ...'" (Ex. 3:7-8)

When God says "I know their sorrows," He means much more than that He is aware of them. Israel is His son, His first-born. Their sorrow is His sorrow, and much more so. By letting us be parents, God enables us to know the pain, as well as the joy, that He feels. "In all their affliction He was afflicted, and the angel of His presence saved them. In His love and and in His compassion He redeemed them; He lifted them up and carried them all the days of old." (Is. 63:9) He is pained, touched in His very being.

He also touches people. Isaiah melted before the holy presence of the Lord. "Woe to me! I am undone! Because I am a man of unclean lips, and I live among a people of unclean lips, and my eyes have seen the King, the Lord of forces." (Is. 6:5)

David was not cleaner than Isaiah, nor was Israel in his day cleaner than in the days of Isaiah, yet He prayed, "Part your heavens, O Lord, and come down; touch the mountains, so that they smoke." (Ps. 144:5) David wanted all of Creation to be touched by God.

When Noah came out of the ark and offered sacrifice to the Lord, "Then the Lord smelled the pleasing aroma, and the Lord said in His heart, 'I will never again curse the ground for the sake of humanity; for the inclination of the heart of humanity is evil from his youth. And I will never again destroy every living thing, as I have done.'" (Gen. 8:21)

The fact that God does not change does not mean that He is without variety of emotion or response. It means that He has always been what He is now, and He always will be. Because of His purpose in creating humanity, He wants us to know what He says in His own heart.

He is unlimited and unaffected by time — eternal, before the beginning and after the end, always the same. He is self-existent, not dependent on anything or anyone. Instead, all things and beings are dependent upon Him for their very existence. "If He were to set His heart on it, if He were to gather to Himself His spirit [*rukho*] and His breath [*nishmato*]; all flesh would perish together, and humanity would return to dust." (Job 34:14-15)

God loans His spirit and His breath to humanity. We have the opportunity to do something with the life we have been given. There comes a time when, "The dust returns to the earth as it was; and the spirit returns to God who gave it." (Eccl. 12:7) All of Creation is dependent upon God.

All of Scripture, God's communication to humanity in language, tells us who the Creator and Judge of all things is. Each piece fits together to give us a view of the whole. There is, however, one section of Scripture in which God specifically describes Himself.

He describes Himself as He wanted Moses, Israel, and all the world to know Him. Moses asked for a greater revelation of God so that he could lead Israel. He said to God, "'Please show me Your glory.'

"And He said, 'I will cause all My goodness to pass before you, and I will proclaim the name of the Everpresent before you. And I will be gracious to whom I will be gracious, and will be compassionate to whom I will be compassionate. 'But,' He said, 'you are not able to see My face [*panai*]; for no one will see Me and live.' Then the Everpresent said, 'Look, there is a place by Me, and you will stand upon a rock. And it will be that when My glory passes by, I will put you in a crevice in the rock, and will cover you with My hand until I have passed by. Then I will take away My hand, and you will see My back; but My face will not be seen.'" (Ex. 33:18-23)

God had told Moses that He Himself would accompany Israel into the land: "My presence [*panai*] will go with you, and

I will give you rest." (Ex. 33:14) Moses had responded: "If Your presence [*panekha*] does not go with me, do not carry us up from here." (Ex. 33:15) I assume that what God said was clear to Moses, especially after he went throught the experience, but it is not clear to me.

1) God says that Moses is able to see His back, but he is not able to see His face/presence. So God has a back which Moses will see and a face/presence which Moses will not see. I don't know exactly what that means, but I know it means something.

2) God tells Moses to stand on a rock by Him, and when God's glory passes by, God will put Moses in a crevice, and cover Moses with His hand. Then, when God has passed by, God will remove His hand which has been covering Moses, and Moses will see God's back. So when God's glory is passing by Moses, God will put Moses in a crevice and cover him with His hand. Then, when God's glory has passed by, God will remove His hand, and Moses will see His back.

I know that God is telling us something about Himself, but I am completely unable to envision what took place, I don't understand what seems to be a separation between God and His glory. And It is God's glory that seems to have a back and a face.

Some things about God are very difficult to understand. God is certainly omnipotent, omniscient, omnipresent, omni-etc., but such words do not really tell us who God is. They do not enable us to know God.

When God came down on the mountain and stood by Moses, He told Moses, Israel, and all humanity how we should know Him. "Then the Everpresent came down in the cloud, and stood with him there, and proclaimed the Name of the Everpresent. And the Everpresent passed by before him, and proclaimed, 'The Everpresent, the Everpresent God, compassionate and gracious, long suffering, and abounding in mercy and truth, keeping mercy for thousands, forgiving iniquity and transgression and sin. Yet He will by no means clear the guilty; visiting the iniquity of the fathers upon the children, and upon the children's children, to the third and to the fourth generation.'" (Ex. 34:5-7)

Traditionally, the Rabbis said that thirteen attributes of God are mentioned here, although they differed on exactly what those attributes were. What is quite evident, however, is that all of these attributes speak of God's faithfulness despite humanity's sinfulness and unfaithfulness.

God is merciful, because we need mercy rather than judgment. We don't deserve mercy, but we need it. God is gracious, in that He does not treat us as our sins deserve. God is slow to anger, though we persist in choosing our own shame.

His mercy and Truth abound, because our hardness and the lies we embrace also abound. He maintains mercy to thousands — or to a thousand generations — but we are unfaithful and never deserve His love. He forgives iniquity, transgression, and sin, because otherwise all humanity would be destroyed in judgment. "If you, O Lord God, were to keep iniquities, who could stand?" (Ps. 130:3)

Nevertheless, there is punishment for sin. There are consequences unto the third and fourth generations. In speaking of these consequences, Maimonides said, "This refers exclusively to the sin of idolatry. This may be inferred from the verse in the Ten Commandments, 'upon the third and fourth generation of My enemies'. None except idolators are called 'enemies'."[1] Perhaps, but people make idols of all kinds of things.

God said, "You are not to make for yourself an engraved image or any likeness of anything in heaven above or on the earth beneath or in the waters below. You are not to bow down to them or serve them; for I, the Lord your God, am a jealous God, visiting the iniquity of the fathers upon the children to the third and fourth generation of those who hate Me, but showing love to a thousand generations of those who love Me and keep My commandments." (Ex. 20:4-6)

God uses the word "God" to indicate that He is the One who has the right to command, the right to be obeyed. By definition, He is the Authority. That's why the first commandment is, "I am the Lord your God..." The first commandment is telling us to recognize the reality of God's authority. It is the foundation for all the other commandments. It is the foundation for all other authority, genuine authority.

When the Lord revealed His nature to Moses, Moses was as close to God as a person can get. He was alone with God in the heights of revelation. But there is no mysticism in the text. This incomparable revelation of God focuses on His gracious forgiving response to humanity's iniquity, transgression, and sin. That is the core of how a person is to know God, because, unfortunately, iniquity, transgression, and sin fill our lives.

It is, however, important to understand that God did not become "merciful and gracious, slow to anger, abounding in lovingkindness and truth" after He created humanity. He has always been that way. It was not only after Adam and Havah rebelled that God could be described as "forgiving iniquity, transgression and sin"; He was always that way, even when there were no creatures given over to iniquity, transgression, and sin. He was that way when He alone existed, and there was no sin or darkness.

In the Scriptures, God tells us what He wants us to know about Himself. How we respond to what He wants us to know is up to us.

In the sight of God, King David was guilty of adultery and murder. God forgave his iniquity, transgression and sin. David knew how and why to praise God. Psalm 103 is a beautiful expression of his appropriate response to God's goodness.

"Bless the Everpresent, O my soul; and all that is within me, bless His holy Name. Bless the Everpresent, O my soul, and do not forget all His benefits — the One who forgives all your iniquities, the One who heals all your diseases, the One who redeems your life from destruction, and the One who surrounds you with mercy and compassion, the One who satisfies your mouth with good so that your youth is renewed like the eagle.

"The Everpresent performs righteous deeds and judgments for all the oppressed. He made known His ways to Moses, His actions to the children of Israel. The Everpresent is merciful and gracious, slow to anger, abounding in lovingkindness. He will not always struggle [with us], nor will He keep anger forever. He has not treated us in accordance with our sins or repaid us according to our iniquities. For as high as the heavens are above the earth, so mighty is His mercy toward those who fear Him. As far as the east is from the west, He has removed our transgressions that far from us.

"As a father has compassion on his children, so the Everpresent has compassion on those who fear Him, for He knows how we are formed. He remembers that we are dust. As for man, his days are like grass. He flourishes like a flower of the field, for the wind passes over it and it is no more, and its place no longer remembers it. But the lovingkindness of the Everpresent is from everlasting and to everlasting upon those who fear Him, and His righteousness to their children's children — to those who keep His covenant and to those who remember to do what He has appointed.

"The Everpresent has established His throne in the heavens, and His kingdom rules over all. Bless the Everpresent, you His angels, you mighty ones who perform His word, who listen to the voice of His word. Bless the Everpresent, all His forces, His servants who do His will. Bless the Everpresent, all His works on all places in His dominion.

"O my soul, bless the Everpresent Lord."

**Footnote**
1. Maimonides, Guide to the Perplexed, 1, 54

# GOD AS AUTHORITY

"His kingdom rules over all. ...Bless the Everpresent, all His works in all places in His dominion." (Ps. 103:19,22)

By definition, "God" is the Authority, the One who has the right to command, and the right to be obeyed. But Pharaoh thought of himself that way. So did many other rulers then and since. Very few people — whether political, religious, artistic, or whatever — recognize God as God.

Many think that God can be easily fooled. "And the Lord said, 'Since this people draw near Me with their mouth, and honor Me with their lips, but have removed their heart far from Me, and their fear of Me is a commandment of men learned by rote. Therefore...'" (Is. 29:13) Many judge God to be guilty and themselves sinless.

So we must respond to the question, "What gives God the right to tell me, or you, what to do?" Or, phrased a little more philosophically, "Who authorized God to command humanity to obey Him?" There are at least six reasons which the Scriptures give for the authority of God.

**1. God is.** "And God said to Moses, 'I AM WHO I AM.' And He said, 'This is what you are to say to the people of Israel, I AM has sent me to you.'" (Ex. 3:14)

"Listen to Me, O Jacob and Israel, My called: I am He; I am the first, I am also the last." (Is. 48:12) Before the beginning, God is; and after the end, He is. There is no existence before Him. There is no other being or thing, and no concepts, whether a Platonic ideal or a theoretical construct, in the beginning. (Gen. 1:1)

Some people choose to believe that God doesn't exist. So they don't like to think about how everything else came into existence. They choose to believe that all living things were spontaneously generated from non-living matter. So they don't like to think about Louis Pasteur, in 1859, showing that spontaneous generation doesn't happen.

So some have conjectured that life on earth came here from

outer space. But that is simply a fanciful evasion of the question: "How did life come into existence?" If life on earth came from outer space, how did life come into existence in outer space? People are free to speculate, but we only observe life coming from life.

And we observe that all living things die. Everything other than God exists only temporarily, only because He created it, and only as long as He sustains it. You and I exist only as long as God wants us to exist. For anyone who values existence, that should provide some incentive to obey God.

**2. God is the head.** King Abiyah, Solomon's grandson, told those who had rebelled against the house of David, "Know that God is with us as head [*rosh*], and His priests with battle trumpets to sound the alarm against you. Children of Israel, do not fight against the Lord God of your fathers; because you will not succeed." (2Ch.13:12) Abiyah, and those with him, became strong and were victorious in the ensuing battle "because they relied on the Lord God of their fathers." (2Ch. 13:18)

In its various forms, *rosh* means "beginning, first, chief, or head". God is the beginning of all that exists; He is the first of all that exists; and He is the chief and head of all that exists.

The head [*rosh*] of a household is the leader of that household. The head of a tribe is the leader of that tribe. The head of a nation is the leader of that nation. God is the head, the ruler, of all that is. The Hebrew word *reshut*, a related form, means "authority".

The first word of the Bible, *b'resheet*, appears five other times in the Scriptures. Four of those times, it refers to the beginning of the reign of a king. (Jer. 26:1, 27:1, 28:1, 49:34) In the beginning, in creating heaven and earth, God began His reign over heaven and earth.

In the Jewish Greek of the Septuagint, Gen. 1:1 begins with *En arche*. *Arche* is a standard translation of *rosh*. In its various forms, *arche* means "beginning, first, principle, ruler, reign, authority, etc." In many passages, the Septuagint uses *eis archas* for the Hebrew *memshelet*, which means "to rule or have dominion". (e.g. Gen. 1:16)

Whatever genuine authorities exist are those that God — the beginning, the ruler, the head — has established. They have only whatever sphere of God's authority He has delegated to them.

**3. God created all that exists.** "The earth belongs to the Everpresent, and all its fullness, the world and those who dwell in it, because He has founded it upon the seas, and established it upon the rivers." (Ps. 24:1-2)

God didn't buy, borrow, or steal anyone else's material to create everything. There was no one else, and there were no materials. Out of nothing, He created all that is. He therefore owns everything and everyone.

Everything exists for His purpose. "The Everpresent has made all things for Himself; even the wicked for the day of evil." (Prov. 16:4)

In addition to creating the content of what exists, God also created the governing order. Everything that exists is governed by His order.

**4. God has power over all people.** He is the Potter, humanity is the clay. (e.g. Jer. 18:1-6) "It is backwards if the Potter is thought of like the clay, because will the thing made say of the One who made it, 'He did not make me'? Or will the thing formed say of the One who formed it, 'He does not understand'?" (Is. 29:16)

God governs all, including the governors. Nebuchadnezzar thought that he himself was the supreme ruler. When God removed both his kingdom and his sanity, he learned otherwise.

"And at the end of the days, I, Nebuchadnezzar, lifted up my eyes to heaven, and my understanding returned to me, and I blessed the most High, and I praised and honored Him who lives for ever, whose dominion is an everlasting dominion, and His kingdom is from generation to generation. And all the inhabitants of the earth are counted as nothing; and He does according to His will in the forces of heaven, and among the inhabitants of the earth. And no one can restrain His hand, or say to Him, 'What are you doing?'" (Dan. 4:31-32)

Nebuchadnezzar learned what many never learn: the

governmental framework of our existence is God's kingdom. "For the kingdom is the Lord's; and He is ruler over the nations." (Ps. 22:29H)

Years later, when Belshazzar was king of Babylon, he "made a great feast for a thousand of his lords, and ...commanded to bring the golden and silver utensils which his father Nebuchadnezzar had taken from the temple which was in Yerushala'im; that the king, and his lords, his wives, and his concubines might drink from them." (Dan. 5:1-2) They indulged themselves, using the holy things that had been set apart for the God of Israel.

"They drank wine, and praised the gods of gold, and of silver, of bronze, of iron, of wood, and of stone. In the same hour the fingers of a man's hand appeared, and wrote opposite the lampstand upon the plaster of the wall of the king's palace; and the king saw the part of the hand that wrote." (Dan. 5:4-5)

No one at the party, nor any of the king's advisors, could read or understand the writing. So they sent for Daniel, who had a reputation for supernatural wisdom. Daniel recounted how God had humbled Nebuchadnezzar,

"But you, his son, O Belshazzar, have not humbled your heart, though you knew all this; but have lifted up yourself against the Lord of heaven; and the utensils of His house have been brought before you, and you, and your lords, your wives, and your concubines, have drunk wine from them; and you have praised the gods of silver, and gold, of bronze, iron, wood, and stone, which do not see, or hear, or know; and the God in whose hand your breath is, and whose are all your ways, you have not glorified. Then the palm of the hand was sent from before Him; and this hand inscribed this writing.

"And this is the writing that was inscribed: *Mene, Mene, Tekel*, and *Parsin*. This is the interpretation of the word; *Mene*: God has numbered your kingdom, and brought it to an end. *Tekel*: You are weighed in the balances, and are found to be lacking. *Peres*: Your kingdom is divided, and given to the Medes and Persians." (Dan. 5:22-28)

Belshazzar and his officials were intoxicated with their own importance. They did not consider what their end would be. But no matter what anyone, or everyone, chooses to embrace, God's power is supreme. There is no way to defeat, escape, or overthrow it.

**5. God created humanity to be His children.** God created humanity in His own image and in His own likeness. We are told that Adam "fathered a son in his own likeness, after his image." (Gen. 5:3)

"Likeness" and "image" are the same words that God used to describe His design for humanity. The use of the same language is intentional. Its purpose is to teach us what kind of relationship God intended for humanity to have with Him. It is one of the ways in which humanity was made in God's image and likeness. Because this is an important theme in the Scriptures, we will look at this relationship in more detail in its own chapter, "God's Children".

Here, we simply need to note that God established a father's role, as head of the household, to entail commanding his children. Before He destroyed Sodom and Gomorrah, "The Everpresent said, 'Shall I hide from Abraham what I am doing, since Abraham will surely become a great and mighty nation, and all the nations of the earth will be blessed in him? For I **have known him so that he may command his children and his household after him...**'" (Gen. 18:17-19)

God commanded us to honor our father and mother. He rebukes Israel for failing to do that. "A son honors his father, and a servant his master. If I am a father, where is my honor? And if I am a master, where is my fear?" (Mal. 1:6)

As our Father, God has the right to command. There is, however, some complexity in our relationship with Him. "But now, O Lord, You are our Father; we are the clay, and You our potter; and we are all the work of Your hand." (Is. 64:7H) On the one hand, God is our father, and, to some extent, we share His nature. On the other hand, He is the potter who made us out of clay, and, to some extent, we are the opposite of what He is. This creates a continual tension.

**6. God will judge all people, and there will be no appeal.**

"I, the Everpresent Lord, search the heart, I test the inwards, to give every man according to his ways, and according to the fruit of his doings." (Jer.17:10) God weighs our motives, our actions, and the consequences of those actions.

We, unfortunately, are not impartial judges of ourselves. "All the ways of a man are clean in his own eyes; but the Everpresent Lord weighs the spirits." (Prov. 16:2) He doesn't judge by our standards of right and wrong, nor does He judge us in comparison to others. Every person will be judged according to God's standard of behavior.

God judges both what we do and what we don't do. "If you forbear to rescue those who are drawn to death, and those who are ready to be slain, if you say, 'Behold, we did not know it'; does not He who ponders the heart consider it? And He who keeps your soul, does He not know it? And will He not give back to every man according to his deeds?" (Prov. 24:11-12)

There are many people who don't recognize God's authority, but God doesn't need their recognition, their vote, or endorsement. As Job found out, "If He snatches away, who can hinder Him? Who will say to Him, 'What are You doing?'" (Job 9:12) God can never be overruled, but He does invite those who know Him to intercede for other people to be spared from the judgment they deserve. And He does invite people to change their own ways so that what has been decreed against them will not happen. All authority remains as His.

Authority is the right to command and to be obeyed, and then the right to judge those who do not obey. God's legal order is completely efficaceous. No crime escapes His notice or His punishment. He has, however, established a system of sacrifice which provides atonement, a system in which an innocent sacrificial animal may be put to death in place of the guilty person.

"The end of the matter, all has been heard: Fear God, and keep His commandments; for this is everything for humanity. For God will bring every deed into judgment, with every secret thing, whether it is good, or whether it is evil." (Eccl.12:13-14)

## *Bara* / CREATED

What does it mean "to create"?

The Hebrew word, *bara* means to cause something to come into existence without any preceding form or natural cause. The Latin phrase, *ex nihilo*, is often used to express the same thing. It simply means "from nothing."

The story is told of a future, friendly contest between God and the top scientists of the earth, in a day in which they have discovered His existence and much more. With all their advances in cloning, biotechnology, and genetic engineering, they challenge God to a contest of making humanity anew, to see who can do a better job.

The terms of the contest are simple: each side is to use their own resources and methods to make a man. The scientists, having gathered several hundred pounds of mineral rich dirt, tell God that they are ready to begin. God's response is simple: "Use your own dirt."

The story is prefigured in the Midrash. "One philosopher asked Rabban Gamliel, saying to him: 'Your God, He was a great artisan, but because He found good materials which assisted Him: *Tohu* [without order], and *bohu* [empty], and *choshekh* [darkness], and *ruakh* [wind], and *mayim* [water], and *tehomot* [the depths].'"

These are all mentioned in the Gen. 1:2, but their existence is not explained there

"He [Rabban Gamliel] said to him... '*Creation* is written for all of them. *Without order and empty*: as it is said (Is. 45): *I make peace and create evil. Darkness*: [In the same verse,] *I form the light, and create darkness. Water*: (Ps. 148) *Praise Him, you heavens of heavens, and the waters that are above the heavens. Why? [The next verse says,] For He commanded, and they were created. Wind*: (Amos 4) *For, know that He forms the mountains, and creates wind. Depths*: (Prov. 8) *When there were no depths, I was brought forth.*'" (Mid. Gen. 1.9)

Only God is able to create in the Biblical sense of the word.

Only He can make something out of nothing. His method of creation is to speak and call into existence what does not exist. He alone even knows what the things are that He speaks and calls into existence.

Only God exists in and of Himself, but He chooses to create things that are other than Himself. Because God chooses to create these things that are other than Himself, their existence tells us something about God. Their nature reveals something about His character and desires. There is a reason, a purpose, for everything that He creates. And also a time. "To every thing there is a season, and a time to every purpose under the heavens." (Eccl. 3:1)

What are "the heavens"? What is "the earth"? What is "light"? or "humanity"? or anything? They are what God created them to be. Nothing more, nothing less. The more clearly we see His purpose in what He has created, the more clearly we will see Him.

### Implications of God creating the heavens and the earth

The chief implication is His unquestionable sovereignty over all. He can do anything in the physical world, or with the physical world, that He chooses to do. He created it. He does not need to obey what He created, owns, and sustains. What He created, owns, and sustains needs to obey Him. He also does not need to justify Himself to what He has created, He Himself is the judge.

Abraham spoke of "God Most High, owner of heaven and earth." (Gen. 14:22) David sang, "The earth is the Lord's, and everything in it, the world, and all who live in it; because He founded it upon the seas and established it upon the waters." (Ps. 24:1-2) Moses told Israel, "To the Lord your God belong the heavens, even the highest heavens, the earth and everything in it." (Dt. 10:14)

Consequently, there are a number of implications to the fact that God created me. I belong to Him. He had His purpose in creating me.

God sent Jeremiah to watch a potter at work. Then He said,

"'Even as this potter does, am I not able to do with you, O house of Israel?' says the Everpresent. 'Know that as the clay is in the hand of the potter, so you, O house of Israel, are in My hand.'" (Jer. 18:6, cf. Is. 29:16, 64:8)

Rashi, following the Midrash Rabbah, points out that the Torah begins by establishing that God is owner of all. That gives God the right to give the land of Israel, which belongs to Him, to the children of Israel. That gives God the right to choose Yerushala'im as His own city, as the capital of Israel, His chosen land and people.

## Other specific things that God created

There are other things which were not created in the first week, and yet the Scriptures say that they are or will be the result of God's creative power. In that their creation is specifically mentioned in Tanakh, each one is worth considering.

1. "But now, this is what the Everpresent says — **He who created you, O Jacob**, He who formed you, O Israel: 'Do not fear, because I have redeemed you. I have called you by your name; you are Mine. ...I am the Everpresent, your Holy One, the Creator of Israel, your King.'" (Is. 43:1,15) Just as God had a purpose in creating all of heaven and earth, so He had a purpose in creating Jacob and the people formed from him. God had a purpose in choosing Israel, the land and the people. A redeemed Israel is an important step in the fulfillment of God's plan for all Creation.

That is why God guarantees Israel's continued existence by pointing to all Creation. "This is what the Lord says: 'Only if the heavens above can be measured and the foundations of the earth below be searched out, then I will cast off all the descendants of Israel for all they have done,' declares the Lord." (Jer. 31:37) The heavens are beyond measurement. The foundations of the earth cannot be searched out. And so, God's continual care and purpose for Israel endure.

As part of His encouragement to Israel to trust in His redemption and not fear, God said, "Do not be afraid, because I am with you; I will bring your descendants from the east and gather you from the west. I will say to the north, 'Give them up!' and to the south, 'Do not hold them back.' 'Bring My sons from afar and My daughters from the ends of the earth — **each one who is called by My name, whom I created for My glory**. I have formed him, truly I have made him.'" (Is. 43:5-7)

It was for His glory that God **created** those who are called by His Name. In the culmination of God's purpose, Israel will yet glorify the Lord throughout the earth, and thereby cause all Creation to break into song. "Sing for joy, O heavens, because the Everpresent has done it. Shout aloud, you lower parts of the earth. Burst into song, you mountains, you forests and every tree in it, because the Everpresent has redeemed Jacob, and glorified Himself in Israel." (Is. 44:23, cf. Is. 49:13; 55:12, Ps. 98:8)

**2.** There is another special act of creation associated with that redemption. "When the Lord washes away the filth of the daughters of Zion, and cleanses the blood of Yerushala'im from its midst by the spirit of judgment, and by the spirit of burning. Then **the Everpresent will create over every dwelling place of mount Zion, and upon her assemblies, a cloud and smoke by day, and the shining of a flaming fire by night**; for there will be a canopy/_huppah_ over all the glory." (Is. 4:4-5)

In these verses, God promises that He will redeem His people. The context is the end of the age and the establishment of the Messianic kingdom. (cf. Is. 4:2) The glory of the Lord, likened to a marriage _huppah_, will be visibly present over Mount Zion.

We can understand some of what that means by looking at Israel's redemption from Egypt, when God led us with a pillar of cloud by day which became a pillar of fire at night. In that cloud, God protected us from Pharaoh's army. In that cloud, He "went before you in the way to seek out places for you to encamp and to show you in fire by night the way you should go, and in a cloud by day." (Dt. 1:33, cf. Neh. 9:12)

He guided us that way all the years we walked through the wilderness. Everyone knew then which way God wanted them to go. The only question was whether or not they would choose to go that way.

Today, many people are confused. They don't know which way God wants them to go; they don't know what God wants them to do. If only God would give them some kind of sign.

In the Messianic Age, the Lord will create such a sign. The cloud and the flaming fire will not move from over mount Zion and over all her assemblies. All the world will be able to know where God wants them to go, and what God wants them to do.

"On the day the Mishkan, the tent of the community, was set up, the cloud covered the Mishkan. From evening till morning there was over the Mishkan the appearance of fire." (Num. 9:15) In the wilderness, everyone knew where God was. No one asked, "How can I find God?" The only question was whether or not they would come to God.

In the Messianic Age, everyone will know where God can be found. God is everywhere, but He invites people to come visit Him at His house. "And many people will come and say, 'Come, and let us go up to the mountain of the Everpresent, to the house of the God of Jacob; and He will teach us from His ways, and we will walk in His paths; because from Zion the Torah will go forth, and the word of the Everpresent from Yerushala'im." (Is. 2:3)

In the cloud, God protected and guided Israel, and caused His presence to be in our midst. The infinite God was in the finite cloud. The glory of God, appearing on earth, was clothed by the cloud. We will look at this again when we examine the Shekhinah, the visible, glorious presence of God on the earth. In the Messianic Age, God will create the cloud and fire anew.

3. **"Know that the One who forms the mountains, creates *ruakh*, and declares to humanity what His thought** is, who makes the morning darkness, and treads on the high places of the earth, the Everpresent Lord, the God of forces, is His Name." (Am. 4:13)

The Hebrew word *ruakh* is translated into English as "spirit," "breath," or "wind," depending upon the context. Here, the proper translation would seem to be "wind," because it is connected to the mountains, part of the physical world; and because the

Scriptures tell us that God has both spirit and breath, which are therefore not created.

For His purposes, God creates the wind, which moves the clouds, and changes the weather. He creates the cool breeze, the stifling hot breath of the desert, and the violent tornado. He creates the wind which, if we are alert, tells us what is coming.

The air around us, which we often don't notice, begins to move. The sun warms the air, land, and water, which heat at different speeds. That results in differences in air pressure, which cause the air to move. Trade winds, jetstreams, and doldrums have played significant roles in human history, as have windmills.

God creates the wind, which may carry the fragrance of fresh bread, new mown grass, or the sounds of destruction. It may fly a kite, overturn a tree or destroy a building. God creates the wind, which appears in a variety of forms and brings a variety of effects.

**4. "Know that I will create new heavens and a new earth.** The first things [*rishonot*] will not be remembered, nor will they arise in the heart. But be glad and rejoice forever in what I will create, for **I will create Yerushala'im a delight and its people a joy.** I will rejoice in Yerushala'im and take delight in My people; the sound of weeping and of crying will no longer be heard in it." (Is. 65:17-19)

Everything that God created was good in His sight. After He created humanity, it was very good in His sight. God, the ruler of all, made humanity to be the ruler of the earth. And that was good.

But Adam and Havah rebelled, and defiled themselves and the rest of Creation. In general, their descendants continued the rebellion and the defilement, generation after generation. "Now the earth was corrupt in God's sight and was full of violence [*hamas*]. God saw how corrupt the earth had become, because all flesh had corrupted its way upon the earth. So God said to Noah, 'The end of all flesh has come before Me; because the earth is filled with violence [*hamas*] through them. So know that I will destroy them with the earth.'" (Gen. 6:11-13)

God did as He said He would, and cleansed the earth with a flood. Noa<u>h</u> and his family were given the opportunity to begin all over again. But it didn't take long for them to defile themselves and the earth. It didn't take long for them to rebel anew against God at Babel. There at Babel, where humanity was united in its rebellion against God, God divided them into different *goyim*/ Gentiles/nations. Since their hearts were set on evil, He set barriers between them.

The history of the Gentiles and the history of Israel are both filled with tragedy and pain. For every spiritual triumph, there are a hundred, a thousand, cases of shame and disgrace. God continued to call out to humanity, to call us back to Himself and His holiness, but we rarely respond.

The earth needs more than cleansing, even as David needed more than cleansing. God will again destroy the earth, but will then create a new heavens and a new earth. And in that day, the cry of David's sinful heart — "**Create** in me a new heart" — will be answered; humanity will have new hearts.

And in that new creation, God will create a new Yerushala'im, which will be to Him a joy and delight. Yerushala'im was always intended to be "the joy of the whole earth". (Ps. 48:3H) But more often than not, in this age, God has wept over Yerushala'im. Neither Israel nor the nations have given Him much cause to rejoice.

When God creates us anew, we will be a joy to Him. We will delight in Him, and He will delight in us. Then He will rejoice over the new Yerushala'im which He will have created.

5. "Know that it is **I who created the metal worker who blows upon the coals in the fire and brings forth an instrument fit for its work. And it is I who have created a destroyer to destroy.**" (Is. 54:16)

God created the metal worker, who heats metal ore dug from the earth and forms suitable instruments for humanity. There are many kinds of metal instruments mentioned in the Scriptures: the sword and the plowshare, the saw, the axe, and the hoe, the mirror and the altar. Each instrument is made for a particular purpose. The heart chooses the purpose, and the hands make the instrument. God created the hands and the understanding.

In this world, where people build what they shouldn't and abuse what they have, there is "a time to plant and a time to uproot what is planted, a time to kill and a time to heal, a time to tear down and a time to build, ... a time for war and a time for peace." (Eccl. 3:2-3,8) There are many different human desires and corresponding actions.

Because all humanity joined together to build the Tower of Babel in rebellion against God, it was necessary to destroy what they had built. In the time of Jeremiah, God promised to destroy Babylon completely for the evil it had brought upon Zion. "The Everpresent says, 'I am against you, O destroying mountain, you who destroy the whole earth. I will stretch out My hand against you, roll you off the cliffs, and make you a burned-out mountain.'" (Jer. 51:25) There is a time for Babylon to prosper, and a time for Babylon to be completely destroyed.

The people of Sodom lived in gross immorality and violence. There came a day when it was necessary to destroy the world of evil which they had built. God had created a destroyer to destroy and a means of destruction.

In Egypt, Pharaoh tried to destroy Israel by killing every male baby. God sent Moses to Pharaoh to say, "My firstborn son is Israel, and I tell you, 'Let My son go, so he may serve Me.' And if you refuse to let him go, know that I will kill your son, your firstborn." (Ex. 4:22-23)

Nine plagues later, when the death of every firstborn in Egypt was imminent, God told Moses to have Israel kill the *pesakh*, the lamb, and put its blood on the lintel and doorposts of their houses. "For the Everpresent will pass through to strike the Egyptians; and when He sees the blood upon the lintel, and on the two side posts, the Everpresent will pass over the door, and will not let the destroyer come into your houses to strike you." (Ex. 12:23)

God sent a destroyer to destroy Egypt. For reasons which made sense to Him, God enabled the people of Israel to secure protection from the destroyer, but only by obediently putting the blood of the *pesakh* on their houses.

Conversely, disobedience made Israel vulnerable to the destroyer. Because of David's sin, "God sent an angel to Yerushala'im to destroy it; but as he was destroying, the Everpresent saw and had compassion beyond the evil. And He said to the destroying angel, 'Enough. Now withdraw your hand.' And the angel of the Everpresent stood by the threshing floor of Ornan the Jebusite." (1Chr. 21:15)

God sent the destroying angel because of the sins of David and Israel. He stopped the destruction because of His compassion. That threshing floor then became the site of the Temple, the place where sacrifices could be offered to atone for the sins of Israel. God created a destroyer to destroy: either to destroy our enemies or to destroy us.

6. "How long will you wander, O unfaithful [hashovevah] daughter? Because **the Everpresent will create a new thing on the earth — a woman will surround [*t'sovev*] a man.**" (Jer. 31:22)

This is an unusual verse, which speaks of an unusual creative act of God. The nature of that special creative act — "a woman will surround a man" — is difficult to discern from the very limited content of the verse and its context. We do know that it will be "a new thing"; it will be something that had not happened before. We also know that it will come about because of a special creative act of the Almighty.

The previous verse, Jer. 31:21, indicates that the "unfaithful daughter" is Israel: "Turn back [*shuvee*], virgin of Israel." It seems that the woman who will encompass a man is presented as a contrast to the unfaithful virgin of Israel. Whatever the special creative act is, it seems to be the means of bringing an end to the unfaithful wandering of the people of Israel. As God promised: "Again I will build you, and you will be built, O virgin of Israel..." (Jer. 31:3H)

"A new thing" is something which has no precedent and is not a natural occurrence. For example, Dathan and Abiram were among the leaders in Korah's rebellion against God, Moses, and Aaron. When Moses called Dathan and Abiram to join the other conspirators in front of the community, they refused to come, and mocked Moses. So Moses went to their tents, and the elders of Israel followed him.

He warned the community: "Now get away from the tents of these wicked men, and do not touch anything that is theirs, so that you are not swept away in all their sins. So they got away from the dwelling of Kora<u>h</u>, Dathan, and Abiram..." (Num. 16:26-27)

Then Moses said: "If these men die as all humanity dies, or if they are visited by the fate of all men; then the Everpresent has not sent me. But **if the Everpresent creates a new thing**, and the earth opens her mouth, and swallows them and all that is theirs, and they go down alive into Sheol; then you will know that these men have despised the Everpresent." (Num. 16:29-30)

As soon as Moses finished speaking, it happened exactly as he had said. "And the earth opened her mouth, and swallowed them up, and their houses, and all the men who belonged to Kora<u>h</u>, and all their goods. They, and all that belonged to them, went down alive into Sheol, and the earth closed upon them; and they perished from among the congregation." (Num. 16:32-33)

That event, though horrendous, was "a new thing". It was unprecedented, and it did not arise solely from natural causes. The Everpresent created this particular judgment for these particular people.

On the more positive side, God promises to do — albeit not *create* — something new for the redemption of Israel. "Behold, **I will do a new thing.** Now it will sprout [*teetzmach*]; will you not know it? I will make a way in the wilderness, and rivers in the desert.... I, I myself, am He who blots out your transgressions for My own sake, and will not remember your sins." (Is. 43:19, 25) In some unprecedented way, God will blot out the transgressions of Israel, in order to restore His people to Himself.

Redemption is God's way of bringing about the same purpose He had in creation. As the means of completing the redemption of Israel, God promises to make something else that is new, a new covenant. This new covenant is presented as the means of transforming the people of Israel.

"'Behold, the days are coming,' declares the Everpresent, 'when I will make a new covenant with the house of Israel and with the house of Judah — not like the covenant I made with their fathers when I strongly took them by their hand to lead them out of Egypt — because they broke My covenant, though I was a husband to them,' declares the Everpresent." (Jer. 31:31-32)

We will look at the details of this new covenant in the next chapter.

# "CREATE IN ME A PURE HEART"

God had blessed and exalted David. One of the reasons He did that was so that David would subdue the enemies of Israel. When David neglected God's purpose in his life, the lustful desires of his heart led him into adultery and murder. That unsubdued internal enemy caused him to commit adultery with Bathsheba, and to then arrange the murder of her husband to try to keep his own sin secret.

When the prophet Nathan confronted David with his sin, the evil of what David had done struck deep. He grieved over it and its consequences. But he did not yet know all the pain he would feel when the child Bathsheba had conceived, the innocent son of David, would die because of David's sin. Nor did David yet know all the evil that would come upon him and his children as his sin continued to be fruitful and multiply.

David did know that he could not undo what he had done to others, to himself, to Israel, and to God. And he could not free his own heart from the evil he had invited in. He knew that unless his heart were purified, he could do the same again, or worse.

So he pleaded with God, "**blot out** my transgressions. **Wash away** all my iniquity and **cleanse** me from my sin. ... **Cleanse** me with hyssop, ... **Hide Your face** from my sins and **blot out** all my iniquity. (Ps. 51:1-2,7,9) Yet he knew that all the cleansing, purifying, and forgiving would still not solve the problem that had caused his fall, the unclean desire in his own heart.

So he asked God for a new heart, a pure heart. "**Create in me a pure heart**, O God, and renew a steadfast spirit within me." (Ps. 51:12) This was not a casual request. It was the desperate cry and terrified longing of a man who loved God, but had dishonored Him.

He knew that if God did not supernaturally change him, he was lost. David feared his own moral impotence, his own inability to change himself at his core. David was not the only one with this problem.

Before Samson was born, his mother was barren, unable to conceive. God supernaturally enabled her to conceive Samson. Samson received his life from God so that "he will begin to save Israel from the hand of the Philistines." (Judg.13:5) When "the spirit of the Lord came mightily upon him," (Judg. 14:6) Samson received supernatural strength to aid him in that task.

Samson was consecrated to God, but he ensnared himself in immorality, with one Philistine woman after another. Instead of saving Israel from the Philistines, he was being overcome by them. "Then Samson went to Gaza, and saw a harlot there, and went in to her." (Judg. 16:1) The Phistines surrounded him, but Samson escaped. He escaped from the Philistines, but not from his own lust.

He next "loved" a Philistine woman named Delilah. You probably know the story. She entrapped him into revealing the consecrated secret of his strength. There came that tragic day, when she betrayed him to the rulers of the Philistines while he slept. She said, "'The Philistines are upon you, Samson.' He awoke from his sleep and thought, 'I'll go out as before and shake myself free.' But he did not know that the Everpresent Lord had departed from him." (Judg. 16:20)

The Philistines overpowered him, gouged out his eyes, and put him in chains. The Philistines overpowered Samson only because the lustful desires of his own heart had overpowered him first.

Samson was Israel's human deliverer; David was Israel's human king. We are all still in the predicament of being called, chosen, and anointed, but nevertheless plagued with the unclean desires of our own hearts.

### Sin and *Yetzer haRa*

The Rabbinic concept of *yetzer hara*, i.e. "the evil inclination," is of something that lives in all people and inclines them to do what is wrong. In general, the Rabbis speak of it as being the hidden cause for the imagination of humanity being evil and unclean, and for their hearts being hard and unclean. "Our

Rabbis taught: 'But I will remove far off from you the hidden one', refers to the Evil Inclination which is constantly hidden in the heart of humanity [Adam]." (Tal. Sukkah 52a)

They speak of it as being our enemy and the thing that causes us to stumble. "Moses called it 'the Uncircumcised,' as it is said, 'Circumcise therefore the foreskin of your heart.' David called it 'Unclean,' as it is said, 'Create in me a pure heart, O Everpresent.' ...Ezekiel called it 'Stone,' as it is said, 'And I will take away the heart of stone out of your flesh and I will give you a heart of flesh.'" (Tal. Sukkah 52a)

If we know that good is good, why are we tempted by evil? Why do we sometimes prefer, and choose, what is evil instead of what is good? Rashi says that, "There was not given to him [Adam] an evil inclination until he ate from the tree." (Commentary on Gen. 2:25) But this view is very problematic. If Adam had no evil inclination before he ate from the tree, then why did he eat from the tree? He knew it was wrong.

In the Talmud, we find a different view. "Why is it written (Gen. 2:7): 'Then the Lord God formed [*vayyitzer*] humanity? [The word *vayyitzer*] is written with two yods, to show that the Holy One, blessed be He, created two inclinations, one the good inclination and one the evil inclination." (Tal. Ber. 61a) In this view, humanity had an evil inclination from the very beginning.

God formed us that way. He didn't compel us to follow evil, but He gave us that possibility. He also gave us the possibility to pursue good. The choices we make determine the direction we go.

"R. Assi said, 'In the beginning, the Evil Inclination is like the thread of a spider, but in the end becomes like cart ropes, as it is said, 'Woe unto those who pull iniquity with cords of vanity, and sin as if by a cart-rope.' [Is. 5:18]" (Tal. Sukkah 52a)

In later chapters, we will look at two more things that God created: "I form the light, and **create darkness**. I make peace, and **create evil**. I, the Everpresent, do all these things." (Is. 45:7) But here we simply note that God created Evil outside of us, and an evil inclination within us.

That tells us something about what God wants from us. And

it tells us that we can't succeed without great effort. Nor can we succeed by our great effort, or by trusting in ourselves.

"This is what the Everpresent says: 'Cursed be the man who trusts in man, and makes flesh his arm, and whose heart departs from the Everpresent. ...Blessed is the man who trusts in the Everpresent, and whose hope is the Everpresent. ...The heart is deceitful above all things, and desperately wicked; who can know it?" (Jer. 17:5,7,9)

That's not the end of the story. "But in the time to come, when I will uproot the Evil Inclination from among you, as it is said, 'And I will take away the stony heart from your flesh (Ezek. 36:26),' I will restore My Divine Presence [*shekhinati*] among you." (Mid. Dt. 6:14)

For an individual who cries out, God will respond. But God is interested in more than individuals. He is interested in a people, and in a redeemed world. He intends to dwell in the midst of that people, and rule over that world. It takes more than one person crying out for God to create new hearts for a whole people. But that day will come.

God has a plan for accomplishing that. "The Holy One, blessed be He, created the *yetzer hara*, but He created the Torah to swallow it up." (Tal. Baba Batra 16a) God gave us the Torah and told us to put its words upon our hearts (Dt. 6:6), i.e. to let it regulate all our desires. We haven't accomplished that, but God will.

### New Hearts for Israel

"'Behold, the days are coming,' declares the Everpresent, 'when I will make a new covenant with the house of Israel and with the house of Judah — not like the covenant I made with their fathers when I strongly took them by their hand to lead them out of Egypt — because they broke My covenant, though I was a husband to them,' declares the Everpresent.

"'Because this is the covenant I will make with the house of Israel after those days,' declares the Everpresent. 'I will put My law within them and write it on their hearts. I will be their God, and they will be My people. And they will no longer teach, a man his neighbor, and a man his brother, saying, *Know the Lord*, because they will all know Me, from the least of them to the greatest,' declares the Everpresent. 'For I will forgive their iniquity and will remember their sins no more.'" (Jer. 31:31-34)

There are many remarkable things in this passage, but four things that God says He will do stand out. **(1)** Though the new covenant is like the covenant made at Sinai in that God's law is central, it is not like the covenant made at Sinai in that God places His law within those who enter into it; and He places it on their hearts, rather than on tablets of stone.

Even as the life of the flesh is in the blood (cf. Gen. 9:4, Lev. 17:11), which is circulated by the heart; so God's Law in a person's heart would circulate through his or her entire being. It would bring nourishment and energy for every part of the body. Every action would be fed from, and therefore in accordance with, God's standard of right behavior.

It will be as God promised: "Then I will sprinkle clean water on you, and you will be clean. I will cleanse you from all your impurities, and I will cleanse you from all your idols. I will give you **a new heart** and put **a new spirit** in you; I will remove the heart of stone from your flesh, and give you a heart of flesh. And I will put **My Spirit** in you and make it so that you walk in My statutes and you will observe and do My laws." (Ezek. 36:25-27)

**(2)** This new covenant is made at two different times. The first time is **in** "the days [which] are coming when..." At that time, it is made with the two houses of Israel and Judah. (v.31) The division between the two houses stems from the time of Solomon's son Rehoboam, and is, apparently, still recognizable the first time the new covenant is established.

The new covenant is then made a second time "**after** those days." At that time, it is made with the house of Israel only, presumably a united house. (v. 33)

This is similar to the covenant at Sinai, which God initially made with our fathers when He brought them out of Egypt. But that generation rebelled and would not trust God. They wandered in the wilderness until they died, except for Joshua and Caleb. When that generation had died, God reconfirmed the covenant with their children, before He brought them into the land. (e.g. Dt. 5:3)

So we can expect that God will make the new covenant, but most will not enter into it. Then, at a later time, He will reconfirm the covenant with a new generation.

**(3)** With this second establishment of the new covenant, everyone who enters into it, whether small or great, will know the Everpresent. This is not an insignificant thing. It is not the same as knowing the system or using the vocabulary. Knowing the Everpresent connects us to Life. It enables us to know ourselves and the purpose of our existence.

It is something to be sought, with heart, mind, and strength. "And you will seek Me and find Me, when you search for Me with all your heart." (Jer. 29:13, cf. Dt. 4:29, Prov. 8:17) We are given the opportunity to do that now. "Seek the Everpresent while He may be found, call upon him while He is near." (Is. 55:6)

Many people want God in their lives, but only as an adornment. He is not interested. God is interested in those who want Him as much as He wants them. Whether we do or not is our own choice.

Wisdom says that there will be distress and anguish for those who scorn and mock now. "When your fear and trembling come like a destroying storm, and your calamity comes like a stormy wind; when distress and anguish comes upon you; then they will call on Me, but I will not answer. They will seek Me early, but will not find Me." (Prov. 1:27-28)

God elaborates: "'Then I will go back to My place until they acknowledge their guilt. Then they will seek My face. In their affliction they will earnestly seek Me.'

"'Come, and let us return to the Everpresent; for He has torn, but He will heal us; He has struck, but He will bind us up. After two days He will cause us to live; on the third day He will raise us up, and we will live before Him. Let us know, let us pursue to know the Everpresent. His going forth is sure as the dawn; and He will come to us as the rain, as the latter rains that water the earth.'" (Hos. 5:15-6:3)

Israel had wandered away. God, in His love, still called her to return. She would not. So God said, "I will return to My place, until they acknowledge their guilt." The time came when David confronted his own sin and sought God for cleansing, forgiveness, and a new heart. "Until they seek My face" — the same time of seeking will come for all Israel.

To return to the Everpresent, and to know Him, we will need to acknowledge that, in some measure, God has struck us and wounded us; and He did that because we were walking contrary to Him. Then, as though pursuing our own way had made us dead, "on the third day He will raise us up." Then we will know the Lord.

All the earth will be at peace when all the earth knows Him. "They will neither hurt nor destroy on all My holy mountain, for the earth will be full of the knowledge of the Everpresent as the waters cover the sea." (Is. 11:9)

When we know God, it is not academic knowledge, it is experiential knowledge. It is life-changing knowledge. God praised Josiah, a righteous king, because his life showed that he knew the Everpresent. "'He did what was right and just, and then it was well with him. He judged the cause of the poor and needy, and then it was good. Isn't this what it means to know Me?' declares the Everpresent." (Jer. 22:15b-16)

**(4)** As part of the new covenant, God will forgive our iniquity and remember our sins no more. A covenant is inaugurated by a sacrificial death. That is why, at Sinai, Moses sacrificed animals as burnt offerings and peace offerings. "And Moses took half of the blood, and put it in basins; and half of the blood he sprinkled on the altar. And he took the Book of the Covenant, and read it in the hearing of the people. Then they said, 'All that the Everpresent has said we will do, and obey.'

"Moses then took the blood, sprinkled it on the people, and said, 'This is the blood of the covenant that the Everpresent has made with you in accordance with all these words.'" (Ex. 24:6-8) In the operation of that covenant, provisions were made for additional sacrifices twice daily, on the holy days, and for the ongoing forgiveness of each sin committed.

There are no such provisions in the new covenant. In the new covenant, God gives forgiveness when the covenant is made and entered into. In some way, the sacrifice that inaugurates the new covenant brings forgiveness of iniquity and removes our sins from God's remembrance.

"'Who is a God like You, taking away iniquity, and passing over the transgression of the remnant of His inheritance?' He does not keep His anger strong forever, because He delights in mercy. He will return and have compassion upon us; He will subdue our iniquities. And You will cast all their sins into the depths of the sea." (Mic. 7:18-19)

# *et*

The Hebrew word *et* has no assigned verbal meaning. So it cannot be translated into another language as a particular word or phrase. It does, however, signify quite a lot.

It indicates a relationship. In general, *et* indicates that what follows is a definite direct or indirect object. The subject performs the action. A direct object is what is directly affected by the action which takes place. An indirect object is what or whom is affected when the direct object is acted upon.

A definite object is a specific entity. It is distinguished by the definite article, by a name, or by some kind of uniqueness.

In the account of the creation of the heavens and the earth, *et* is very important. It indicates that whatever was created was an object, not the subject. God is the subject. He is the one doing the creating. No one else. Nothing else.

"God created *et* the heavens and *et* the earth." Creation is not God. It is neither equal to nor equivalent to God. It is what God made. In different ways, Creation reveals things about the Creator, but it is not the same as God. It is not part of God. It was made from nothing. It will continue to exist as long as God sustains it, and no longer than that.

R. Akiba said that if the *et* had been left out, "we might say the heavens and the earth are divinity.... '*et* the heavens' includes the multitude of sun, moon, and stars; '*v'et* the earth' includes the multitude of trees, vegetation, and the Garden of Eden." (Mid. Gen. Rabbah 1.14) There are some people who exalt the physical world to make it equal to God, or to replace God. That's a mistake. Everything that currently exists is simply something which God made.

In the first chapter of Genesis, *et* appears many times to indicate the objects that God made.

v.7 "God made *et* the firmament..."

v.16 "God made *et* two great lights... *et* the great light... and *et* the small light... and *et* the stars also."

v. 21 "God created *et* great sea creatures and *et* every living thing that moves, ...and *et* every winged bird."

v.25 "God made *et* the beast of the earth according to its kind, *et* cattle according to its kind, and *et* everything that creeps on the earth..."

God is the subject; the heavens and the earth and all they contain are the created objects. Therefore the purpose of heaven and earth, and all that they contain, does not come from themselves. The purpose of all things that currently exist comes from the Subject, the One who created them.

The climax of Creation is given in v.27, "God created *et* the human in His own image; in the image of God He created him, male and female He created them." Humanity is also the object of God's creative actions. God is the Creator; humanity is the created.

That tells us something important about the nature of the relationship. Humanity is not equal to God, nor the equivalent of God. Humanity was created by God for His purposes. That does not, however, mean that the relationship is impersonal or exploitative.

If we observe that John loves Mary, or that Yohanan loves *et* Miriam, we see that Yohanan is the subject and Miriam is the object. But Miriam is the object of Yohanan's love, and if it is real love, then Yohanan will seek to serve Miriam, not exploit her. The existence of Miriam explains, at least partially, the purpose of Yohanan's life.

As part of His purposes, God created humanity in His own image and likeness. As part of being made in the image and likeness of God, humanity was given the responsibility to rule over the earth and all of its creatures. That rulership is to be characterized by service, not by exploitation.

As part of that responsibility, Adam was given the opportunity to name all the creatures. "And out of the ground the Everpresent God formed every beast of the field, and every bird of the air; and brought them to Adam to see what he would call them. And whatever Adam called every living creature, that was its name." (Gen. 2:19)

God brought the creatures to Adam to see what he would

name them. This indicates that Adam was empowered to bring definition and order to the Earth. He was created to make his own choices, choices with consequences, and to make them before God. In this way, humanity was created to be like God.

*Et* indicates a definite object. Without overemphasizing the grammatical aspect, we can say that all of Creation, and especially humanity, is a definite object for God. He called it all into being, and He has a definite purpose for all of it, especially for the creature He created in His own image and likeness.

Having said that, it should also be said that sometimes the Biblical Hebrew concept of a "direct object" goes beyond the English concept. For example, "And Adam knew *et* Havah his wife; and she conceived, and gave birth *et* Ka'in, and said, 'I have acquired a man *et* the Everpresent Lord.'" (Gen. 4:1)

In this verse, the first two uses of *et* are understood to indicate what we understand as a direct object: Havah is the one Adam knew; Ka'in is the one to whom Havah gives birth. But the third use of *et* is different, though the Targum Yonatan[1] has "I have acquired a man, the Angel of the Lord."Neither the Angel of the Lord (following the Targum) nor the Everpresent Lord Himself (following the Hebrew) is the one that Havah acquired.

Havah was acknowledging the role of God in the creation and formation of her son, Ka'in. God was not the one upon whom the action took place; He was the one by whom the action took place. That is why most translators put something like: "I have acquired a man from (or with) the Everpresent Lord."

Here are two other examples: "And Hanoch walked *et* God; and he was not, because God took him." (Gen. 5:24) "Noah was a just man and whole in his generations, and Noah walked *et* God." (Gen. 6:29) Unlike the sense of a direct object in English, God is not the one to whom the walking was done. But in a Biblical sense, He is. Hanoch and Noah did their walking, i.e. lived their lives, unto God.

## Command *et* the children of Israel

A slightly different, but equally important, sense is given when God tells Moses, "You are to command *et* the children of Israel, that they bring you pure beaten olive oil for the light, to raise up a lamp always [*ner tamid*]. In the Tent of Meeting, outside the veil which is before the Testimony, Aaron and his sons shall order it from evening to morning before the Everpresent. It is a statute forever throughout their generations *me'et* the children of Israel." (Ex. 27:20-21)

Both usages of *et* indicate that the children of Israel are the ones who are commanded: "command *et* the children of Israel... It is a statute... *me'et* the children of Israel." A statute is a legal command. Both usages indicate a relationship between God, the ultimate Subject, and Israel, the commanded people.

The Midrash on these verses notes that God compares Israel to many different kinds of trees: the olive tree, the fig tree, the palm, the cedar, etc. And it then suggests reasons why God compares Israel to an olive tree. The first reason given relates the history of Israel to the process of making pure olive oil.

The olive "is brought down from the tree and beaten, and after it has been beaten is brought up to the vat and they are placed in a grinding-mill. And after that they are ground, and after that they are tied up with ropes, and then stones are brought, and after that they give their oil. it is like that with Israel: the idolators come and beat them from place to place, and imprison them and bind them in chains, and surround them with officers, and after that they make repentance. Then the Holy One, blessed be He, answers them." (Mid. Ex. 36.1)

With this understanding, there are deep reasons for God's command to Israel to make the pure, beaten olive oil and keep it burning continually. It is His way of making Israel a light to the nations, a *ner tamid*.

Though *et* cannot be translated as a particular word or phrase, it is a very powerful word. It indicates that a certain relationship exists between the Subject and the direct or indirect object of His actions.

**Footnote**
1. Revised English by Jeremy Kapp

# GOD'S DELEGATED AUTHORITY

This discussion of *et* leads to the relationship between a particular subject and object: God and those He has created. We looked at the basis for God's authority over humanity. Since God delegates some of His authority to humanity, we should look briefly at the way in which God's authority is to be exercised.

In creating the world, God spoke, and what He spoke became physical reality. No authority was delegated. No one else could exercise or refuse to exercise that authority.

When God created humanity, He delegated a portion of His authority, saying, "Rule over the fish of the sea, and over the birds of the air, and over every living thing that creeps upon the earth." (Gen. 1:28) "And the Lord God took the man, and put him into the garden of Eden to cultivate it and to watch over it." (Gen. 2:15) In the Scriptures, authority and responsibility are intertwined. Adam had the responsibility to cultivate and watch over the Garden and to exercise God's dominion over the animals, so he was given the authority to fulfill that responsibility.

Adam's rebellion brought negative consequences for himself, his descendants, the animals and the earth. God said to Adam, "...Cursed is the ground for your sake. All the days of your life, you will eat of it in sorrow. And it will sprout thorns and thistles for you, and you will eat the plants of the field. You will eat bread by the sweat of your face, until you return to the ground; for out of it you were taken; for dust you are, and to dust you will return." (Gen. 3:17-19)

By the time of Noa<u>h</u>, those negative consequences had passed the point of no return. God said, "I will destroy from the face of the earth humanity which I created; from humanity to the domesticated animal, to the creeping thing, and to the bird of the heavens; for I am grieved that I have made them." (Gen. 6:7) "All flesh had destroyed its way on the earth." (Gen. 6:12)

Accordingly, God destroyed all flesh. Only a small remnant of people and animals were preserved on the ark. But after the flood, people continued their rejection of God's authority and their rejection of their own responsibility.

Those who had power claimed that it gave them authority. Those who had real authority failed to exercise it in accordance with God's ways. Though there have been exceptions, this has been a constant throughout human history.

### k'negdo

How then should God's delegated authority be exercised? With an understanding of God's purpose in delegating the authority. Let's look at an example.

The marriage relationship between a husband and wife is presented as part of Creation. It is the first Scriptural example of God delegating to one human being some of His authority over another human being: Havah was created to be a help to Adam. Given that, their relationship serves as a primary example of how such authority should be exercised.

Marriage is a source of great joy and great pain. It is very controversial in modern western society. And it is commonly misrepresented in traditional Biblical translations as well as in various religions and cultures. So it seems like a good example to examine.

Instead of the hypothetical case where Yohanan loves *et* Miriam, let's switch to the first couple, Adam and Havah. Initially, God created only one human, *ha'Adam*. Here is what came next, according to different translations.

"And the Lord God said, It is not good that *ha'Adam* should be alone; I will make him a help to match him." (Gen. 2:18, JPS, 1917)

"And the Lord God said, It is not good that the man should be alone; I will make a fitting helper for him." (JPS, 1985)

"And the LORD God said, 'It is not good that the man should be alone; I will make him an help meet for him.'" (KJV)

I searched through many English translations and found that they almost all translate this verse the same way. In other words, they almost all mistranslate this verse in the same way. There is no Hebrew word in the verse that means "matching," "fitting," "appropriate," or "suitable".

There is at least one English exception to the ubiquitous mistranslation. Robert Young, in Young's Literal Translation (YLT), translates the last phrase as: "I do make to him an helper — as his counterpart." This is accurate. The pivotal part is the last phrase of the verse, which describes the relationship to be established between Adam and his companion. God said, *e'eseh-lo ezer k'negdo*.

I searched through many translations in a few different languages, and found that almost all of them also mistranslate the text of this verse. Several French translations, however, present something similar to what is given in YLT. For example, Andre Chouraqui's <u>La Bible</u> renders it "*je ferai pour lui une aide contre lui*," i.e. "I will make for him a help against him."

The problem that so many translators have had with this verse concerns the last Hebrew word. In Gen. 2:18,20, the text does not say only *ezer*, which means "a help"; it says *ezer k'negdo*, which means "a help as opposite him". *Neged* is a positional word which means "opposite".

The Rabbis, in both Talmud and Midrash, comment on this odd combination. "R. Eleazar further stated: 'What is the meaning of the Scriptural text, I will make him a help meet for him? If he was worthy she is a help to him [*ezrato*]; if he was not worthy she is against him [*k'negdo*]. Others say: R. Eleazar pointed out a contradiction: 'It is written *k'negdo* but we read *k'neegdo*! — If he was worthy she is meet for him; if he was not worthy she chastises him.'" (Soncino Tal. Yebamoth 63a, cf. Mid Gen. 17:3, Rashi on Gen. 2:18)

In these passages, Chouraqui and the Rabbis understood that *neged* carries the meaning of "opposite," but their understanding seems to have been skewed by a few prominent passages in Tanakh where the word appears. The angel with a drawn sword in his hand told Balaam that Balaam's way was *neged* to him. (Num. 22:32) The angel then said, "The donkey saw me, and turned from me these three times; if it had not turned aside from me, surely now also I would have slain you, and let her live." (Num. 22:33)

That was a hostile encounter. Balaam was going the wrong

way, to do the wrong thing. If it hadn't been for the donkey, Balaam's wrong-headedness would have gotten him killed. (As it happened, his wrong-headedness did get him killed later, because he refused to change. [Num. 31:8])

Likewise, "It happened when Joshua was by Jericho, that he lifted up his eyes and looked, and, behold, a man stood opposite him [*l'negdo*] with his sword drawn in his hand. And Joshua went to him, and said to him, 'Are you for us, or for our adversaries?'

"And he said, 'No. Because I am prince of the army of the Everpresent. Now I have come.'

"And Joshua fell on his face to the earth, bowed down, and said to him, 'What does my lord say to his servant?'" (Josh. 5:13-14)

This also was a life-and-death encounter. Joshua, the leader of Israel, realized that he wasn't in charge. The Everpresent was in charge. Joshua was merely His servant.

But the Rabbis of the Talmud and the Midrash, Rashi, and almost all Jewish and Christian translators have failed to comprehend what the text says.

"What?!! They don't understand, but you do?!!"

Yes, and you can understand, too. It's not hard. (And it's not the only place where traditional translators and commentators are wrong.)

All one needs to do is look at all the places where the word *neged* appears in Tanakh. If you do that, you will find that the word does not carry the meaning of standing in hostile opposition, but rather of standing opposite in position. I'll start you out with a few examples.

Hagar sat *neged* her son Ishmael, fearing that he would die. (Gen. 21:16)

After Laban had searched through all of Jacob's possessions for his teraphim, Jacob told him to set what he had found *neged* their brethren. (Gen. 31:27)

The tribes of Israel were to camp *neged* the Tabernacle. (Num. 2:2)

Joshua led the people across the Jordan *neged* Jericho.

(Josh. 3:16)

David said, "*sh'viti adonai l'negdi tamid.*" (Ps. 16:8) "I have set the Lord *l'negdi* [before me] always."

"I will pay my vows to the Lord now *neged* [in the presence of] all His people." (Ps. 116:14,18)

In these, and in the other places in Tanakh where *neged* appears, it means opposite in position, rather than any kind of hostile opposition. This is very important for understanding the relationship which God established for Adam and Havah. God created the woman to stand opposite, and therefore see opposite, the man.

Very often, a husband and a wife think they are supposed to see things the same way. This causes much friction, because they don't actually see things the same way. By God's design, they are not supposed to. It is by combining their opposite points of view that the correct understanding can be reached. In that way, the wife is a help to her husband.

With two eyes, we have stereoscopic vision, two slightly different images which the brain combines into a composite image and then interprets. Though the human brain can make mistakes in interpretation, the two different images give it more information with which to work. Usually, we can see more clearly and accurately with two eyes than with one. We can also perceive depth better.

God designed marriage with binocular, i.e. stereoscopic, vision in mind. The design, when followed, produces a complementary relationship. Because that relationship isn't static, but must move through time and space, God built a steering mechanism into it.

That's the function of the authority that God delegated. It is a way of directing the marriage to the fulfillment of His purposes. That also applies to the authority that God gives to parents, civil government, etc. The one who exercise the authority has the responsibility of decision-making, and will therefore give account for those decisions to the One who delegated His authority.

As I write this, the Winter Olympics are taking place.

Marriage, I suppose, is somewhat like a two-person bobsled team, except that the course isn't smooth or predictable, and sometimes things happen much more quickly.

## Understanding Priorities

God made for Adam *ezer k'negdo* and brought her to him. "And Adam said, 'This time, it is bone of my bones, and flesh of my flesh. She shall be called Woman [*eeshah*], because she was taken out of Man [*eesh*].' Because of this, a man is to leave his father and his mother, and stay close to his wife; and they will be one flesh." (Gen. 2:23-25)

Neither Adam nor Havah had a father or a mother. When they were in the Garden, they didn't have children either. It wasn't then possible for them to understand what God had designed: "a man is to leave his father and his mother, and stay close to his wife". Nevertheless God was expressing the prioritization of the marriage relationship over other human relationships.

When a man gets married, his relationship with his wife becomes his most important human relationship. Though he must still honor his father and his mother, he must leave them in order to stay close to his wife. Regardless of what geographic change takes place in his life, a change in priorities takes place. His closest relationship and greatest responsibilities were to his parents; now they are to his wife. Having the authority creates the responsibilities.

And it creates a symbiotic relationship. "They will be one flesh." Each becomes dependent upon the other. Each becomes part of a living organism that is bigger than either one of them.

In God's design, if you want a strong marriage, you have to spend a lot of time working on it. You have to do a lot of reps, i.e. repetitious exercise. You have to choose to do those things that will keep the "one flesh" healthy, and choose to abstain from those things which will be harmful.

In every case where God has delegated authority, its purpose is the well-being of those subject to it.

## *ha* / the

The Hebrew *ha* is the equivalent of "the" in English. It is a definite article, indicating something specific that is, to some extent, known, rather than something general. The purpose of using a definite article is to distinguish the particular something from all other things which belong to the same category, or to distinguish it from other categories.

The heavens and the earth are both created realms, but they are distinguished one from the other. They are paired, even as light and darkness are (1:4), the water below the firmament and the water above it (1:7), the dry land and the gathering of the waters (1:10), the greater light and the lesser light (1:16), etc. The pairing indicates both a connection and a distinction.

The text does not tells us that "God created heavens and earth," speaking of two general things; rather it tells us that "God created **the** heavens and **the** earth," speaking of two specific things. This doesn't mean that God did not create any other worlds, but it does indicate that what we read will be about these specific heavens and this specific earth.

In this first verse, and in thousands of other places, "God" appears without a definite article. He does not belong in any category. "Then to whom will you liken God? Or what likeness will you compare to Him?" (Is. 40:18) This passage in Isaiah then goes on to describe how people foolishly make their own gods, instead of recognizing the One who is God.

Categories are conceptual rather than concrete. People are therefore able to categorize God, or anything in the created world, however they want to. In a very real sense, humanity's problems come from adopting false categories or from placing the things that exist into the wrong categories.

There are therefore passages in the Scriptures where *ha'elohim*, i.e. "**the** God," appears, to distinguish the One true God from the many vanities that people serve. As other people walked after their own desires and imagination, "Hanokh walked with **the** God" (Gen. 5:22,24). Noah also "walked with **the** God"

(Gen. 6:9) at a time when "the earth was corrupted before **the** God..." (Gen. 6:11)

On particular occasions, to emphasize that it is God and no other, the definite article is used in the Hebrew text. It is, however, usually left out in English translations. "Then it was that after these things **the** God tested Abraham..." (Gen. 22:1; cf. vv.3,9) It was **the** God who told Abraham to sacrifice Isaac. It was **the** God to whom Moses spoke at the burning bush. (Ex. 3:11,13)

It is interesting how the account of creation speaks of the days of the week. After morning and evening, there was "one day." It is "**one** day," not <u>the first</u> day, when there were no other days to which it was related nor to which it could be compared.

This is very different from what God said when He established the first month for Israel. At that time, just before our redemption from slavery, He said, "This is **the** month that is the beginning of months for you; it is the first month of the year for you." (Ex. 12:2) The months were already known, but not the beginning and end of their cycle. God was emphasizing that it's the month of redemption that marks the beginning.

Of the following days of the week, we are told: "a second day... a third day... a fourth day... a fifth day..." There was a sequence following a beginning, but not yet an end to the sequence, not yet a weekly cycle.

Then the text speaks of "**the** sixth day," when the end of the sequence was approaching, and "**the** seventh day" when the end of the sequence had arrived. The definite article is used only for **the** sixth day and **the** seventh day. The other days are not distinguished in this way.

After the redemption from Egypt, the importance of the seventh day was highlighted. In the wilderness, Moses told the people, "the Lord has given you **the** sabbath, therefore He gives you on **the** sixth day the bread of two days. Let every man of you abide in his place, let no man go out of his place on **the** seventh day." (Ex. 16:29)

In the Ten Commandments, Israel is commanded to observe the sabbath of **the** seventh day. The other six days are for work, **the** seventh is to be set apart, even as God rested on **the** seventh day of the world's existence. (Ex. 20:8-11) As a special covenant in itself, the observance of the sabbath rest of **the** seventh day is Israel's way of commemorating God's creation of the world. (Ex. 31:12-17)

As a definite article, *ha* has another function. It sometimes serves to indicate a question. God asked Adam, "Have you eaten of the tree...?" [**ha**'min ha'etz... achalta?]

When Ka'in says, "Am I my brother's guardian?" [**ha**'shomer a_hi_, ano_hi_?], the *ha* serves two purposes: 1) it indicates that he is asking a question; and 2) that he is not asking "Am I **a** guardian?" — i.e., one of many — but "Am I **the** guardian?" — i.e., the one who is primarily responsible.

The Hebrew definite article, though it is indicated by a single letter, can carry a lot of meaning. It refers to something specific, distinguishing it from all other things.

## *haShamayim* / THE HEAVENS

In creating the heavens, God created space and place. Before God created the heavens, there was no "where." "Where" only has meaning when there are different locations. Before Creation, there were no different locations.

God existed without location, without reference to anything else. The only "place" to be was God. One of the rabbinic names for God is *haMakom*, **the** Place. God was all there was.

There was no place else to go, nothing else to do. God had no need to go anywhere. He is.

Space is something, not nothing. It defines place. Where there is no space, there is no place. Astrophysicists tell us that the universe is expanding, and space is expanding with it. The universe is not expanding to fill empty space; there is no such thing as empty space. Space itself is something. As the universe expands, new space is created. There is no space outside, or around, the universe.

Almost all of space, in Biblical language, is the heavens. In the Scriptures, only the earth is not part of the heavens. In the next chapter, we will look at the earth and God's purposes for it, but first the heavens.

The Hebrew word *shamayim* is a plural, i.e. heavens. There is more than one heaven. Solomon spoke of "heaven and the heaven of heavens". (1Kin. 8:25) In rabbinic tradition, there are seven heavens. (cf. Tal. Hagigah 12b-13a; Tal. Menachot 39a; Tal. Pesachim 94b) Or sometimes the Rabbis spoke of a division into the lower sphere, which is visible, and the upper sphere, which is not. (cf. Tal. Rosh HaShanah 24b)

God is the Creator, and the heavens are the created. God is the One who acts, and the heavens are the object of His action. For His own reasons and purposes, God created the heavens. What are those reasons and purposes? The Scriptures tell us of at least five functions which God has assigned to the heavens.

1. **To mark divisions in Time**
2. **To testify of who God is**
3. **To signify and witness God's dealings with humanity**
4. **To give light dominion over darkness**
5. **To provide a habitation in Creation for God**

### 1. To mark divisions in time

"And God said, 'Let there be lights in the expanse of the heaven **to divide the day from the night**; and let them be **for signs**, and **for seasons**, and **for days and years**; and let them be lights in the expanse of the sky **to give light on the earth**.' And it was so." (Gen. 1:14-15)

These divisions of time take place upon the earth, but they are primarily marked, or determined, by the heavens. God existed before what we call time, and He continues to exist outside of what we call time. But He distinguishes between one moment in time and another.

The earth rotates all the way around on its axis in relationship to the sun, and a day passes. In that day, the sun and moon mark the time that belongs to the day, and the time that belongs to the night. Together, the daytime and nighttime make up one complete day. There is a purpose for the day and a purpose for the night.

A (Biblical) month is the time it takes the moon to complete its orbit around the earth. During that orbit, it goes through a full cycle of phases as the light of the sun shines upon it. There are times of great brightness, and there are times when the earth blocks some of the light from the sun to the moon. There are also times of total eclipse, when the sun, earth, and moon are in a straight line, with the moon behind the earth. The earth then blocks all sunlight from reaching the moon.

The day, the month, and the year are visible in the physical world. The week is not. In commemoration of Creation, there is the first day, the seventh day, and the five days in between. Together, the six days of Creation and Shabbat form a complete unit, a week.

This package of seven days is a concept that is not

determined by the movement of the earth, the moon, the sun, or the stars. Nor is it visible in the lives of the animals which God made. It is only visible in the nature of that one creature on the Earth who was made in the image and likeness of God.

God commanded Israel to keep and observe Shabbat (Ex. 31:12-17) to signify that He sets us apart for Himself. The nations/Gentiles are not commanded to keep and observe Shabbat, but they are invited to do so. (Is. 56) In a future time, they all will. "'For as the new heavens and the new earth which I will make will remain before Me,' says the Everpresent, 'so will your descendants and your name remain. And it will be from one new month to another, and from one Shabbat to another, all flesh will come to bow down before Me," says the Everpresent." (Is. 66:22-23) All of humanity has six days of work and one day of rest in their future.

But as for the present, the earth completes its orbit around the sun, and a year has passed. Spring, summer, autumn, and winter. Everything is a year older: a year to look back, remember, and learn; and a year to look ahead and make new choices. There is a cycle of seasons that makes a year, and a cycle of years that make a life.

We read: "And there was the life of Sarah, a hundred years and twenty years and seven years, the years of the life of Sarah." (Gen. 23:1) We don't know how she measured her own life, what she thought of it in terms of accomplishments and failures. But God says: "Listen to me, you who pursue righteousness, you who seek the Everpresent; look to the rock from where you have been cut, and to the hole of the pit from where you have been dug. Look to Abraham your father, and to Sarah who gave birth to you..." (Is. 51:1-2) God presents the life of Sarah as a model for all those after her who will pursue righteousness and seek Him.

We also don't know how Abraham measured his own life, what he thought of it in terms of accomplishments and failures. "And these were the days of the years of the life of Abraham which he lived, a hundred years and seventy years and five years." (Gen. 25:7) But we know what God thinks of Abraham,

His friend, an example of faithfulness for all who come after him.

God measures their lives according to His standard, what it is that He desires of humanity. Some day, every life will be complete; every life will be weighed in God's balances. Much of what is valued now will be worthless then; much of what counts for very little now will be of great value then.

As we get older, we sometimes wonder where the time went. But that's what time is, going from one moment to the next. Sunrise, sunset. A week, a month, a year. A childhood, raising a family, the prime of life, a time of declining abilities, and a time when we "gather in our labors from the field," and are "gathered to our fathers."

I am continually reminded of the Amish proverb, "We get too soon old, and too late smart." I have no control over the passage of time — the rotation of the earth, the orbits of the moon and the sun. Unless I die before my time, I will get old. But when will I become smart?

Moses prayed: "You have set our iniquities opposite You [*l'negdekha*], and the things we conceal in the light of Your countenance. For all our days have turned away in Your wrath. We finish our years like a sigh. There are seventy years in the days of our years, and eighty years if in strength. Yet their pride is trouble and iniquity. For it is soon cut off, and we fly away. Who knows the power of Your anger? For as the fear of You, so is Your wrath. So teach us to number our days, and a heart of wisdom will come." (Ps. 90:8-12)

God placed lights in the heavens to separate the day from the night, and to mark seasons and days and years. He gives us the opportunity to learn from what He has done. One of the things we can learn is that "There is a time for everything, and a season for every activity under heaven." (Eccl. 3:1)

Even as that is true in individual lives, so there are also times and seasons in the history of peoples and nations. And even as God gave Moses signs to perform before Pharaoh, so God uses the lights in the expanse to signify times that are coming upon the earth.

The "day of the Lord" is a time when God uses the physical elements of this world to bring judgment upon nations. He uses the heavens to signify the coming of that judgment, when nations are weighed in the balance.

The prophet Joel describes the coming day of the Lord. "The earth quakes before them; the heavens tremble; the sun and the moon are dark, and the stars withdraw their shining. ...And I will show wonders in the heavens and on the earth, blood, and fire, and pillars of smoke. The sun will be turned into darkness, and the moon into blood, before the great and the awesome day of the Lord comes." (Joel 2:11, 3:3-4H)

Am I smart enough to understand what the events in the heavens signify? Do I have a heart of wisdom to know the message that God is communicating? Following His promise of judgment on the earth, He makes a promise to Israel. "So you will know that I am the Lord your God dwelling in Zion, My holy mountain; then Yerushala'im will be holy, and no strangers will pass through her any more." (Joel 4:17H) Who will learn from the signs in the heavens?

### 2. To testify of who God is

"The heavens declare the glory of God; the expanse proclaims the work of His hands. Day after day they pour forth speech; night after night they display knowledge. There is no speech or language where their voice is not heard. Their voice goes out into all the earth, their words to the ends of the world...." (Ps. 19:1-4)

The heavens are continually speaking in a language that few take the time to understand, but everyone can. If we want to know what God has done, all we need to do is listen. If we listen, and see what God has done, then we will know some important things about Him.

When I look at the stars, and I have done so from every inhabited continent, I feel small. But, having the privilege of seeing what is so immense, so beautiful, so peaceful, I don't feel insignificant. I think I feel somewhat like David felt: "When I consider your heavens, the work of your fingers, the moon and the stars, which You have set in place, what is man that You are mindful of him, the son of man that You care for him? ...For as high as the heavens are above the earth, so great is His love for those who fear Him." (Ps. 8:3-4; Ps. 103:11)

I am in awe of what God has made, and I wonder how and why He cares for me. Because when I look at the beauty and immensity of what God has made, I know He cares for me, but I don't understand why. And at the same time, I don't understand why I have to endure the things I have to endure.

David heard a lot when he listened to the heavens. They clearly reveal the glory and majesty of God. Yet many do not want to listen, or do not think they have the time. The watchword of our relationship with God is "**Hear**, O Israel..." Listening to the voice of God comes first. If a person is unwilling to listen, the other things he or she chooses are disconnected from Life itself.

One of God's rebukes of our fathers through the prophets is that they had ears to hear but did not. (e.g. Jer. 5:21; Ezek.12:2) At Sinai, the people said, "Let me not hear again the voice of the Everpresent my God, nor see again this great fire, so I will not die." (Dt.18:16) That was a choice they made, but it had lasting consequences for their descendants.

Moses told their children before they went into the land, "And to this day, the Everpresent has not given you a heart to know and eyes to see and ears to hear." (Dt. 29:4) God told Isaiah to tell his generation, "Keep on hearing, but do not understand; keep on seeing, but do not know." (Is.6:9) What futility.

I want God to open my eyes to see, and my ears to hear. But sometimes I know that what He's going to say is not what I want to hear. His ways and His thoughts are not the same as mine. (Is. 55:8) God doesn't submit Himself to my desires or understanding. He expects me to submit myself to His desires and understanding.

I don't always like what God has to say, but I know He's always right. And I know He's always more loving and righteous than I am.

### 3. To signify and witness God's dealings with humanity

God called a Gentile named Abram to leave his homeland, his family, and his people. (Gen.12:1-3) God called him to go to a land he did not know, to become the father of a people who did not yet exist. When Abram arrived in the land, he possessed none of it, and he had no children.

And yet God had told Abram, "*lekh lekha.*" "Go for yourself." As Rashi comments, "for your own benefit and for your own good." In other words, 'For your own good, leave everything and everyone with whom you've lived and grown up, and follow Me to the unknown.'

Years later, the situation hadn't changed much. Abram had become rich, but he was still childless. He questioned God concerning this futility in light of what God had promised. God said to him, "'Look up at the heavens and count the stars — if you are able to count them.' Then He said to him, 'So will your seed be.'" (Gen. 15:5)

God hadn't yet fulfilled what He had previously promised. Now He was adding this promise as well: 'Your descendants will be as numerous as the stars of the heavens.' It was a great promise, but God hadn't yet given Abram any children at all. Abram had to choose whether to believe God or not.

Unlike the later testing of the *akedah* in which God called Abraham to sacrifice his son Isaac, there was no particular action that Abram was told to do. It was all about his heart. He could have said, "When I see it, I'll believe it." That would have been the safe way to go. To believe God for more, when He hadn't yet delivered on His previous promises, was risky. It meant being vulnerable, responding to daily disappointment by trusting God for the impossible.

"And he believed in the Everpresent Lord, and He considered it as righteousness for him." (Gen.15:6) Abram chose to believe what God had signified in the heavens, even though he couldn't see it on the Earth. The stars were to be his daily antidote to unbelief and hopelessness, even if their multitude seemed to mock the unfulfillment of God's promise.

In a similar way, the heavens testify of God's faithfulness

to Israel, the people created from Abraham, despite what may be happening upon the earth. At a time when the land of Israel was devastated by foreign armies, and almost all the people of Israel had been taken into exile, God pointed to the heavens. "'Only if the heavens above can be measured and the foundations of the earth below can be searched out will I reject all the descendants of Israel because of all they have done,' declares the Everpresent." (Jer. 31:37)

God uses the heavens to communicate His pleasure and displeasure with what people are doing. He opens the heavens, He shuts them, He sends warnings from them. He uses the heavens as a highly visible message board.

Moses told Israel what would happen in the land if their hearts turned away from the Everpresent. "Then the anger of the Everpresent will burn against you, and He will shut the heavens so that it will not rain and the ground will yield no produce, and you will soon perish from the good land the Everpresent is giving you." (Dt. 11:17)

But Moses also told them what would happen if they did listen to the voice of the Everpresent, and obey His commandments. "The Everpresent will open the heavens, the storehouse of His bounty, to send rain on your land in season and to bless all the work of your hands...." (Dt. 28:12) The heavens will be open when Israel is faithful, but closed when Israel is unfaithful.

God also speaks of the time when He will restore Israel to Himself, and pour out His Spirit. "And I will show wonders in the heavens and on the earth, blood and fire and billows of smoke. The sun will be turned to darkness and the moon to blood before the coming of the great and dreadful day of the Everpresent." (Joel 3:3-4H)

The heavens will signify the judgment of God that is coming upon all the earth. The Talmud comments on the moon, saying, "If its face is red as blood, the sword is coming to the world; if it is like sackcloth, the arrows of famine are coming to the world; if it resembles both, the sword and the arrows of famine are coming to the world." [Tal. Sukkah 29a. In the final part, the Tosephta (2:7) has "the sword, and pestilence and famine".]

As Israel is designated by God as His witnesses to the peoples of the earth, so the Heavens (and the Earth) — because they have seen the actions of generations — are designated by God as His witnesses concerning Israel. "He summons the heavens above, and the earth, that He may judge His people." (Ps. 50:4) "I call *et* the heaven and *et* the earth to witness against you that I have set before you life and death, blessing and cursing. Therefore choose life, that both you and your descendants may live." (Dt. 30:19)

Much of what the heavens have seen, and what is recorded in the Scriptures, is not good. As God said in the time of Isaiah, "Hear, O heavens! Listen, O earth! For the Everpresent has spoken: I reared children and brought them up, but they have rebelled against Me." (Is. 1:2)

Fortunately, that is not the whole story. The heavens will also see the restoration of the people of Israel to the God of Israel. "Sing for joy, O heavens, for the Everpresent has done this. Shout aloud, O earth beneath. Burst into song, you mountains, you forests and all your trees, for the Everpresent has redeemed Jacob, He displays His glory in Israel." (Is. 44:23) In that day, "Shout for joy, O heavens; rejoice, O earth; burst into song, O mountains! For the Everpresent comforts His people and will have compassion on His afflicted ones." (Is. 49:13)

### 4. To give Light dominion over Darkness

"God made two great lights —the greater light **to govern the day** and the lesser light **to govern the night**. He also made the stars. God set them in the expanse of the sky to give light on the earth, to govern the day and the night, and to separate light from darkness. And God saw that it was good." (Gen. 1:16-18)

God set the great lights for the earth: the sun and the moon, in the heavens to determine day and night upon the earth. There is a time for darkness as well as a time for light. Each has its purpose. (We'll look at that in more detail in later chapters.) But God wanted them to be separate.

Though clouds and other atmospheric conditions have their effect, when a particular part of the earth is facing the sun, i.e.

daytime, that part receives light. Light enables us to see, work, and avoid dangers. It is the source of life and energy. It shows us what is before us.

When a particular part of the earth is facing away from the sun, i.e. nighttime, the earth itself blocks direct light from the sun. Direct light can still come from the stars, and reflected light from the moon, depending upon where the moon is in its orbit around the earth. Darkness has different aspects for humans. It can bring rest, physical renewal, and protection from the sun's heat. It can also be a time of anxious waiting, a time of fearing known and unknown dangers.

In the world God created, Light is to rule, to govern, both the day and the night. Even when darkness predominates, Light is still supposed to rule on the earth, from the heavens. Darkness is to be subservient to Light. Darkness envelops light, but Light has the power to drive back Darkness.

When God led us through the wilderness between Egypt and the land He had promised to our fathers, He gave light at night as well as in the day. "And the Everpresent went before them by day in a pillar of cloud to lead the way, and by night in a pillar of fire to give them light, so as to go by day and night." (Ex. 13:21) It was still nighttime, but the darkness did not rule, and it did not prevent Israel from following the Everpresent Lord.

When we were still back in Egypt, the next to the last plague that God sent was darkness, a thick darkness which the Egyptians could feel. "They did not see one another; nor did anyone rise from his place for three days. But all the children of Israel had light in their dwellings." (Ex. 10:23)

God wanted us to learn that He is greater than any darkness. As David said, "The Everpresent is my light and my salvation; whom shall I fear? The Everpresent is the strength of my life; of whom shall I be afraid?" (Ps. 27:1) There is a time for darkness, but Light is still to have dominion.

David knew that wherever he was, God was there too, even when David, like Adam, wanted to hide. "Where can I go from Your Spirit? Where can I flee from Your presence? If I go up to the heavens, You are there; if I make my bed in the depths, You are there. If I rise on the wings of the dawn, if I settle on the far side of the sea, even there Your hand will guide me, Your right hand will hold me fast. If I say, 'Surely the darkness will hide me and the light become night around me,' even the darkness will not be dark to You; the night will shine like the day, for darkness is as light to You." (Ps. 139:7-12)

The heavens are over the earth, and light comes from the heavens to the earth. So Light is supposed to rule upon the earth, whether in the day or in the night.

### 5. To provide a place in Creation for God

"He who builds his lofty palace in the heavens and sets its foundation on the earth, who calls for the waters of the sea and pours them out over the face of the land — the Everpresent is His Name." (Amos 9:6)

God did not make the universe as one makes a clock, start it up, and then leave it on its own. He is very interested in and very involved in what takes place upon it. Though He still exists eternally outside of Creation, He has taken up residence within it — a second home if you will — in the heavens.

"The heavens of heavens belong to the Everpresent, but He has given the earth to the children of Adam." (Ps. 115:16) God did not transfer ownership of the earth to humanity, He simply entrusted to us the privilege of living on it, and the responsibility of caring for it. "To the Everpresent your God belong the heavens, and the heavens of heavens, the earth and everything in it." (Dt. 10:14)

Humanity lives on the limited earth; God lives in the much more spacious heavens. Humanity's vision of themselves and their surrounding is limited and obstructed by natural features; God sees humanity exactly as we are. "Do not be rash with your mouth, and do not let your heart utter anything hastily before God, because God is in heaven, and you are on earth. Therefore let your words be few." (Eccl. 5:1H)

The earth is almost infinitesimally small compared to the heavens. That is meant to tell us something about our own strength and wisdom. We and the great things we do are minuscule to God. We and our devices control very little, "But our God is in heaven; He does whatever He pleases." (Ps. 115:3)

If we question or even challenge the way God runs the universe, it does not make Him nervous. But for our own sake, we need to be willing to listen to His responses; we need to understand that we are the ones who lack understanding. The more wisdom we have, the humbler we will be. Looking at the heavens should remind us of the infinite distance between who and where we are and who God is.

And yet, God walked in the Garden with Adam and Havah. He appeared to Moses in a bush. And He told Israel to build Him a very small, movable home in the wilderness, the Mishkan, i.e. the place of His dwelling.

When Solomon built the Temple, he was aware of both the inestimable greatness and the patent absurdity of what he had done. He prayed and asked, "But will God really live on earth with humanity? The heavens, even the heavens of heavens, cannot contain You. How much less this house I have built!" (2Chr. 6:18)

God answered him very clearly. "When Solomon had finished praying, then the fire came down from the heavens and consumed the burnt offering and the sacrifices; and the glory of the Everpresent filled the house." (2Chr. 7:1) The glorious presence of the infinite God filled the little building, and then remained there in a small room, where the High Priest would come, once a year.

God lives in the infinite heavens, but He also came down to live in accordance with the very small stature of humanity. He is not far off; He is very near. "...'Do I not fill *et* the heaven and *et* the earth?" says the Everpresent." (Jer. 23:24) There is no place too small for God to live, except for some human hearts.

### Inhabitants of the Heavens

There are two other things worth noting about the heavens. The first is that there are inhabitants other than God in the heavens. "You alone are He, the Everpresent. You made the heavens, the heaven of heavens, and all their forces, the earth and all that is on it, the seas and all that is in them. You give life to everything, and the forces of heaven bow down to You." (Neh. 9:6) "Praise him, all His angels, praise him, all His forces." (Ps. 148:2)

Heaven is the domain of the angels, but the Scriptures portray numerous instances when they appear to people on the earth. Abraham was visited by angels who ate and drank with him, and then went on to deliver Lot from Sodom. (Gen.18-19) The Scriptures record many instances when people — Jacob, Joshua, Daniel, Isaiah, Ezekiel, Bala'am and others — encounter beings from heaven.

Just as there are those in heaven who worship and serve God, there are also those who do not. The troubles of Job began when "Then there was the day when the sons of God came to present themselves before the Everpresent, and the Adversary also came with them. And the Everpresent said to the Adversary, 'Where are you coming from?' Then the Adversary answered the Everpresent and said, 'From going to and fro on the earth, and from walking back on it.'" (Job 1:6-7)

Judging from what he did to Job, we can say that the Adversary had been on the earth seeking to destroy. Though Job was faithful to God, God permitted the Adversary to destroy everything and everyone he had, and to afflict him physically. But God would not let the Adversary kill Job.

The Scriptures tell us that God sometimes lets ungodly people afflict the godly, but He promises to right the accounts. Likewise, God promises to judge those heavenly beings who do evil. "In that day the Everpresent will punish in the heavens the powers in the heavens and the kings of the earth on the earth." (Is. 24:21) To the Adversary, He says, "Your heart was lifted up because of your beauty, and you corrupted your wisdom because of your splendor. So I threw you to the earth; I made a spectacle of you before kings." (Ezek. 28:17)

The creatures of heaven sometimes come to earth, and interact with human beings. People do not usually see them, but they can become visible. They sometimes appear in physical form and converse with people.

## New Heavens

The second additional thing we should know is that the present heavens will be destroyed and replaced with new heavens. "Know that I will create new heavens and a new earth. The former things will not be remembered, nor will they come to mind." (Is. 65:17)

Even as humanity has made the earth unclean by their choices, so also some of the inhabitants of heaven have made the heavens unclean. They can be cast out of heaven, but that does not remove the uncleanness of what they have done.

"How you are fallen from heaven, O Shining One, son of the morning! how you are cut down to the ground, you who ruled the nations! For you have said in your heart, I will ascend to heaven, I will exalt my throne above the stars of God; I will sit also upon the mount of assembly, in the farthest north. I will ascend above the heights of the clouds; I will be like the most High.'" (Is. 14:12-14)

This evil heavenly being was thrown down to the earth. The two realms are not totally separate. To some degree, they are connected, and those in the heavens can exist upon the earth.

In one of the visions given to Daniel, a mighty ruler "became great up to the powers of the heavens, and some of the powers and the stars fell down to the earth. And it trampled them." (Dan. 8:10)

Eliphaz, in wisdom without compassion, said to Job: "What is man, that he could be pure? and one born of a woman, that he could be righteous? See that God does not trust in His holy ones, and the heavens are not pure in His sight. What then of man, abhorred and corrupted, who drinks iniquity like water!" (Job 15:14-16)

The heavens are part of the created world. They are no more eternal than the earth. "All the forces of the heavens will be dissolved and the sky rolled up like a scroll; all their forces will fall like withered leaves from the vine, like shriveled figs from the fig tree." (Is. 34:4)

# THE FIRST VERSE

"Lift up your eyes to the heavens, and look at the earth beneath; because the heavens will vanish like smoke, and the earth will become old like a garment, and those who dwell in it will die in like manner; but My salvation will be forever, and My righteousness will not be abolished." (Is. 51:6) God's salvation is connected to His righteousness, not to the heavens. There will be righteous judgment for all of Creation, but there will also be salvation.

In the midst of the promise to destroy, God also promises to renew. "'As the new heavens and the new earth that I make will endure before Me,' declares the Everpresent, 'so will your name and descendants endure.'" (Is. 66:22) Heaven and earth will be destroyed, but made new. And in that newness is the confirmation of God's everlasting promise to renew and restore Israel. He has joined Himself to His people forever.

# *v'* / And, But, Or

"God created the heavens '**and**' [*v*] the earth.

The Hebrew letter *vav* functions as a conjunction, joining items or phrases together. It is, by far, the most common word in the Bible, appearing more than 50,000 times. In the first three verses of the Bible, it is used seven times. In the 31 verses of the first chapter, it is used 99 times. It is a small but important word.

Depending upon the context, it is translated into English as "and," "but," "or," "then," or some other conjunctive word. It indicates a relationship between two or more things which are differentiated from each other; it indicates that they are to be considered together. It may be that the two or more things are connected, or that they stand in opposition to one another, or that they exist as alternatives, or have some relationship that requires understanding both together.

Some people apparently believe that the whole of something is equal to the sum of its parts, nothing more. The error of that belief is that it disregards relationship, the way in which two or more things are joined together. The relationship does not exist when the parts are isolated; it only exists when the two or more things are connected together.

There is a difference between one thing in isolation and that same thing in relationship. Consider Adam, then consider Adam and the *adamah*/earth from which he was made. Now consider Adam and God, Adam and Havah, Adam and Ka'in, Adam and all Adamkind, i.e. humanity. Each connection brings with it a multitude of associations and issues. The nature of a relationship necessarily enters into what is communicated when two things are joined together.

Or think of the difference between a single note and a series of notes that are sequentially connected. A single note can be beautiful, but the joining of notes together creates something that none of the notes is by itself. Likewise, think of the difference between that single note or series of notes being played on one instrument and the same note or series of notes being played on different instruments at the same time, or at different times in the same piece. Or by a particular musician or group of musicians. The whole is something much more than simply the sum of the parts.

The same is true of words. Joining them together produces meaning that none of the individual words contains alone. The proper translation of a word or a phrase is necessarily dependent upon the context in which it appears, i.e. the words around it.

It is also dependent upon how the translator understands the word or phrase in its context. A translator must try to retain the meaning of the words in their original context while bringing them into a different linguistic and cultural context.

When we read that God created "the heavens **and** the earth," there is an evident syntactical relationship between "the heavens" and "the earth". They are both objects created by the same Being. They share some things in common, but they are distinguished by the differences that attend the different purposes for which they were ceated.

Many translators don't understand the importance of the *vav*, and so they often leave it out when it appears at the beginning of a sentence. They don't understand that the sentence itself is connected to something which preceded it.

Disconnecting anything that follows from its origin in God's purpose will lead to a skewed understanding. What we read in Deuteronomy or Psalms or Hosea cannot be separated from "In the beginning, God..." We might not understand the connection that God makes between one thing and another, but the vav is powerful in that it holds all things together.

The thing that follows is to be understood in relation to the thing that preceded it. In this sense, the whole Bible is one long run-on sentence. It all flows from the beginning; it flows from God. Whatever comes after that must be understood in terms of that origin. There actually is neither punctuation nor paragraphing in the Scriptures, no marks to divide any of the text. It is all connected.

# *ha'Aretz* / THE EARTH

The Scriptures give at least four functions for which God designed the earth.

**1. To be the Great Stage for the Drama of human existence**

**2. To be a legal witness to the actions of humanity**

**3. To provide a contrast to the eternal**

**4. To provide a place for humanity to encounter God**

**1. To be the Great Stage for the Drama of human existence**

"The earth and what fills it, the world and those who inhabit it: it all belongs to the Lord, because He laid its foundation upon the seas and established it upon the rivers." (Ps. 24:1-2) The earth belongs to God because He created it (out of nothing) and gave it form. If anyone can own anything — if there is any basis for ownership — then certainly God owns everything.

And of all that God owns, He created the earth to be that stage on which all of human history (except for an occasional trip into orbit or beyond) has been, and will be, played out. "The heavens are the heavens of the Everpresent Lord, but the earth He has given to the children of Adam." (Ps. 115:16)

It's a very elaborate stage, with mountains and valleys, forests and fields, deserts and glaciers, rivers, lakes, seas, and oceans. And overhead are the sun, the moon, and the stars. God is a Stage Designer beyond compare, with an unlimited budget.

He is a Dramatist with a purpose. He expressed that purpose in the beginning. "Let us make Adam in Our image, in accordance with Our likeness, and let them rule over the fish of the sea and the birds of the air, over the livestock, over all the earth, and over all the creatures that move along the ground." (Gen. 1:26)

Since that beginning, everything has gone wrong, terribly wrong. Humanity as a whole is rushing away from God, determined to define itself however it chooses, determined to define itself in opposition to God.

God grieves, but He will not be mocked, even though life on the earth will become more and more degenerate. "R. Levi said: 'The son of David will not come except in a generation which is brutal and deserves to be destroyed.' R. Yannai said: 'If you see generation after generation cursing and blaspheming, be watching for the feet of King Messiah, as it is written (Ps. 89:52), *which Your enemies have mocked, O Lord, which Your enemies have mocked the footsteps of Your Messiah*, and immediately afterwards it is written, *Blessed be the Lord forever, Amen and Amen.*'" (Mid. Song of Songs 2.33)

It will be hopeless. "When the foundations are destroyed, what can the righteous do?" (Ps. 11:3) Yet God will deliver those who hope in Him. He has established a foundation for His Kingdom. "Righteousness and justice are the fixed foundation of Your throne; lovingkindness and truth go before You." (Ps. 89:15H)

With many twists, turns, and trials along the way, from beginning to end, the excruciating drama is proceeding towards its climax.

### 2. To be a legal witness to the actions of humanity

As Abraham said, God is the judge of all the earth. (Gen. 18:25) God sees all, knows all, and judges all. But a judge listens as witnesses relate what they have seen, heard, and experienced.

God established a principle in Torah that there must be at least two witnesses for crimes deserving the death penalty. "There is not to be one witness against a person concerning any iniquity or any sin which one sins. A matter will be established by the mouth of two witnesses or three witnesses." (Dt. 19:15, cf. Dt. 17:16, Num. 35:30) Since God will be deciding the guilt or innocence of every individual for crimes that He considers to be deserving the death penalty, there will be witnesses.

Throughout the Scriptures, inanimate objects are called to be witnesses of human actions. Jacob and Laban piled up a mound of stones to be a witness between them. (Gen. 31:48,52) The two and a half tribes settling on the east side of the Yarden River built a replica altar to be a witness to their connection to the rest of the people of Israel. (Josh. 22)

Before his death, Moses told the people, "..this book of the Law will be a witness against you." (Dt. 31:26) What was written in it, its commandments and admonitions, would remain and would testify on the day of judgment. God told Moses to teach the people a song, saying, "...this song will be My witness against the descendants of Israel." (Dt. 31:19)

Joshua called the people to decide whether or not they would serve the Everpresent Lord. The people said they would, and Joshua told them that they were therefore witnesses against themselves. (Josh. 24:22) Then Joshua set up a large stone. "And Joshua said to all the people, 'See that this stone will be a witness for us because it has heard all the words of the Everpresent Lord which He spoke to us and will be a witness of them so that you do not not deny your God." (Josh. 24:27)

Ka'in killed his brother in secret, and Hevel's blood sunk into the earth. God said that from within the earth that blood cried out against Ka'in. (Gen. 4:10) This may be more than a metaphor, for the earth actually contained physical evidence of what Ka'in had done. Sensitive chemical and DNA analysis of the soil would show that it contained the blood of Hevel.

The earth also witnessed the sight and sound of what took place. When sound waves encounter an object, some waves are reflected, some are absorbed. The waves that are absorbed contain the sound of what took place. With special equipment, we can record sound in a compound of iron and oxygen on magnetic tape. The iron oxide compound doesn't make any sound, it simply preserves the original sound. One only needs to be able to play back what was recorded. If the tape is kept in good condition, the sound can be played back years later.

The same is true of light. When light encounters an object, some is reflected, and some is absorbed. The light that is absorbed contains the images of what took place. The earth absorbs light and sound from every event that takes place upon it. With special equipment, we can record and preserve visual images in silver compound on film. Years later, one only needs to be able to play back what was recorded in order to see the images of what originally place.

A CD, or dvd, is made of polycarbonate plastic thinly coated with aluminum or gold. With special equipment, e.g. a computer, we can preserve sound and images on a CD. If you hold the CD next to your ear, you won't hear the preserved sounds; if you look at it, you won't see the preserved images. But if you have the right equipment, shining laser light on the CD will make the sound audible and the images visible. What is heard and seen is a faithful record of the original event.

Sound that is reflected continues to travel in a straight line. As long as the sound continues to travel, it can still be heard at another place along that line at a later time, by anything sensitive to that frequency and intensity. An echo is sound that has bounced off an object back towards the original source of the sound. That reflected sound continues to travel in a straight line past the original source. A mile farther on, 5 seconds later, someone with sensitive ears will hear the sound. Because it takes time for sound to travel, whenever we hear something, we hear it after it has happened.

Because light travels faster than sound, we see an event sooner than we hear it. We see lightning before we hear the thunder that accompanies it. Knowing the speed of sound, we can calculate how far off the lightning was by the length of time it takes for the sound to reach us.

What a person sees and hears is somehow recorded in the living tissue of his or her brain. Somehow the brain is able to play back what was recorded, making those original images visible, and those original sounds audible. All kinds of data can be recorded in the brain and played back — a language, a concerto, an equation, or a philosophical proposition — and it's portable. Some brains, of course, do this better than others.

When we see something, we always see it after it has happened. Light travels amazingly fast at 186,000 miles per second, but it still takes time to travel. It takes a little more than

8 minutes for light to travel from the sun to the earth. When we see the sun, we are seeing it as it was 8 minutes earlier.

It takes about 80 minutes for light from the sun to reach Saturn. If we were on Saturn, we would see the sun as it had been 80 minutes earlier. When we see stars in the night sky, we are seeing them as they were years before. We are always and only seeing and hearing what has already taken place in the past.

In that one respect, we are all living in the past. We react in the present to events that are past. Only if perception takes place at the exact location, and therefore at the exact time, at which an event occurs, can it be said that one is fully living in the present. [And likewise, only then is One not subject to any quantum effects.] Perhaps this is another reason why God, Who is everywhere at all times, tells Moses that He is "I Am".

"But maybe a man will say, 'Who will witness against me?' The stones of the house of the man and the walls of the house of the man will witness against him. As it is said, 'A stone from a wall will cry out and a beam from a tree will answer.' [Hab. 2:11]" (Tal. Ta'anit 11a, cf. Tal. Chagigah 16a)

The sights and sounds of every event are contained in absorbed and reflected light and in absorbed and reflected sound waves. So it may be, when that final legal proceeding takes place, when the earth and the heavens are both called as witnesses, that there will be a preserved record of everything that was said and done. "I set the heavens and the earth to be witnesses against you..." (Dt. 4:26, 30:19,31:28)

It is worth noting that the word *aretz*, which is translated as "earth" in the first verse of the Bible, often signifies a land or country. In particular, it often signifies the land of Israel.

God told Abram to go to *"ha'aretz* which I will show you." (Gen. 12:1) God told Moses to tell the people of Israel, "I will bring you in to *ha'aretz* which I swore to give to Abraham, to Isaac, and to Jacob; and I will give it to you for a heritage; I am the Lord." (Ex. 6:8) God told Joshua to lead the people to *"ha'aretz* which I give to them, to the descendants of Israel." (Josh. 1:2)

There are some passages in which it is not clear which meaning is intended. There are some passages in which it seems clear that God is dealing with *ha'aretz* Israel as He intends to do with the whole earth [*ha'aretz*]. The people and the land of Israel will also be called as witnesses.

### 3. To provide a contrast to the eternal
As we live our lives on the earth, we naturally focus our attention and our desires on what our senses bring to us. But all that is on the earth, the good and the bad, the beautiful and the ugly, the pleasure and the pain, all of it will, with the passage of time, pass away and be no more. In the simple, but straightforward words of Isaiah the prophet: "The grass withers, the flower fades, but the word of our God will stand forever." (Is. 40:8)

Every human life will come to an end; its time will run out. What will be accomplished? What will be left? The lives of some people are consumed in their pleasure, pain, or work, and they never stop to consider what the purpose of their lives is. "There is one without a second — he has neither son nor brother — but there is no end to all his laboring. Yet his eye is not satisfied with riches. 'And for whom am I laboring and depriving my soul of good?' This also is vanity, and it is an evil occupation." (Eccl. 4:8)

From the beginning, God gave humanity work to do upon the earth. (Gen. 1:28) But God is not operating a work farm or a factory. He is looking for humanity to embrace its identity in the image and likeness of God. He is looking for humanity to embrace Him.

The heavens are beautiful, and the earth is amazing, but they are merely realms that God created, realms that will disappear. God is more magnificent than all that He has created. "Before everything, You laid the foundations of the earth, and the heavens are the work of Your hands. They will perish, but You remain; they will all wear out like a garment. Like clothing You will change them and they will be discarded. But You are He, and Your years will never end." (Ps. 102:26-28H)

The heavens and the earth will come to an end, but God IS forever and ever. God is life, and to find Him is to find life. "Lift up your eyes to the heavens, look at the earth beneath; the heavens will vanish like smoke, the earth will wear out like a garment and its inhabitants die like flies. But My salvation will last forever, My righteousness will never fail." (Is. 51:6)

No matter how disgusting or painful something or someone is, there is an end. No matter how attractive something or someone is, death and decay are waiting. The earth and everything and everyone on it belong to the Lord (Ps. 24:1), but it will all be destroyed. There is, however, something that God calls "My salvation" which will last forever. Whatever that salvation is, God makes it available to humanity.

### 4. To provide a place for humanity to encounter God

From the earth, we can look and see that "The heavens declare the glory of God, and the firmament tells of His handiwork." (Ps. 19:1) In different places around the world, I have seen a clear night sky filled with awe-inducing stars; a sky that has humbled and quieted me with its magnitude and magnificence.

And the earth itself is filled with wonders. With the wisdom that God had given him, Solomon "spoke three thousand proverbs, and his songs were one thousand and five. And he spoke about the trees, from the cedar which is in Lebanon even to the hyssop that comes out of the wall; he spoke about animals, and about birds, and about the creeping things, and about fish. And from all the peoples, they came to hear the wisdom of Solomon, from all the kings of the earth who had heard his wisdom." (1Kings 5:12-14H/4:32-34)

We cut up trees and build with them, or burn them to stay warm in the winter. But a tree is amazing in itself. The chlorophyll in its leaves or needles takes energy from sunlight and uses it to produce the chemical energy that sustains the tree and, through the food chain, so much else.

I drink cold juice on a hot day and feel refreshed. What takes place at a subatomic level is incomprehensible. What and where is the consciousness and the thought that triggers the purposeful muscle movement? How is the chemical interaction of whirring particles and force fields transformed into a relaxed smile that communicates emotion? Where, at a molecular level, is satisfaction?

Existence is filled with fantastic mysteries. Everything on the earth, from the smallest to the largest, bears the intriguing imprint of its Maker and His purposes. Everything on the earth can teach us something about God; everything on the earth can draw us closer to God.

But God draws us to Himself so that we can actually encounter Him. He walked in the Garden to seek out Adam and Havah. When He asked the first question in the Bible — "Adam, where are you?" — it was not because He did not know where Adam was. It was because He wanted Adam to face up to where he was. Having turned away from God, Adam was being given the opportunity to turn back to Him.

The Bible, taken at face value, exists because God spoke to people and what He said was recorded. He spoke to Adam, and He spoke to Ka'in. He spoke to Noah, and He spoke to Abraham. He spoke to Moses. God spoke to the judges, the prophets; He spoke to priests, and kings. At Sinai, He spoke to all the people of Israel. God wants people to hear His voice. That's why He commanded Israel to "Hear..."

Moses heard the Lord, and he also saw the Lord. According to the Scriptures, he was not the only one who did. In the next three chapters, we look at the patriarchs and others who encountered God upon the earth in this way. Then, in the following chapters, we will look at some of the other ways in which God enabled people to encounter Him.

# THE PATRIARCHS SAW GOD

The Scriptures tell us that God appeared to Abraham, to Isaac, and to Jacob. The various passages don't give much detail about how God appeared to them, but they make it clear that He did. It seems that God appears when He wants to emphasize what He has to say. Certainly that is the impact it has.

Humans retain a certain amount of what they see, and a certain amount of what they hear. They retain more if they both see and hear. God's appearance makes the experience and the message hard to forget.

"Great is the power of the prophets, inasmuch as they compare the likeness of the Almighty on high to the form of Adam." (Mid. Num. 19:4, cf. Mid. Gen. 27:1, Mid. Kohelet 2.26, 8.1) The Midrash, however, misses the point here. The "form of man" was made in "the likeness of the Almighty on high," not vice versa. The prophets, the patriarchs, and others were seeing the original, from which the likeness was made.

God called **Abraham** to leave his country, his people and his father's house. "And the Everpresent Lord said to Abram, 'Get out from your country, and from your family, and from your father's house, to a land that I will show you.'" (Gen. 12:1) God led Abraham to the land of Canaan.

"Then the Everpresent Lord appeared [*vayera*] to Abram and said, 'I will give this land to your offspring.' So he built an altar there to the Everpresent Lord, who had appeared [*ha'nireh*] to him." (Gen.12:7) This was the beginning of an ongoing relationship.

God created everything that we see, and He created the ability to see. Sometimes, He enables a person to see Him. God made himself visible to Abraham, the father of the Jewish people, to accentuate His setting apart the land of Canaan for the people who would come from Abraham. We are not told in what form God appeared to Abraham, but only that He spoke to him and appeared to him.

This incident is not presented as something that only took place in Abram's mind. (Though in actuality, all 'normal' vision takes place in the mind in response to physical stimuli.) The incident is presented as a physical event. In some way, at a particular point in time, God made Himself visible to Abraham. Abraham heard God and saw God.

And this was not the only time. God made a covenant with Abraham to give him and his offspring all the land of Canaan. (Gen. 15:16) In God's plan and purpose, the land was very important, and His appearing to Abraham emphasized that.

He appeared again to Abraham, when He confirmed the covenant by the sign of circumcision. "Then when Abram was 99 years old the Everpresent Lord appeared [vayera] to Abram and said, 'I am God Almighty; walk before Me and be blameless. I will confirm My covenant between Me and you and will greatly increase your numbers.... And I give to you and your offspring after you the land of your sojournings, all the land of Canaan to possess forever; and I will be their God.'" (Gen.17:1-2,8)

"When Abram was 99 years old" — The text tells us that God appeared to a particular person at a particular time, at a particular point in his life. God appeared to him upon the earth, at a particular place, for two reasons.

1) God established the covenant of circumcision, indicating the setting apart of Abraham and the covenant people who would come from him. Circumcision indicates that all that we are physically must be submitted to God.

"Great is circumcision, for there is none among you who is as occupied with the commandments as Abraham, our father; yet he was not called whole except on account of circumcision. As it says (Gen. 17), 'Walk before Me and be whole'. And it is written, 'And I will give My covenant between Me and you.'" (Tal. Nedarim 32a)

2) God wanted Abraham to know that with Him, nothing is impossible. Sarah was past menopause, but God would cause her to conceive and give birth to Isaac. When He appeared to Abraham, God, in His purposes, had already chosen Isaac to inherit the calling, the covenant, the land, and the promises.

At that time, Abraham had a son, Ishmael. Abraham pleaded with God to accept Ishmael, instead of a nonexistent "Isaac" who was supposed to be born some day to Sarah, who was physically no longer able to conceive. God rejected Abraham's plea, saying, "'Nevertheless, I will establish My covenant with Isaac, whom Sarah will bear to you by this time next year.' When He had finished speaking with Abraham, God went up from him." (Gen. 17:21-22)

"God went up from him" — The text tells us that God had been with Abraham in a certain location upon the earth. Then He ascended to heaven. A little later in this study, we'll look at other passages in Tanakh where the text tells us that "God came down".

God appeared to Abraham a third time as one of three men. Abraham received the three visitors hospitably, bringing them water so they could be refreshed in the shade of a tree, and providing them with an abundant meal. (Gen.18:1-8)

After they ate and were refreshed, two of the men went towards Sodom, where we find out that they were angels. (Gen. 18:22; 19:1). The Midrash says, "When the Shekhinah [the abiding, visible presence of God] was over them, they are called 'men' [Gen. 18:2]; but when the Shekhinah departed from over them they appeared as angels. [Gen. 19:1]" (Mid. Genesis 50.2)

Rashi says, "He [God] brought the angels to him [Abraham] in the form of men." (Gen. 18:1) Perhaps angels have a different form, or no form at all, when they are in the presence of God. But when they appear to humanity, they have a form which is like the form of men.

God appeared to Abraham this third time to tell him of the imminent fulfillment of the promise of the miraculous birth of Isaac; and God appeared to him to tell him of the imminent destruction that would be coming upon Sodom. (Gen. 18:20-21) God tested Abraham so that Abraham could show his character.

"And the men turned their faces from there, and went toward Sodom; but Abraham still stood before the Lord." (Gen. 18:22, cf. 19:1) The third man did not go to Sodom, but remained with

Abraham. We are told that this One was the Everpresent Lord Himself. "'And he [Abraham] lifted up his eyes and looked... (Gen. 18:2) He saw the Shekhinah and he saw the angels." (Mid. Genesis 48.9)

"And Abraham drew near and said, 'Will you also destroy the righteous with the wicked?'" (Gen. 18:22-23, cf. 19:1) Here is the sequence that is described: the Lord was in a particular place and Abraham stood before Him. Then Abraham came closer to the place where the Lord was, to speak to Him. Closer to God, Abraham interceded with Him to spare the city.

When their conversation ended, "Then the Everpresent Lord went His way, as soon as He had finished talking with Abraham; and Abraham returned to his place." (Gen. 18:33) God left the place where He was, the place where Abraham could see Him and speak with Him. Then Abraham left that particular place also. From that meeting on the earth, Abraham went his way, and God went His.

### The Lord Appeared to Isaac and also to Jacob

It was not only to Abraham that God appeared. The Scriptures tell us of two occasions when God appeared to **Isaac**. The first time He appeared was to declare that the promise of the land to Abraham was confirmed to Isaac and his descendants.

Because of a famine in the land, Isaac had gone to live in Gerar. "And the Everpresent Lord appeared to him and said, 'Do not go down to Egypt; live in the land which I tell you. Sojourn in this land, and I will be with you and I will bless you. For to you and to your descendants I will give all these lands and will confirm the oath I swore to Abraham your father. I will make your descendants as numerous as the stars of the heavens, and will give to your descendants all these lands. And all nations of the earth will be blessed through your descendants, because Abraham listened to My voice, and kept My requirements, My commandments, My statutes and My laws." (Gen. 26:2-5)

God appeared to Isaac to affirm that all that was promised to Abraham was promised to Isaac as well. And it was promised because Abraham was faithful to listen to God's voice and obey. Before Israel received the Law at Mt. Sinai, before Israel existed, Abraham had kept God's commandments, statutes, and laws. (That is a full topic for another time.)

When the famine abated and Isaac was able to move to Beersheva, that very night, the Everpresent Lord appeared to him and said, "I am the God of your father Abraham. Do not be afraid, for I am with you. I will bless you and will increase the number of your descendants for the sake of My servant Abraham." (Gen. 26:24)

And in the place where God appeared to him, Isaac "built an altar there, and called on the Name of the Everpresent Lord. And he stretched out his tent there, and the servants of Isaac dug a well there." (Gen. 26:25) Isaac saw God on the earth in a particular place in the land of Canaan, and then built an altar in that place. His servants dug a well in that same place. Isaac lived in the land where God appeared to him.

God appeared to **Jacob** on at least three occasions. The first time was when he was fleeing from his brother Esau, who planned to kill him. Jacob lay down to sleep at night in a desolate place. "And he had a dream in which a ladder stood on the earth, and its top reached to the heavens. And there were angels of God ascending and descending upon it.

"There above it stood the Lord, and He said: 'I am the Lord, the God of Abraham your father and the God of Isaac. I will give to you and to your descendants the land on which you are lying. And your descendants will be as the dust of the earth, and you will spread abroad to the west, and to the east, and to the north, and to the south. And in you and in your descendants, all the families of the earth will be blessed. And know that I am with you, and will keep you in all places where you go, and will bring you back to this land; for I will not leave you, until I have done what I have spoken to you.'" (Gen. 28:12-15)

God appeared in order to assure Jacob of his safety, his future, and his inheritance of all that God had promised to Abraham and Isaac. And He showed Jacob angels ascending and descending close to him. (cf. 2Kings 6:17)

The Scriptures don't tell us a lot about angels, but from what we are told, it doesn't seem likely that they would need a ladder or staircase to go from heaven to earth or from earth to heaven. But in the dream, God showed Jacob a ladder, or stairway, something that connects heaven and earth. God showed Jacob that there is a way to ascend or descend from one realm to the other.

The rabbis note that some of the angels were ascending, and take that to mean that those angels had been with Jacob up until that time, protecting him while he was in the land. And now God was sending other angels to take their place as he journeyed outside the land. (cf. Mid. Gen. 68.12) Long before Jacob saw the Everpresent Lord, long before Jacob knew Him, He was watching over him. God was protecting him, and blessing him.

Jacob saw God "standing". That means that God appeared to Jacob in a particular posture, in a recognizable living form. Others, like Isaiah and Daniel, saw God sitting. (e.g. Is. 6:1, Dan. 7:9)

The second time God appeared to Jacob was years later, when Jacob was returning to the land with his large family. He left Laban, "and Jacob went on his way, and the angels of God met him." (Gen. 32:1) He had seen the angels when he left the land, and now he saw them again as he was returning.

Jacob knew that Esau, who had planned to kill him, was coming towards him with four hundred men. Jacob was afraid, so he sent messengers with lavish gifts to his brother. He organized his family, servants, and flocks, and then crossed over a brook to spend the night alone.

"And a man wrestled with him until the coming of the dawn." (Gen. 32:25H) Jacob held onto "the man," and demanded a blessing. "And he [the man] said, 'Your name will no longer be called Jacob, but Israel ["a prince with God"]; for as a prince you have power with God and with men, and have prevailed." (Gen. 32:29)

When the man let him go, Jacob "called the place *Peniel* [face of God], saying, 'It is because I saw God face to face, but my soul has been delivered.'" (Gen. 32:31H) Perhaps the "man" was an angel, maybe even the Angel of the Lord, but what Jacob said is, "I saw God face to face." God had appeared to him before, and Jacob believed that God had appeared to him again.

The Scriptures record that God appeared to Jacob a third time as he journeyed to Bethel and beyond. "God appeared to him again and blessed him. God said to him, 'Your name is Jacob, but you will no longer be called Jacob. Your name will be Israel.' So He named him Israel. And God said to him, 'I am God Almighty; be fruitful and increase in number. A nation and a community of nations will come from you, and kings will go forth from your body. The land which I gave to Abraham and Isaac I will give it to you, and I will give this land to your offspring after you.' Then God went up from him at the place where he had spoken to him." (Gen. 35:9-13)

God appeared to Jacob to affirm that Jacob would be known as Israel, a prince with God. God again confirmed that the land and the promises spoken to Abraham and Isaac were to be carried out through Jacob. He spoke to Jacob in a particular place, and when God finished speaking to him, He ascended from that place.

The Scriptures tell us that the Everpresent Lord appeared to Abraham, Isaac, and Jacob in a specific, visible form. He appeared to them at specific geographical locations. He appeared for specific purposes: to promise, affirm, and confirm His plans for them.

Almost every time that God appeared to the patriarchs, it is somehow connected to the physical land of Canaan, soon to be called "Israel". It is the one land on the face of the earth that God had promised to give to them and to their offspring forever. It is the land where God promised to live in the midst of His people.

# MOSES SAW GOD

We naturally see only a small range of the spectrum of what could be seen. There are infrared and ultraviolet frequencies that we cannot see. If we could see them, we could watch the microwaves that cook our food. We could watch the radio waves that fill the air. We could watch the frequencies entering and leaving our cell phones or routers. But if we saw the whole range of electromagnetic frequencies, there would be no night.

Our eyes are also limited in terms of the intensity of light they can safely endure. If we stare at the sun, we can damage or destroy our retinas. That will happen even when the sun is 99% eclipsed. To safely watch an eclipse, we can look away from the sun to a shadow image of what is taking place.

And God is a brighter, more intense light than any star which He has made. (e.g. Is. 60:19) We are not naturally well equipped to see Him. Nevertheless, the Scriptures tell us that there are several occasions when Moses saw God.

The first time Moses encountered God, he didn't see Him; he looked away so that he wouldn't see Him. "And the Angel of the Everpresent Lord appeared to him in a flame of fire in the middle of the bush. And he saw the bush was burning with fire, but the bush was not consumed." (Ex. 3:2) Moses turned aside to get a closer look at the burning bush.

Then God spoke to him from within the bush, and said, "'Don't come any closer. Take off your sandals, because the place where you are standing is holy ground. I am the God of your father, the God of Abraham, the God of Isaac and the God of Jacob.' At this, Moses hid his face, because he was afraid to look [habeet] upon God." (Ex. 3:5-6)

This is a little confusing. The text says, "the Angel of the Everpresent Lord appeared to him," but "Moses hid his face, because he was afraid to look [habeet] upon God." Who was visible in the bush, an angel or God?

The Midrash says, "At first, God did not descend, but one angel which came from Him and stood in the middle of the fire.

Then afterwards the Shechinah descended and spoke with him from within the bush." (Mid. Exodus 2.5) God said, "Don't come any closer." That means that God was in a physical location. Moses was forbidden to come closer to that location. In some way, God was present in a particular bush in a particular location. Therefore the physical area around it became holy ground.

"Moses hid his face, because he was afraid to look at God." This means that Moses could have looked at God — he was able to do so — but he was afraid to do so. God was speaking to him from the bush.

At that time, the people of Israel were in bitter slavery in Egypt. "God said to Moses: 'Are you aware that I live in trouble just as Israel lives in trouble? From the place I speak to you — from the middle of a thorn-bush — know that I am able to share in their trouble." (Mid. Ex. 2.5)

Though it's difficult to understand how it can be, God suffers with His people, even if the suffering is a result of their own disobedience. "In all their affliction He was afflicted, and the angel of His presence [*panav*] saved them. In His love and in His pity He redeemed them; and He bore them, and carried them all the days of old." (Is. 63:9)

Moses hid his face rather than look at God. It's similar, though quite different in spirt, to what Adam and Havah did after they had rebelled against God. "Then they heard the voice of the Lord God walking in the Garden in the breeze of the day. And Adam and his wife hid themselves from the presence [*p'nay*] of the Lord God among the trees of the garden." (Gen. 3:8)

Adam and Havah heard God walking in a particular location. They hid themselves so that, in their own estimation, He couldn't see them from that location. The text doesn't say they saw God; it simply says that they hid so they wouldn't have to.

In Mid. Gen. 19.7, R. Halapay understands the verse to mean that the voice of the Lord was walking in the Garden. This is similar to the text in Targum Yonatan: "And they heard the voice of the Word of the Lord God walking in the garden..."

Genesis 3:8 can also be translated as "They heard the sound of the Lord God walking in the Garden..." That translation raises the very interesting question: What would be the sound made by God walking in the Garden? What would make the sound? God's feet stepping on the ground? His hands brushing against the branches?

When the Philistines heard that David had been anointed king of Israel, they came up to attack him. David asked God what he should do. God replied, "And it shall be, when you hear a sound of marching in the tops of the mulberry trees, that you should then go out to battle, for God has gone out before you to strike the army of the Philistines." (1Chr. 14:15)

God Himself went out against the Philistines, making "a sound of marching in the tops of the mulberry trees". God can be heard, and God can be seen.

Adam and Havah hid from God; Moses "was afraid to look [*habeet*] upon God." The Hebrew word translated in Ex. 3:6 as "look at" is *habeet*. It appears in some other interesting places which, like that passage, are related to redemption, deliverance, or salvation. Here are some of them.

1) Because of their rebellion in the wilderness, many in Israel were being bitten by snakes, and dying. "And the Everpresent said to Moses, 'Make a venomous serpent, and put it upon a pole; and it will be that everyone who is bitten, when he looks upon it, will live. So Moses made a bronze snake and put it up on the pole. And if the serpent bit anyone, if he looked [*habeet*] upon the bronze snake, then he lived." (Num. 21:8-9)

2) Jonah had run away from the Lord, ending up in the belly of a large fish. As stubborn as he was, after three days and three nights in the belly of the fish, he began to pray. "From the belly of Sheol I cried, and You heard my voice... I said, 'I have been driven away from before Your eyes; yet I will again look [*habeet*] upon Your holy temple.'" (Jonah 2:5H)

3) "And I will pour out upon the house of David and upon those who live in Yeushala'im a spirit of grace and supplication. And they will look [*habeet*] upon Me, the one they have pierced, and they will mourn for him as one mourns for an only child, and grieve bitterly for him as one grieves for a firstborn son." (Zech. 12:10)

These instances have something in common. Looking up to the serpent is the way to healing. Looking up to the Temple is the way to deliverance. Looking up to the one who was pierced is the way to salvation. In Tal. Sukkah 52a, the one who is pierced is identified as the Messiah.

## At Mt. Sinai

When Israel was at Mt. Sinai, God told Moses, "Come up to the Everpresent Lord, you and Aaron, Nadab and Abihu, and seventy of the elders of Israel, and bow down from far off. But Moses alone is to come near to the Everpresent Lord, but they are not to come near; and the people are not to come up with him." (Ex. 24:1-2)

God invited these seventy-four men to come up to Him, because He had come down to the mountain. (cf. Ex. 19:18-20) "Then Moses went up, and Aaron, Nadab and Abihu, and the seventy elders of Israel. And they saw [yiru] the God of Israel. Under His feet was something like a paved work of sapphire, like the heaven itself for purity. But God did not raise His hand against these leaders of the children of Israel; they gazed upon [yehezu] God, and they ate and drank." (Ex. 24:9-11)

The passage is interesting because we are first told that these seventy-four men saw [yiru] God as one sees anything else. It is presented as a physical event. They saw His feet, and they saw a pure sapphire surface underneath His feet. The text describes something that physically happened in this world.

We are also told that they gazed upon [yehezu] God, or saw Him as in a vision. The Hebrew word can also be translated as "envisioned". Did they see God in the physical world, or did they see Him in a vision? There is no indication in the text that 74 men simultaneously saw an identical vision, one which included each of them actually doing things in real time in a specific place.

Their seeing God is immediately connected to the very physical act of eating and drinking. They didn't have a vision of each other eating and drinking while seeing God; they actually ate and drank.

The text also points out that "God did not raise His hand against these leaders of the children of Israel". Before this incident at Mt. Sinai, God had told Moses to "warn the people so that they do not destroy [the boundary] to the Everpresent Lord to see [lir'ot], and many from them fall." (Ex. 19:21) For looking at God, Aaron, Nadav, Avihu, and the 70 elders could have been put to death, even as, in the time of Samuel, God put to death many men of Beth Shemesh for looking into the ark of the covenant. (1Sam. 6)

God never said that no one could see Him; He said that, "humanity cannot see Me and live." Why then did He not put to death those who saw Him? God had told them to come and meet with Him. Rashi, following the Midrash Tanhuma, explains that God did not want to diminish the joy of the Torah having been given. So He delayed until later His judgment of death upon each one of them.

If God had given these seventy-four men an identical vision of Himself, there would be no need to point out that He didn't punish them. There would be no reason for God to punish anyone for seeing what He Himself caused them to see. The event is described as a physical, not a metaphysical or mystical one.

But even so, what does it mean to see God in a vision? God caused some of the prophets to see Him in a vision. That means that they saw some kind of representation of God, but one that did not actually appear in this physical realm. They saw God in another realm. But they did see God; God appeared to them in a visible form.

God appears in whatever form He chooses, at whatever particular location He chooses. "R. Joseph said: 'Man should always learn from the mind of his Creator; see that the Holy One, blessed be He, ignored all the mountains and high places and caused His Shekhinah to remain upon Mount Sinai, and ignored all the beautiful, tall trees and caused His Shekhinah to remain in a bush.'" (Tal. Sotah 5a) In R. Joseph's understanding, God chooses to appear to humanity in humble settings.

We see because a visible frequency of light enters our eyes.

If no light enters our eyes, or if the frequency of light is higher or lower than what our eyes perceive, then we do not see anything. When there is visible light, it is focused by the eye and interpreted by the brain. Sight takes place in our heads. That is where the image is. The brain interprets the image as to size, shape, color, depth, etc., and, amazingly, gives us a sense of the location of the object external to ourselves. But the images are always in our heads.

We can dream or daydream with our eyes closed or open, seeing images that are not caused by reflected light. But even what is seen in a dream or a daydream is still an image. We can re-envision something we have seen before. These images, too, are all in our heads. Even a vision provides a visual image that is seen in the mind, the same place where all vision takes place.

Does God have an image? Of course He does. "God created humanity in His own image, in the image of God He created him; male and female He created them." (Gen. 1:27)

Can an image of God be seen? The question makes sense when asked by someone who hasn't read the first chapter of the Bible. But it's absurd when asked by anyone who has. Adam and Havah were visible.

I don't know exactly what it means that humanity is made not only in the likeness, but also in the image of God, but it means something. When God appeared to Moses and the 73 others, they saw His feet. Does God have feet? I don't know, but the text says that this recognizable appearance of God had feet.

I suppose that God is able to appear anyway He wants to. Sometimes, according to Tanakh, He appeared in a human form. This is not anthropomorphic language, ascribing human attributes to God; it is the opposite of that. It is theomorphic language, ascribing God's attributes to humanity.

If humanity has been made in the image and likeness of God, then the question here becomes, "Is God able to appear in His own image and likeness?" There is no reasonable or logical reason to ask this question. The answer is obvious and inescapable. Of course.

## Back to Mt. Sinai

After the seventy-four men saw God, Moses went up the mountain alone, coming near to God. God appeared in a particular physical location, to which Moses drew near. Moses said to God, "'Please show me Your glory.'

"And He responded, 'I will cause all My goodness to pass in front of you, and I will proclaim My Name, the Everpresent Lord, in your presence. ... But,' He said, 'you are not able to see My face because man does not see Me and live.' ...

"Then the Everpresent Lord said, 'There is a place with Me where you may stand on the rock. And it will be that when **My glory** passes by, I will put you in a crevice in the rock and cover you with **My hand** upon you until I have passed by. Then I will remove **My hand** and **you will see My back**; but **you will not see My face**.'" (Ex. 33:18-23)

God said that His glory has a face and a back. And until the face of His glory passes Moses, God will cover Moses with His hand. Moses will see the back of God's glory, but not the face.

God did as He had said to Moses. Because of this very close encounter with God, the face of Moses became radiant with light, a light that all Israel could see when he returned. "And when Aaron and all the people of Israel saw Moses, behold, the skin of his face shone; and they were afraid to come closer to him." (Ex. 34:30)

The brightness of the light was too much for the people, so Moses covered his face with a veil. The face of Moses was irradiated with the light of God's face. In the wilderness, God gave Aaron a blessing to pronounce over Israel. It included: "The Lord make His face shine upon you, and be gracious to you. The Lord lift up His face upon you, and give you peace." (Num. 6:25-26)

Before Israel was to enter the land, Moses recounted God's dealings with the people during the time in the wilderness. He reminded them of the time when they stood before the Everpresent Lord at Horeb to receive the Ten Commandments.

"Then the Everpresent Lord spoke to you out of the fire. You heard the sound of words but saw no form [*tmunah*]; there was only a voice." (Dt. 4:12)

Some people assume, because of this verse, that the Scriptures teach that God has no form, and therefore cannot be seen. The verse, however, does not say that God has no form. It simply says that, on that day, Israel saw no form.

Earlier in the wilderness, God had said, "With Moses I speak face to face, clearly and not in ways hard to understand. He sees the form [*tmunah*] of the Everpresent Lord...." (Num.12:8, cf. Ex. 33:11) If God says that Moses sees His form, then God must have, or be able to adopt, a form that can be seen.

The Scriptures say there are many people who heard God's voice — all the prophets and more. God confined His infinite, Creation creating, tree shattering voice (Ps. 29:5) to a particular locality, in a frequency within the limited range humanity can hear, and with the reduced volume that humanity can endure. We naturally hear only a small range of the spectrum of what can be heard. Many animals hear a higher range than what is inaudible to man. Some children can hear frequencies that adults cannot.

God spoke to Moses and instructed him on how to build the Mishkan, the place for God's presence, and why. "And there I will meet with you, and I will talk with you from above the cover of atonement, from between the two cherubim which are upon the ark of the Testimony, of all things which I will give you in commandment to the people of Israel." (Ex. 25:22, cf. Num. 7:89) All the commandments were spoken by God to Moses.

"And the Lord spoke to Moses after the death of the two sons of Aaron, when they came near the Lord, and died; And the Lord said to Moses, 'Speak to Aaron your brother, that he come not at all times into the holy place inside the veil before the cover of atonement, which is upon the ark; that he die not; for **I will appear** in the cloud upon the cover of atonement.'" (Lev. 16:1-2)

Two of Aaron's sons had come into the holy place when they should not have come, and presented an offering which

God had not commanded. (Lev. 10:1-7) It's possible that they were drunk when they did it. (Lev. 10:8-11) God put them to death.

So Aaron understood the reality of God's warning. In some way, God would make Himself visible above the cover of atonement. Once a year, on Yom Kippur, Aaron was commanded to come before the visible presence of God. If he came when he was not commanded to, then he also would be put to death.

The Scriptures say there are people who saw God. Some of them saw Him in a dream; some saw Him in a vision; but most saw Him, we are told, without any such qualification. But in every case, God appeared to them in such a way that they knew it was He. He limited Himself, or His image, to a particular locality, a suitable frequency range, and an endurable intensity.

# OTHERS SAW GOD

There is much about God that is beyond our understanding, even when we have first-hand experience. Towards the end of his suffering, Job saw God, and said, "With the hearing of the ear, I had heard of You, but now my eye sees You. Therefore I reject myself and repent in dust and ashes." (Job 42:5-6)

Job had heard about God with his ear. Now he was seeing God with his eye. He speaks of both the hearing and the seeing as physical events.

Solomon saw God twice in dreams. He recognized that what he saw was God. "At Gibeon the Everpresent Lord appeared to Solomon in a dream of the night, and God said, 'Whatever you ask, I will give you.'" (1 Kings 3:5) Solomon asked for the wisdom to govern Israel, and God granted his request. That wisdom enabled him to pursue justice.

"Then the Everpresent Lord appeared to Solomon a second time, as He had appeared to him at Gibeon. The Everpresent Lord said to him, 'I have heard your prayer and your entreaty which you have made before Me. I have consecrated this Temple, which you have built, by putting My Name there forever. My eyes and My heart will always be there.'" (1 Kings 9:2-3)

God gave Solomon great wisdom: he knew about plants and animals; he knew how to discern the motives of human hearts. But his greatest wisdom was in seeking God. And his greatest foolishness was in following his own desires. Either one or the other becomes our greatest priority.

God has His own priorities. His eyes and His heart are always on Yerushala'im. Israel is the apple of His eye. (Dt. 32:8-10, Zech. 2:12H)

Micaiah the prophet prophesied: "I saw [ra'iti] all Israel scattered upon the hills, as sheep that do not have a shepherd... I saw [ra'iti] the Everpresent Lord sitting on His throne with all the forces of the heavens standing by Him on His right and on His left.... And the Everpresent Lord said, 'Who will persuade Ahab so that he goes up and falls at Ramot Gilead?'..." (1 Kings

22:17,19,20)

In the same way that Micaiah saw "all Israel scattered," so he saw "the Everpresent Lord sitting on His throne". In the same way he saw the Everpresent Lord, so he heard Him also. And what Micaiah saw and heard turned out to be an accurate description of what then happened to Israel after the battle. Micaiah had seen and heard God. He had seen how the conflict between human and divine purposes works out.

The text says "all the forces of heavens stood by Him, on His right and on His left." In the vision Micaiah saw, God was in a particular, limited locality and in a particular posture; He was sitting on His throne. And some of the forces of heaven stood on His right and other forces stood on His left. Micaiah saw God and the forces of heaven.

Isaiah also saw God in His glory. "In the year that King Uzziah died, then I saw [er'eh] the Everpresent Lord seated on a throne, high and exalted, and the hem of His robe filled the Temple. ... 'Woe to me!' I cried. 'I am ruined! For I am a man of unclean lips, and I live among a people of unclean lips, and my eyes have seen [ra'u] the King, the Everpresent Lord Almighty.'" (Is. 6:1,5)

Isaiah said that his eyes saw God sitting on a throne, wearing a huge robe. Like Job, Isaiah was overwhelmed when he saw God. He knew that he was unworthy and unclean, but nevertheless, as he simply recorded, "my eyes have seen the King, the Everpresent Lord Almighty." The language is simple to understand.

Amos also saw God. "I saw [ra'iti] the Everpresent Lord standing by the altar, and He said: 'Strike the tops of the pillars so that the thresholds shake. Cut off all of them by the head; I will slay the last of them with the sword. None of them will be able to flee, and a fugitive of them will not escape.'" (Am. 9:1)

God was warning Amos of the judgment that would come upon the northern kingdom of Israel. Generation after generation had rejected Him. Amos saw God standing by the altar, which God had given for mercy and forgiveness, but the people had rejected that too. When a prophet says that he heard God, that is what he means; when he says that he saw God, that also is what he means.

Daniel saw God in a human form in a vision. "As I looked, thrones were set down, and the Ancient of Days sat. His clothing was white as snow; the hair of His head was pure wool. His throne was flames of fire, and its wheels flaming fire. A river of fire was flowing, coming out from before Him. A thousand thousands served Him, and ten thousand times ten thousand stood before Him. He sat for judgment, and the books were opened." (Dan. 7:9-10)

Daniel describes what God caused him to see: God clothed in white, having white hair, and sitting down on a fiery throne. A little later, we will look at the continuation of Daniel's vision, after we look briefly at the visions of Ezekiel.

Ezekiel saw the image of the Glory of God in a human form, and he described God's appearance. "Above the expanse over the heads [of the winged creatures] was the likeness of a throne of sapphire, and high above on the throne was the likeness [d'moot] and appearance of a man [adam]. I saw that from the appearance of his waist up, he looked like glowing amber all around. And from his waist down, I saw his appearance as fire, and brilliant light surrounded him. Like the appearance of a rainbow in the clouds on a day of rain, so was the appearance of the radiance around him. This was the appearance of the likeness of the glory of the Everpresent Lord. When I saw it, I fell facedown, and I heard the voice of One speaking." (Ezek. 1:26-28, cf. Ezek. 3:23, 8:2-3, 43:2-4)

Ezekiel saw the glory of God in the form of a man, as the appearance of a radiant Adam. God had shown Moses the back of His glory, but not the face of His glory.

After Moses had been in the presence of God for 40 days, his face was radiant with light. (Ex. 34:29-35) That was reflected glory. Obviously there was much more radiance and glory to the appearance of God Himself.

The Rabbis say that Adam was greatly diminished after he rebelled against God. "Six things were taken away from the first Adam, and will be restored in the future through the son of Nahshon — he is the Messiah — and these are they: his glorious brightness, his life [without death], his stature, the fruit of the earth, the fruit of the trees, and the lights." (Mid. Num. 13:12, cf. Mid. Gen. 12:6)

In this view, humanity was created to be radiant with the glory of God. The rebellion of the first Adam deprived his descendants of that glory. It is, therefore, the obedience of another Adam, the Messiah, which will restore that glory, as well as life without death. Messiah will be a radiant Adam in the image and likeness of God.

Every person appears as a visible likeness of God, though we are far from radiant. "Listen to Me, you stubborn of heart, who are far from righteousness. I am bringing near My righteousness; it will not be far off, and My salvation will not delay. And I am placing salvation in Zion, for Israel My glory." (Is. 46:12-13)

The nations make images of their gods and bow down to them, but Israel is prohibited from making any image of the one true God. God has already made an image of Himself, Adam, but it is to the Everpresent Lord alone that we bow down. In serving Him, however, we are to serve those who are made in His image.

As it says in Talmud, "'in His image' [b'tzalmo]: in the image of the likeness of His pattern [b'tzelem d'moot tavneeto]." (Tal. Ketubot 8a) As it says in the Midrash: "In the hour that the Holy One, blessed be He, created the first Adam, the ministering angels erred and sought to say 'Holy' before him." (Mid. Genesis 8.10) I.e., the angels saw the first Adam as though he were God.

On several other occasions, Ezekiel saw this same image of the glory of God. He fell facedown before this radiant man, who stood before him. (Ezek. 3:23) The radiant man stretched out his hand and grabbed Ezekiel. (Ezek. 8:2-3) The radiant man spoke with a voice like the roar of rushing waters, his radiance caused the earth to shine, and he entered the Temple. (Ezek. 43:2-4)

When Isaiah saw God, he heard the seraphim say "Holy, holy, holy, is the Everpresent Lord of forces; the fullness of all the earth is His glory." (Is. 6:3) That helps to explain why God caused Ezekiel to see the glory of the Everpresent Lord in the form of a man. God makes His glory visible in the earth.

So if God chooses to appear to humanity, and the Scriptures say that He does, then certainly He can appear in His own likeness and image. It could even be expected that He would likely appear that way. The prophets say that He did. Echoing his own experience — "my eyes have seen the King" — Isaiah the prophet said to Israel: "Your eyes will see the King in His beauty." (Is. 33:13,17)

Even when God appeared to a prophet in a vision, or especially when God appeared to a prophet in a vision, He appeared in a form similar to that of Adam. God caused the prophets to see Him that way.

But God cautioned Ezekiel: "Son of Adam, you are living among a people in rebellion. They have eyes to see but they do not see. They have ears to hear but they do not hear, because they are a people in rebellion." (Ezek. 12:2)

Daniel's vision — what God showed Daniel and wanted him to record — continued. "In my vision at night, I looked and there before me was one like a son of Man, coming with the clouds of heaven. He approached the Ancient of Days and was led near to Him. He was given honor, authority to rule, and a kingdom; and all peoples, nations, and men of every language were to serve him. His authority to rule is an everlasting authority that will not pass away, and his kingdom is one that will never be destroyed." (Dan. 7:13-14)

In an argument in the Talmud about the thrones mentioned in this section of Daniel, we read, "'one was for Himself, one for David.' This is R. Akiba's view." (Tal. Sanh. 38b) The Talmud is not explicit, but either Akiba believed that God would raise David from the dead to rule again, or he said "David" to indicate, as is often done, a future descendant of David who would rule on his throne. Whichever it was, other rabbis rejected Akiba's view, even as R. Yohanan b. Tortha rejected Rabbi Akiba's claim that Bar Kokhba was the Messiah. (Mid. Lamentations 2.4) But Akiba was not alone in his understanding of the passage in Daniel. R. Joshua b. Levi applied "the son of Adam" in that passage to Messiah. (Tal. Sanhedrin 98a)

In terms of God's purposes for the earth, the prophets clearly say that God will raise up a descendant of David who will rule from his throne and over his kingdom. That son of David is understood to be God's Anointed King who will establish God's kingdom over all the earth, i.e. the Messiah.

God intends for this son of David to establish a righteous government that will spread over all the earth. Other passages in the prophets speak about this son of David, the Messiah, to tell us the things God wants us to know about how He has purposed to work on the earth.

In Jer. 23:5-6, we are told "'Be aware that days are coming,' says the Everpresent Lord, 'and I will raise up to David a righteous branch and a king will reign, act wisely, and do judgment and righteousness in the earth [aretz]. In his days, Judah will be saved and Israel will dwell in security. And this is his name which he will be called, *the Everlasting Lord, our Righteousness.*'"

In Is. 9:5-6H, we are told, "For a child is born to us, a son is given to us. And the government will be on his shoulder. And his name will be called 'Wonderful, counsellor, mighty God, everlasting Father, prince of peace. There is no end to the increase of the government and peace, on the throne of David and over his kingdom, to establish it and sustain it in judgment and in justice, from now until forever. The zeal of the Everpresent Lord of all forces will do this."

All the names in the various passage indicate a close relationship between God and this king. God created the earth for His purposes, and that includes establishing His kingdom, ruled by His King.

# "THE LORD CAME DOWN"

After the flood, God told Noah and his descendants to "Be fruitful and become many, and fill the earth." (Gen. 9:1) A few generations later, however, the descendants of Noah said to each other, "Come, let's build a city and a tower with its top in heaven, and let's make a name for ourselves so that we are not scattered abroad on the face of all the earth." (Gen.11:4) Instead of spreading abroad, they wanted to stay in one place. Instead of filling the earth, they wanted to ascend into heaven. Humanity continued in rebellion against God.

"So **the Everpresent Lord came down** to see the city and the tower which the descendants of Adam had built. And He said, '...Come, let us go down there and confuse their speech so that a man will not understand the speech of his neighbor." (Gen. 11:5,7) Instead of letting men ascend into heaven, God came down to earth.

Why did God come down from heaven to earth? Certainly He could already see quite clearly what humanity was doing. "The Everpresent Lord is in His holy temple; the throne of the Everpresent Lord is in heaven. His eyes observe [*yehezu*], His eyelids examine the children of Adam." (Ps. 11:4) [*Yehezu* would usually be understood to denote a vision.]

God has a temple in heaven. God has a throne in heaven. From there, He sees all that humanity is doing. "From heaven the Everpresent Lord looks [*hibeet*]] and sees [*ra'ah*] all the children of Adam; from His dwelling place He gazes [*hishgi'ah*] on all the inhabitants of the earth — the One who creates the hearts of each individual, the One who understands everything they do." (Ps. 33:13-15) Expressed in many different ways, God sees everything from heaven.

So why would God come down to earth? Was someone hiding something from Him, as Adam and Havah had tried to do? Perhaps some people thought they were hiding something from God; often, people think they can do that, but it's foolish. "'Is it possible that a person can hide in secret places so that I will not see him?" asks the Everpresent Lord. 'Do I not fill the heaven and the earth?' declares the Everpresent Lord." (Jer. 23:24)

God fills heaven and earth. So what does it mean that He came down to earth? We are cautioned, "Do not be hasty with your mouth; and do not let your heart hurry to bring forth a word before God; because the God is in heaven and you are on the earth. Therefore let your words be few." (Eccl. 5:1H)

Though we don't know exactly how far it is from heaven to earth, we know there is a great distance between God and humanity. Though we don't know exactly how far down God came, we know that He came down to our level to be close to humanity. God bridges the distance. The Scriptures give us several reasons why He does this.

### To Be a Witness

In Gen. 11:5-7, God came down to be present at the site of a rebellion, a criminal act. God is the judge of all the earth, and this was a fact-gathering mission. He then pronounced and enforced His judgment to make future rebellions more isolated. He scattered humanity to different locations, dividing people into different language groups.

God came down for a similar purpose before the destruction of Sodom and Gomorrah. "Then the Everpresent Lord said, 'The outcry against Sodom and Gomorrah is so great and their sin so very heavy, that **I will go down** now and see [*ayradah na v'er'eh*] if what they have done is as bad as the outcry that has come to Me. And if not, I will know." (Gen. 18:20-21)

God already knew, but He came down anyway. Rashi says that when God says, "I will go down now," He is teaching judges that they are not to decide capital cases if they have not seen [the evidence]." (commentary on Gen. 11:5, citing Midrash Tanhuma) Because God came down, no one could say that He didn't really know what it was like on the earth.

### To Deliver Israel

God spoke to Moses from the burning bush in the wilderness.

He said, "I have surely seen the affliction of My people who are in Egypt, and I have heard them crying out because of their oppressors, and I know their pain. So **I have come down** [va'ayrayd] to deliver them from the power of Egypt and to bring them up out of that land into a good and spacious land, a land flowing with milk and honey — to the place of the Canaanites, Hittites, Amorites, Perizzites, Hivites and Jebusites." (Ex. 3:7-8)

At the end of this age, the nations will unite to come against Israel. Their goal will be to forcibly divide Yerushala'im and expel the Jewish people from half of it. They will succeed. "Then the Everpresent Lord will go out and fight against those nations, as in the day He fights, in the day of war. And on that day **His feet will stand on the Mount of Olives** which is before Yerushala'im to the east. and the Mount of Olives will be split in two from east to west, forming a great valley, with half of the mountain moving north and half moving south." (Zech. 14:3-4)

On that day, God will come down to the earth to fight for His city, His people, and His land. "And I will gather all the nations and bring them down to the valley of Yehoshaphat. And I will judge them there because of My people, My inheritance, Israel, whom they have scattered among the nations, and they divided My land." (Joel 4:2H)

That land has been and will be the site of many battles. The rulers of the nations do not recognize God's authority in the earth. God lets their rebellion become fully ripe, then He will come down to Yerushala'im to settle the issue.

## To Make Himself Known

The most common phrase in the Bible is, "And the Everpresent Lord spoke to Moses..." It appears exactly that way more than one hundred times, and in variations many times more. The task which God gave to Moses was very difficult, and Moses therefore needed to hear often from God.

For the same reason, God appeared to Moses. He appeared to him first in the burning bush, but at various other times after that. Some of those times, the text explicitly states that God "came down" to meet with him or with the people.

At Mt. Sinai, God said to Moses, "Go to the people and consecrate them today and tomorrow. Have them wash their clothes and be ready by the third day, because on the third day **the Everpresent Lord will come down** on Mount Sinai in the sight of all the people." (Ex. 19:10-11)

God, infinite in power and dimensions, planned to come down on a small mountain in a forsaken wilderness. When He did, "Mount Sinai was all in smoke, because **the Everpresent Lord descended** [*yarad*] on it in fire. And its smoke went up like smoke from a furnace. And all the mountain trembled greatly. And the sound of the shofar went forth and became very loud. Moses spoke and God answered him in a voice. Then **the Everpresent Lord descended** [*va'yayred*] to the top of Mount Sinai, and called Moses to the top of the mountain. So Moses went up." (Ex. 19:18-20)

As much as it may be contrary to what we expect, the God of the Bible, the God of Israel, comes down to earth so that people may encounter Him. Surely He is beyond what we can know or understand, but He comes down to make Himself known.

With Moses, He made Himself known in a special way. "Then **the Everpresent Lord came down** [*va'yayred*] in the cloud and stood there with him and proclaimed His Name, the Everpresent Lord. And the Everpresent Lord passed in front of him and proclaimed, 'The Everpresent Lord, the Everpresent Lord, compassionate and gracious God, slow to anger, and great in lovingkindness and truth; maintaining lovingkindness to thousands, removing iniquity and transgression and sin, but assuredly not leaving these unpunished; visiting the iniquity of the parents upon the children and upon the children's children to the third and fourth generations." (Ex. 34:5-7)

God came down to the top of an insignificant mountain to identify Himself in this way, so that Moses, Israel, and all who would read what Moses recorded could know what He is like. In telling us what He is like, God tells us what we should be like. There are some ways in which we are supposed to be like God, because we were made in His image and likeness; and there are other ways in which we are to recognize that we are not God.

## To Provide

Besides Himself, there are other things which God brings down from heaven to earth. "Then the Everpresent Lord said to Moses, '**I will rain down bread from heaven** for you. The people are to go out each day and gather enough for that day. In this way I will test them and see whether they will walk in accordance with My Torah or not." (Ex. 16:4)

God said the manna was bread that came down from heaven. The people gathered it every day off the ground. It sustained them every day, year after year in the wilderness.

At the end of those years, Moses explained why God provided for them in that way. "So he humbled you and let you be hungry. He fed you with the manna — which you didn't know and your fathers didn't know — so that He could make you understand that humanity is not to live by bread alone, but humanity is to live by all that goes out of the mouth of the Everpresent Lord."(Dt. 8:3) What God says, His Word, is what truly gives us life.

Years later, through Isaiah the prophet, God explained this in terms of His purposes. "For **as the rain comes down, and the snow from heaven**, and do not return, but water the earth, and make it sprout and bear fruit, so that it gives seed to the sower and bread to the eater; **My Word** that goes forth from My mouth is like this. It will not return to Me empty, but it **will accomplish My purpose, and will succeed in what I sent it to do.**" (Is. 55:10-11)

God sends His Word, like the rain, down from heaven to accomplish His purpose on the earth. When we get to Gen. 1:3, where God says, "Let there be light," we will look at His Word more. God begins the creation of all things on the earth by speaking. He speaks, and His Word accomplishes His purpose.

When we get to Gen. 1:2, where we are told that "the Spirit of God hovered over the waters," we will look more deeply at the Spirit of God in terms of God's purposes on the earth. But here, we should mention one more thing that God brings down from heaven to earth, His Spirit. God told Moses, "Gather to Me seventy men from the elders of Israel, whom you know are elders and officials among the people. And take them to the Tent of Meeting, and have them stand there with you. Then I **will come down** [*yaradti*] and speak with you there. And I will take of the Spirit that is on you and put it on them, so that they will carry the burden of the people with you, so that you will not carry it alone." (Num. 11:16-17) God came down to put His Spirit on the leaders of Israel.

The manna, God's Word, and God's Spirit are for life, but sometimes death comes down from heaven. After Lot was safe, "Then the Lord rained upon Sodom and upon Gomorrah brimstone and fire from the Lord out of heaven." (Gen. 19:24)

Three times, King Aḥaziah sent an army captain with fifty soldiers to arrest Elijah the prophet. The first and second captains said, "You man of God, the king has said, 'Come down.' And Elijah answered and said to the captain of fifty, 'If I am a man of God, then let fire come down from heaven, and consume you and your fifty.' And there came down fire from heaven, and consumed him and his fifty." (2Kings 1:9-10, 11-12) The third captain pleaded for mercy for himself and his fifty soldiers. Elijah did not call down fire from heaven.

## To Live

God created and called Israel to be a people set apart to Himself. The generation that He brought out of Egypt lived in tents in the wilderness. Even so, God told them to build the Mishkan, the place of dwelling, a tent for God in the midst of His people.

"Let them now make for Me a holy place, and I will dwell [*shekhanti*] among them." (Ex. 25:8) "Then I will dwell [*shekhanti*] among the descendents of Israel and will be their God. They will know that I am the Everpresent Lord their God, who brought them out of the land of Egypt so **that I might dwell among them**. [*l'shakhni*] I am the Everpresent Lord their God." (Ex. 29:45-46)

God came down and lived in that tent. At the same time,

He was still enthroned in heaven, and He still filled heaven and earth. At the same time, He existed outside of Creation.

And that tent, with the presence of God inside, travelled with Israel across the wilderness and into the land He had promised to them. God could have travelled with Israel without having His own tent. For some reason, He wanted a place on the earth with people. For some reason, He wanted a place made of physical things of the earth — minerals (gold, silver and bronze), skins of animals, and products of vegetation (cloth and boards). (cf. Ex. 25:3-8) God is saying something about Himself that He wants us to understand. He demonstrated that He could live within the same physical framework in which His people lived.

Solomon built and dedicated a Temple for God. The Temple was more solid than the Mishkan and stayed in one place, but it too was made from things of the earth. Why would an infinite God want people to build Him a little house? "Then Solomon said, 'The Everpresent Lord has said that He would dwell in thick darkness. [Ex.20:21, Ps. 97:2] I have surely built an exalted house for You, **a place for You to live** [*l'shivtekha*] forever." (1Kgs. 8:12-13, cf. 1Chr. 23:25, Ex.20:21, Dt. 4:11) "But will God truly live [*yayshayv*] on the earth? The heavens, even the heavens of the heavens, cannot contain You. How much less this house which I have built!" (1Kgs. 8:27)

Solomon knew that all of Creation was too small to contain God. So it was obvious that the house he built, no matter how grand by human standards, was too small for God. But God had told him to build the house, and had promised: "This house which you are building, if you will walk in My statutes, and execute My judgments, and observe all My commandments to walk in them, then I will establish My word with you which I spoke to David your father. Then I will dwell [*shekhanti*] among the descendants of Israel and will not forsake My people Israel." (1Kings 6:12-13)

When Solomon's Temple was dedicated, the glory of God, His abiding Shekhinah, came down and filled the house with His presence. "And it happened that when the priests came out of the holy place, the cloud filled the house of the Everpresent

Lord, and the priests could not stand to minister because of the cloud; because the glory of the Everpresent Lord had filled the house of the Lord. Then Solomon spoke: 'The Everpresent Lord said that He would dwell in the thick darkness. **I have surely built You a house to dwell in**, a settled place for You to abide in forever." (1K. 8:10-13)

The same thing had happened when the Mishkan was set up for the first time, the glory of God came down. (cf. Ex. 40:34-35) From the beginning, God had made it clear that He intended to make His presence known on the earth. He had walked in the Garden.

The Mishkan in the wilderness, in the center of the people of Israel, was replaced by the Temple. But the Temple didn't last forever. Instead of the Temple taking away our sins, our sins took away the Temple.

But God has promised that in the Age to Come, He will come down again to live in the midst of Israel. He showed Ezekiel visions of a restored Israel with a new Temple at its center. "Son of Adam, this is the place of My throne and the place of the soles of My feet, where **I will dwell** [*eshkan*] there among the descendants of Israel forever." (Ezek. 43:7a)

God will have a throne on which He will sit. And He says He has feet, which have soles, and which will stand in Yerushala'im. God created language. He brought the universe into existence by speaking. So He certainly knows what He is communicating. The words must signify something. When God says He will dwell in Yerushala'im, He means something that He wants us to understand.

"This is what the Everpresent Lord says: "**I will return to Zion and dwell** [*shekhanti*] in Yerushala'im. Then Yerushala'im will be called the City of Truth, and the mountain of the Everpresent Lord of all forces will be called the Holy Mountain." (Zech. 8:3) God will be present in such a way that "the name of the city will be 'the Lord is there'." (Ezek. 48:35)

## To Establish a Just Society
There is an interesting comment in the Midrash on this

124

name —'the Lord is there' — for Yerushala'im. "What is the name of King Messiah? R. Abba b. Kahana said: 'His name is *the Everpresent Lord*; as it is stated, *And this is his name by which he will be called, 'The Lord our righteousness'* (Jer. 23). For R. Levi said: 'It is good for a society when its name is as the name of its king, and the name of its king is as the name of its God. It is good for a society when its name is identical with that of its king,' as it is written, *And the name of the city from that day will be the Lord is there* (Ezek. 48). And the name of its king as the name of its God, as it is said, *And this is his name by which he will be called, 'The Lord our righteousness.'"* (Mid. Lamentations 1.51)

God intends to establish a permanent residence in Yerushala'im. It is there that He intends to establish His throne, the capital of His government. Messiah will be king in the city of the great king. And the city and the kingdom will be righteous. All the nations are commanded to then come to Yerushala'im to acknowledge His sovereignty. (Zech. 14:16-19)

God gave humanity the responsibility to exercise His authority, in His image and likeness, over the earth and all its creatures. God did not abdicate His responsibility and authority; He delegated them. And He intends to see them properly exercised.

In the Garden, Adam and Havah chose to go their own way, seeking to become their own standard of good and evil. They were exiled from the Garden. Their descendants, from Ka'in on, then filled the earth with violence and ungodliness.

God waited and waited upon a humanity that refused to change, and then He sent a flood as judgment. Only eight humans survived the flood. After it subsided, God told those who survived, "Be fruitful, and become many, and fill the earth."

Humanity's response was to say, "Let's stay here and build a tower to heaven." Different goals, different views of what life should be. As a judgment, God separated humanity into languages and nations.

Then God created Israel as a means of bringing the nations back to Himself. He entreated the descendants of Israel to live as His sons and daughters, but, like the goyim, they too embraced the rebellion of Adam. "He looked for judgment, but behold oppression; for righteousness, but behold a cry." (is. 5:7)

The pattern persists throughout humanity's history. Yet the Scriptures present God as One who has not abandoned His purpose for the earth.

What God wants for humanity is not difficult to understand. "He has told you, Adam, what is good and what the Everpresent Lord seeks from you: that you do justice, love mercy, and walk in humility with your God." (Mic. 6:8)

But people can be very strange. Sometimes they think they know more than God does, love more than God does, and are more righteous than God is. So, unfortunately, God will have to do what He has had to do countless times throughout human history. He will have to bring judgment upon those who reject His standard of good and evil, those who refuse to recognize His right to rule over what He created.

"Why do nations rage and the peoples meditate on what is futile? The kings of the earth take their stand and the rulers take counsel together against the Everpresent Lord and against His Messiah. 'Let us tear off their restraints,' they say, 'and throw away their cords from us.'" (Ps. 2:1-3)

Human rulers reject God's authority to place constraints upon them, but God has appointed His own ruler for the earth. "The One who sits in the heavens laughs; the Everpresent Lord ridicules them. Then He will rebuke them in His anger and terrify them in His fury, saying, 'I have installed My King on Zion, the mountain of My holiness.'" (Ps. 2:4-6)

God declares Yerushala'im to be the capitol of His kingdom on the earth, ruled over by His own King. Though human rulers rage against him even as they rage against God, God has appointed him to establish His kingdom upon the earth.

"Know that days are coming,' says the Everpresent Lord, 'when I will raise up to David a righteous offshoot — a king will reign, act wisely, and execute judgment and righteousness in the earth.'" (Jer. 23:5) "He will judge the poor with righteousness, with integrity he will give decisions for the afflicted of the earth.

He will strike the earth with the rod of his mouth; he will slay the wicked with the breath of his lips. Righteousness will be his belt and faithfulness the sash around his waist. (Is. 11:4-5)

In the age to come, God's King will establish God's government over all the earth. It will be a different kind of government, a different kind of justice. "Your throne is fixed upon righteousness and justice; lovingkindness and Truth come together in front of You." (Ps. 89:14, cf. Ps. 97:2) Messiah will rule with God. "The Holy One, blessed be He, will put His crown on King Messiah." (Mid. Ex. 8:1)

God will have come down to stay. "And many people will go and say, 'Come, and let us go up to the mountain of the Everpresent Lord, to the house of the God of Jacob; and He will teach us of His ways. And we will walk in His paths, because Torah will go from Zion, and the word of the Everpresent Lord from Yerushala'im. And He will judge among the nations and give decisions many people. And they will beat their swords into plowshares, and their spears into pruning hooks. Nation will not lift up sword against nation, nor will they learn war any more." (Is. 2:3-4)

"Many Gentiles will be joined to the Everpresent Lord in that day, and they will become a people for Me. And **I will dwell** [*shekhanti*] in your midst. Then you will know that the Everpresent Lord of all forces has sent Me to you." (Zech. 2:15H)

# GOD'S CHILDREN

In different mythologies, certain gods and goddesses had sexual relations with each other and produced children who were gods. Other gods or goddesses had sexual relations with humans and produced offspring which were half-human, half-divine.

It is quite clear in the Scriptures that the God of the Bible does not have any children produced in this sexual way. But the Bible does teach that God has children who share in some of His characteristics, children who can hear His voice and know His presence. They differ from each other, but are nevertheless presented as His children.

**1) Angels are called the sons of God.** "Now there was a day when the sons of God came to present themselves before the Everpresent Lord, and Satan [the Adversary] also came among them. ...Again there was a day when the sons of God came to present themselves before the Everpresent Lord, and Satan also came among them to present himself before the Everpresent Lord." (Job 1:6, 2:1)

In this passage, "the sons of God" are heavenly beings, because the scene takes place in heaven. They are generally understood to be angels, because Satan is an angel, though one who rebelled against God.

"And the Everpresent Lord said to Satan [the Adversary], 'Where are you coming from? Then Satan answered the Everpresent Lord and said, 'From roaming upon the earth, and from walking upon it.'" (Job 1:7) He had been upon the earth, but he was now before God in heaven.

It's never made explicit why these heavenly beings are called "the sons of God". We are not told that they were created in His image and likeness. We do not know what characteristics of His they share.

When God appeared to Job, He challenged him concerning the earth. "Upon what are its foundations fastened? Or who laid its corner stone when the morning stars sang together, and all the sons of God shouted for joy?" (Job 38:6-7) Job is silent, because he had not witnessed that event. But these sons of God had.

Gen. 6:2-4 says: "The sons of God saw the daughters of humanity, that they were beautiful, and they took wives for themselves from all whom they chose.... The *Nephillim* were in the earth in those days, and also after that, when the sons of God came to the daughters of humanity and bore children to them. Those were the mighty of old, famous men."

Some people think that in this passage "the sons of God" refers to angels, who had sexual intercourse with women, producing the giants. Josephus records this view. (Antiquities 1:73 [1.3.1]) Philo does also. ("On the Giants" II. [6]) It appears in some of the Pseudopigrapha. (e.g. 1Enoch, Section 1, chapters 7, 9, 15 *passim*)

Other people think that "the sons of God" are certain human leaders, the elite of that age, in distinction from the common people. This is the view presented in the Midrash. (Mid. Genesis 26:5,7)

The text itself doesn't provide a lot of information. What is clear is that there are some who are called "the sons of God," and they procreated with human women.

Nebuchadnezzar demanded that all the inhabitants of his kingdom bow down to his image of gold. Some of the exiles from Judea — Hananiah, Mishael, and Azariah — refused to do so. The three of them — more commonly known by their Babylonian names: Shadrach, Meshach, and Abednego — were tied up and thrown into a fiery furnace. But God sent a heavenly being to protect them.

Nebuchadnezzar looked into the furnace and said, "Behold, I see four men unbound, walking in the midst of the fire, and they are not hurt; and the appearance of the fourth is like a son of the gods." (Dan. 3:25) He calls this heavenly being an angel. (Dan. 3:28)

**2) God calls Israel His son.** God's love for humanity is of a different nature. It is presented as the love of a Father for His children. That is how God presents Himself in His relationship with Israel. God told Moses to tell Pharoah, "Israel is My son, My firstborn. So I tell you, send out My son so that he can serve Me. And if you refuse to send him out, know that I will kill your son, your firstborn." (Ex. 4:22, cf. Hos. 11:1; Is. 63:16, 64:8; Jer. 3:4,14,19; 31:9) Israel is just as much God's son as Pharaoh's firstborn was his.

King David prayed, "Blessed are You, Everpresent Lord God of Israel. our Father forever and ever." (1Chr. 29:10) God calls the redeemed of Israel His sons and daughters. "Don't be afraid, because I am with you. I will bring your descendants from the east and I will gather you from the west. I will say to the north, 'Give [them up]!' and to the south, 'Do not hold [them back]! Bring My sons from far off and My daughters from the ends of the earth!'" (Is. 43:5-6)

In the wilderness, Moses said to the people, "You are children of the Everpresent Lord your God..." (Dt. 14:1) Many centuries later, God said, "Surely they are My people, children who will not lie; so He became their Savior." (Is. 63:8) God doesn't save His people because they are righteous — since they aren't righteous — He saves them because they are His children.

In response to our sin and rebellion, God promised to scatter Israel across the earth. But He also promised to redeem and forgive us. (Is. 43:25) "And the number of the children of Israel will be as the sand of the sea, which cannot be measured or counted. And it will be that in the place where it was said to them, 'You are not My people,' they will be called 'children of the living God.'" (Hos. 2:1H)

### 3) Adam is presented as the son of God.
"This is the book of the generations of Adam. In the day when God created Adam, in the likeness [b'dmoot] of God He made him; male and female He created them; and blessed them, and called their name Adam, in the day when they were created. And Adam lived a hundred and thirty years, and fathered a son

in his own likeness, after his image [*b'dmooto k'tzalmo*]; and called his name Seth." (Gen. 5:1-3)

God created living beings in such a way that physical offspring receive their genetic characteristics from their parents. That is why Adam "fathered a son in his own likeness, after his image." That is God's design for humanity.

God's design for humanity tell us something about Himself. The specific words used in Gen. 5:3 were chosen intentionally to connect them to Gen. 1:26: "And God said, Let us make man in our image, after our likeness... [*b'tzalmenu, k'dmootenu*]" The father-son relationship between Adam and Seth is intended to illustrate the Father-son relationship between God and Adam.

The fact that God calls Israel "My firstborn son" indicates that God has other children among the nations. And there is a clear sense in which all of humanity is presented as the children of God. For we are told that: "Adam lived one hundred thirty years and fathered [a son] in his image and according to his likeness, and called his name 'Seth'." (Gen. 5:3) The child bears the image and likeness of the father. Humanity was created in the image and likeness of God. To the extent that we bear God's image and likeness, to that extent He is our Father and we are His children.

The Midrash goes beyond this in saying, "He called them 'gods,' as it is written, 'And you will be like God (Gen. 3:5)" (Mid. Lev. 11.1). That, however, is an inappropriate combination of verses. In Gen. 3:5, it is not God who calls Adam and Havah "gods"; it is the Serpent, who is seducing them to believe that they will become like God by disobeying God and eating the fruit of the tree of the knowledge of good and evil.

Given the tragic history of humanity, it would seem that Adam and Havah must have been more like God before they rebelled than they and their descendants have been since. Nevertheless, sometimes someone will behave in such a good or gracious way that he or she must bring joy to their Father.

**4) God calls Messiah His son.** God promised King David, "Solomon, your son will build My house and My courts; for I have chosen him to be My son, and I will be his father. And I will establish his kingdom forever, if he is constant to do My commandments and My judgments, as at this day." (1Chr. 28:6-7) God chose Solomon, the son of David, to be His own son; but Solomon wasn't faithful. He followed his own eyes and his own desires, even as Adam had done. So God took the kingdom away from him. (e.g. 1Kings 11:1-11)

But His promise remained to be fulfilled through a future son of David. "I will tell of the decree: the Everpresent Lord has said to me, 'You are My son; this day I have begotten you. Ask of Me, and I will give you the nations for your inheritance, and the uttermost parts of the earth for your possession.'" (Ps. 2:7-8)

Virtually all commentators apply these verses to the Messiah, because it is explicit in the Biblical text. For example, the Talmud does in Sukkah 52a: "Our Rabbis taught, 'The Holy One, blessed be He, will say to the Messiah, the son of David — may he reveal himself speedily in our days! — *Ask of me anything, and I will give it to you,* as it is said, *I will tell of the decree etc. this day I have begotten you, ask of Me and I will give the nations for your inheritance.*'"

As the Midrash says, "All these goodly promises are in the decree of the King, the King of kings who will fulfill them for the lord Messiah. ...God, speaking to the Messiah, says: 'If you ask for dominion over the nations, already they are your inheritance; if for the ends of the earth, already they are your possession.'" (Mid. Ps. 2:9,10)

The text of the psalm says, but does not explain, that there is some way in which Messiah is begotten by God as His son. This is different than God adopting Solomon as His own son. The Midrash comments: "When the time comes, the Holy One, blessed be He, will say: 'I must create the Messiah — a new creation.' As Scripture says: 'This day I have begotten you (Mid. Ps. 2:9) — that is, on the very day of redemption, God will create the Messiah."

Elsewhere, the Midrash says: "The Holy One, blessed be He, spoke to Moses saying, 'Even as I made Jacob a firstborn, for it says, *Israel is My son, My firstborn* [Ex. 4:22], so I will also make King Messiah My firstborn, as it is written, *I will make him My firstborn.'* [Ps. 89:28H]" (Mid. Ex. 19:7)

When the rebellion of Adam's children becomes fully ripe, and all the nations rage "against the Everpresent Lord and against His Messiah," then God will install Messiah, His Son, as King in Yerushala'im. God will declare to him, "You are My son; today I have become your Father. Ask of Me, and I will make the nations your inheritance, the ends of the earth your possession." (Ps. 2:7-8)

God challenged the priests of Israel: "A son honors his father, and a servant his master. If I am a father, where is My honor? And if I am a master, where is My fear?" (Mal. 1:6) He commanded and promised: "Honor your father and your mother; that your days may be long upon the land which the Lord your God gives you." Our days will be much longer if we honor the Father who created us.

"R. Haninah said, 'The son of David will not come until there are no more conceited men in Israel, as it is written (Zeph. 3), *And then I will take away out of your midst those who rejoice in your pride.* Then it is written, *I will also leave a remnant in your midst, an afflicted and poor people, and they will take refuge in the Name of the Lord.*" (Tal. Sanh. 98a)

God called Solomon His son, but Solomon did not humble himself to honor his Father. God calls Messiah, son of David, "My King" and "My Son". In humility, Messiah will thoroughly honor his Father. Then the children of Adam, whom God created to be His son, and the children of Israel, whom God also created to be His son, will be brought under the rule of Heaven upon the earth.

There is another passage that speaks of God and His son, but it is not clear what the identity of that son is. "Who has ascended to heaven and come down? Who has gathered the wind in His fists? Who has bound the waters in a garment? Who has established all the ends of the earth? What is His Name, and what is His son's name? Certainly you know." (Prov. 30:4)

We have seen that God comes down to earth (e.g. Gen.

11:5) and ascends into heaven (e.g. Gen. 17:22). He gathers and limits the winds and the waters. (e.g. Job 38:8-11, Ps. 104:2-6) And it is He alone who establishes "the ends of the earth." (Is. 40:28)

"What is His Name?" We know what God's Name is because "God further said to Moses, 'This is what you are to say to the people of Israel: *The Everpresent Lord God of your fathers, the God of Abraham, the God of Isaac, and the God of Jacob, has sent me to you; this is My Name forever, and this is My memorial to all generations.'*" (Ex. 3:15) This is a "name" in that it declares who God is.

But "What is His son's name?" To answer that question, we need to know of which son the passage speaks. Maybe it is Messiah, maybe it is Israel. Maybe it is another son.

Whether or not we can identify which son of God is spoken of in Proverbs 30:4, it is clear that the Scriptures teach that God has a son, even many sons. God created humanity to be His children, and He created humanity with the ability to have children, so that we could better understand what that means.

# THE ARM OF THE LORD

The Rabbis say that "The Torah speaks in the language of the descendants of Adam." (Tal. Baba Metzia 31b) The Torah was written by humans for humans, and therefore it uses language that humans can understand. But language and the ability to understand it are things which God gave to humanity so that we could understand Him and each other, and so that we could describe the world around us and inside us.

Because of the infinite distance between God and humanity, there are some things about God which words cannot properly or wholly express, or, at least, humans cannot wholly comprehend. It is therefore customary to speak of passages that describe God according to the nature of humanity as being "anthropomorphic" references. This customary practice, however, begins with and centers on humanity as the standard from which the Scriptures should be understood.

That is irredeemably backwards. The Scriptures themselves present a different view, a theocentric view. They begin and end with God. "So says the Everpresent Lord, King of Israel, and His redeemer the Everpresent Lord of forces: 'I am first, and I am last; and beside me there is no God." (Is. 44:6) All things, including humanity, begin and end with God. From that perspective, there are no Biblical passages that describe God according to the nature of humanity.

As previously mentioned, Samuel Butler observed: "Every man's work, whether it be literature or music or pictures or architecture or anything else, is always a portrait of himself." Neither what is written nor played nor drawn nor built is the same as its author, composer, or designer; but each work presents a picture of the one who created it.

Nor is every element in a work a mirror reflection of the creator. The work must be seen as a whole, because individual elements are often used to bring out a theme. By demonstrating values opposite to those of the author, a villain serves to clarify the author's values and their importance. The villain serves as a concrete illustration of what the author does not approve.

The values of the creator also determine the design of the work. Those who are skilled in understanding the genre, whether a painting or a computer program, are able to delineate the design and then work backwords to identify the values.

God created the heavens and the earth. "...And on the seventh day God ended His work which He had made; and He rested on the seventh day from all His work which He had made." (Gen. 2:1-2) God did not rest because He was tired. He rested because he was establishing something, Shabbat, for humanity. The heavens and the earth, time and space, are God's work. And all His work illustrates who He is.

The Scriptures teach that humanity is a "theomorphic" species, one designed and defined by God according to His own nature. That design communicates information about God, information which He wants humanity to know.

God hears, and so He created the human ear. He sees, and so He created the human eye. He speaks, and so He created the human mouth. "He who planted the ear, will He not hear? He who formed the eye, will He not see?" (Ps. 94:9)

These physical parts of the human form are "theomorphic" expressions of the attributes of God. They are all imperfect representations of what God calls "My ears" (e.g. 2Kings 19:28), "My eyes" (e.g. 2Chr. 7:15), "My mouth" (e.g. Is. 45:23), and "My nose" (e.g. Is. 65:5). After all, "He [God] made him [Adam] in the likeness of God." (Gen. 5:1)

Perhaps the most well known "anthropomorphic" reference in the Scriptures is to "the arm of the Lord". The human arm was created to represent something in the nature of God. It is part of the theomorphic nature of humanity. It is part of God's design to enable us to know Him.

Jeremiah said, "Ah, Everpresent Lord, You have made the heavens and the earth by Your great power and outstretched arm! Nothing is too hard for You." (Jer. 32:17) This is, of course, figurative language. We do not understand it to mean that God has an arm like that of a human, only infinitely bigger and stronger. But we should understand it to mean that the arm of a human is a finite, physical representation of something that God has. Since we were made in His image and likeness, the way we are made illustrates who He is.

The human arm is the means by which we make things, the way our creativity becomes tangible. It is the means by which we touch and interact with the physical world. The human arm is the way by which we exert force and get things done.

Jeremiah ascribed the work of creation to God's outstretched arm, but God's arm is more often connected to His work of deliverance, redemption, and salvation. As God told Moses, "Therefore, say to the descendants of Israel: 'I am the Everpresent Lord, and I will bring you out from under the yoke of the Egyptians. I will free you from being slaves to them, and I will redeem you with an outstretched arm and with mighty acts of judgment." (Ex. 6:6, cf. Dt. 4:34 26:8)

And Moses told all Israel before the crossing into the land of Canaan: "Remember that you were slaves in Egypt and that the Everpresent Lord your God brought you out of there with a mighty hand and an outstretched arm." (Dt. 5:15) God delivered Israel by His outstretched arm — by the exertion of His strength and power.

In a sequence of passages in Isaiah, the arm of the Lord indicates God's future faithfulness and power. "The people will dwell in Zion, in Yerushala'im. You will surely no longer weep, because He will surely be gracious to you at the sound of your cry. When He hears it, He will answer you.... The Everpresent Lord will cause the splendor of His voice to be heard, and will make them see His arm coming down with raging anger and a flaming, consuming fire, with a storm of rain and hail." (Is. 30:19,30) The arm of the Lord will execute God's vengeance on those who attack Yerushala'im.

Yerushala'im is to be comforted from all her warfare, which God will bring to an end. "Console the heart of Yerushala'im, and cry to her that her warfare has ended, that her iniquity is pardoned; because she has received double for all her sins from the hand of the Everpresent. A voice cries in the wilderness, 'Prepare the way of the Everpresent Lord, make straight in the

137

desert a highway for our God. ...Know that the Everpresent Lord comes with power, and His arm rules for Him. Know that His reward is with Him, and His recompense is before Him." (Is. 40:2-3,10)

The arm of the Lord will rule over the earth. Much of the language of this promise is repeated later as confirmation that God will surely do this. "Know that the Everpresent Lord has proclaimed to the end of the earth: 'Say to the daughter of Zion, *Know that His reward is with Him and His recompense is before Him.'*" (Is. 62:11) God will give back to the nations what they have done to Zion.

"Awake, awake! O arm of the Lord; clothe yourself with strength. Awake, as in days gone by, as in the days of old, in ancient generations. Was it not you who cut Rahab to pieces, who pierced the serpent?" (Is. 51:9) No power can stand before the arm of the Lord.

"You deserted places of Yerushala'im, break forth and sing together for joy, because the Everpresent Lord has comforted His people, He has redeemed Yerushala'im. The Everpresent Lord will lay bare His holy arm in the sight of all the Gentiles, and all the ends of the earth will see the salvation of our God." (Is. 52:10) The arm of the Lord will be revealed to all the Gentiles, and they will see that He brings salvation to Yerushala'im.

When God decreed judgment on King Belshazzar of Babylon, He did it by sending a hand from heaven. At the end, He wll send His Arm to bring judgment on all the kingdoms of this world.

A few verses later in Isaiah, however, two changes become evident in the way the arm of the Everpresent Lord is portrayed. 1) The arm of the Everpresent becomes personified as a theomorphic reality. 2) The salvation which the arm of the Everpresent brings is now salvation from sin rather than salvation from physical enemies.

"Know that My Servant will act with wisdom. He will be exalted and extolled, and be very high. Just as many were astonished at you, so His appearance is too marred for a man and his form for the descendants of Adam. So he will startle many Gentiles.

Kings will shut their mouths at him, because they will see what they had not been told; and they will understand what they had not heard. Who has believed our message and to whom has the arm of the Lord been revealed? ...Surely he has carried our sicknesses and carried the weight of our pains. But we thought he was struck and beaten by God and afflicted. But he was pierced for our transgressions, crushed for our iniquities; the chastisement for our peace was upon him, and we are healed by the beating he received. We all have wandered astray as sheep, we have each turned to his own way; but the Everpresent has caused the iniquity of us all to come upon him. ...And it pleased the Everpresent to crush him, making him weak. When You will present his soul as a guilt offering, he will see his seed, his days will be extended, and the desire of the Everpresent will succeed in his hand." (Is. 52:13-53:1, 53:4-6,10)

Traditionally, this portion was understood to refer to Messiah. "Messiah ...what is his name? ...The Rabbis said. 'His name is the leprous one, as it is written *Surely he has carried our sicknesses and carried the weight of our pains. But we thought he was struck [nagua] and beaten by God and afflicted.*' (Is. 53)" (Tal. Sanhedrin 98b) *Nagua* has the same root as *nega*, meaning "plague," sometimes specifically what is usually translated, though incorrectly, as "leprosy". The rabbinic understanding here is that God struck Messiah with the equivalent of "leprosy," which would make him unclean and cause people to exclude him from the camp of Israel. The arm of the Everpresent Lord will be revealed, but the message will not be believed.

And the Midrash comments on Boaz's invitation to Ruth in Ruth 2:14: "And at the mealtime Boaz said to her, 'Come here, and eat of the bread, and dip your morsel in the vinegar. And she sat beside the reapers; and he passed to her parched grain, and she ate, and was satisfied, and left."

Here is the rabbinic commentary in the Midrash: "He is speaking of King Messiah: 'Come here' — come near to the kingdom; 'and eat of the bread' — this is the bread of the kingdom; 'and dip your piece of bread in the vinegar,' this refers to his chastisements, as it is said (Is. 53), 'But he was pierced for our transgressions'; 'and she sat besides the reapers' — because the kingdom prepared for him will be kept from him for a short time, as it is said (Zech. 14), 'For I will gather all the nations against Yerushala'im to battle; and the city will be captured.' 'And he held out to her roasted grain,' means that the kingdom will be restored to him, as it is said (Is. 11), 'And he will strike the earth with the rod of his mouth.' R. Berekiah said in the name of R. Levi: 'The last Redeemer will be like the first Redeemer, in that the first Redeemer revealed himself, then returned and was hidden from them... so the last Redeemer will be revealed to them, then return and be hidden from them.'" (Mid. Ruth Rabbah 5.6)

The rabbinic understanding here seems to be that Messiah — identified as "the arm of the Lord" in Is. 53 — will be excluded from his people and his kingdom when he is first revealed, but will in the future be brought near to his people and into his kingdom.

In the extended Kedushah for the Yom Kippur Musaf service, we read: "Our righteous Messiah is turned away from us; we shudder in horror, and there is no one to justify us. He carries the load of our iniquities and the yoke of our transgressions. And he is wounded because of our transgressions. He bears the heaviness of our sins on his shoulder, that he may find forgiveness for our iniquities. There is healing for us in his wound." (Hebrew text in The Complete Artscroll Machzor, Yom Kippur, Mesorah Publications, 1986, Pp. 827-828)

Some today say that this passage is not about Messiah but about Israel, and that it is the Gentile kings who are speaking about Israel. There are at least three problems with that view.

1) The text says that the Gentile kings will be startled and shut their mouths concerning him. It is difficult to imagine how that could possibly mean that they immediately start talking about him.

2) Nowhere in Tanakh is Israel called "the arm of the Lord". To the contrary, in the twenty specific references, as well as in the numerous general references, the arm of the Lord acts on behalf of Israel. Israel is not expected to save itself; it cannot.

For example, Is. 59:1-2 says, "Surely the arm of the Lord is not too short to save, nor is His ear too dull to hear. But your iniquities have separated you from your God; your sins have hidden His face from you, from hearing you." (cf. Num. 11:23) The arm of the Lord has the power to save His people. His ear is able to hear their cry. But the iniquities and sins of Israel have made it impossible for them to see His face.

During the time in the wilderness, God had already asked Israel: "Is the arm of the Lord too short? You will now see whether or not what I say will come true for you." (Num. 11:23) At that time, God put His Spirit upon 70 of the elders of Israel and they prophesied.

This foreshadows God pouring out His Spirit on all Israel. "And it will be that I will afterward pour out My Spirit upon all flesh; and your sons and your daughters will prophesy, your old men will dream dreams, your young men will see visions. And also upon the servants and upon the maidservants in those days I will pour out My Spirit. And I will show wonders in the heavens and blood, fire, and pillars of smoke on the earth. The sun will be turned into darkness, and the moon into blood, before the great and the awesome day of the Everpresent Lord comes. And it will be that whoever will call on the Name of the Everpresent Lord will be saved; for in Mount Zion and in Yerushala'im there will be those who escape, as the Everpresent Lord has said, and among the remnant those whom the Everpresent Lord will call.'" (Joel 3:1-5H)

The book of Isaiah begins with a declaration of Israel's sins (e.g. Is. 1:1-31), and continues that way through the end (e.g. Is. 66:3-4,24). But it also contains God's promises to take away that sin, restore Israel to Himself, and glorify His city, His land, and His people. It is the arm of the Lord that will save Israel from her enemies and her sins.

3) Though "the servant of the Everpresent" is primarily used in Isaiah to refer to Israel, there are a few passages where it cannot be understood that way. In these passages, it designates someone other than Israel.

For example, Isaiah 49:5-7: "And now, the Everpresent

Lord, who formed me from the womb to be His Servant, to bring
Jacob back to Him, so that Israel is gathered to Him — for I
was honored in the eyes of the Everpresent Lord and My God
will be my strength — indeed He says: 'It is too easy a thing
that You should be My Servant to raise up the tribes of Jacob
and to restore the preserved ones of Israel. So I will also give
You as a light to the Gentiles, that You should be My salvation
to the ends of the earth.' This is what the Everpresent Lord
says — the Redeemer of Israel, his Holy One — to him whom
man despises, the one whom the nation loathes, to a servant of
rulers: 'Kings will see and rise up, princes also will bow down,
because of the Everpresent Lord, who is faithful, the Holy One
of Israel, who has chosen you."

In this passage, the Servant of the Everpresent gathers
Israel and brings Jacob back to God. So the Servant of the
Everpresent cannot be Israel. The Servant of the Everpresent
was formed in the womb to bring Jacob back to God; so the
Servant of the Everpresent cannot be Jacob. The content of this
text does not permit equating "the Servant of the Everpresent"
with Israel.

In Isaiah 52:13-53:12, the Servant of the Everpresent
(52:13) is presented as the arm of the Lord (53:1).The arm of
the Everpresent Lord raises up the tribes of Jacob, and restores
those of Israel whom God has kept. In this passage also, neither
the Servant of the Lord nor the arm of the Lord can be Israel.

That is why the question is asked: "Who has believed our
report, and to whom is the arm of the Lord revealed?" The arm
of the Lord has been revealed and is therefore knowable. Its
identity and purpose are revealed to the one "who has believed
our report".

# THE ROLE OF WISDOM IN CREATION

Of all that we can seek in life, the Scriptures most highly recommend wisdom. "There is good for the man who finds wisdom, and the man who gets understanding. For the profit from it is better than the profit from silver and the increase from fine gold. She is more precious than rubies; and all that you desire does not compare to her. Length of days is in her right hand; and in her left hand riches and honor. Her ways are ways of pleasantness, and all her paths are peace. She is a tree of life to those who strongly hold onto her; and there is good for everyone who holds her fast." (Prov. 3:13-18)

Wisdom enables us to know how to do something, or how to discern the correct way to go, or how to speak in difficult circumstances. It is something that, in a frantic age, we do not value enough. We have so much to do that we don't have the time to find out whether or not it is what we should do.

Sometimes God gives Wisdom to a particular person by His Spirit. "See, I have called by name Betzal'el son of Uri, the son of Hur, of the tribe of Judah, and I have filled him with the Spirit of God, with wisdom, understanding, and knowledge in all kinds of work." (Ex. 31:2-3, cf. Ex. 35:30) God filled Betzal'el with His Spirit of Wisdom to enable Betzal'el to oversee the building of the Mishkan, a place for God to live on the earth.

God commanded Moses: "Now you are to speak to all who are wise hearted, whom I have filled with the Spirit of Wisdom, that they may make Aaron's garments to consecrate him, that he may minister to Me in the priest's office." (Ex. 28:3) The Mishkan and what God's presence required were built by Wisdom, through people.

Moses passed on the leadership to Joshua, who needed more than strength to fulfill that task. "Now Joshua son of Nun was filled with the Spirit of Wisdom because Moses had laid his hands on him. So the descendants of Israel listened to him and did what the Everpresent Lord had commanded Moses." (Dt. 34:9) God filled Joshua with His Spirit of Wisdom to enable him to bring the people of Israel into the land that God had prepared for them.

At the beginning of Solomon's reign, God appeared to him and said, "Ask! What shall I give you?" And Solomon replied, "'Give me now wisdom and knowledge, that I may go out and come in before this people; for who can judge this great people of Yours?'

"And God said to Solomon, 'Because this was in your heart... The wisdom and the knowledge is given to you; and I will give you riches, and wealth, and honor, such as none of the kings have had who have been before you, nor will there be any after you who have it.'" (2Chr. 1:10-12) Solomon was wise enough to desire wisdom, even though he later was not always wise enough to follow it.

In a more consistent way, with the wisdom of God upon him, Messiah will establish justice in the earth. "The Spirit of the Everpresent Lord will rest upon him, the Spirit of Wisdom and understanding, the Spirit of counsel and might, the Spirit of knowledge and of the fear of the Everpresent." (Is. 11:2, cf. Is. 11:3ff, Mid. Ruth 7.2, Tal. Sanhedrin 93b) In the Messianic Age, all the nations will come to Yerushala'im to learn to walk in the ways of the Everpresent. (Is. 2:1-5)

In the book of Proverbs, after the opening exaltation of wisdom in chapter 3, the next verse says: "By wisdom the Everpresent founded the earth, by understanding He set the heavens in place." (Prov. 3:19) Wisdom is an attribute of God which characterizes the way in which He works. "How numerous are Your works, O Everpresent! By wisdom You made them all; the earth is full of what belongs to You." (Ps. 104:24)

It is God's own wisdom that He gives, and He gives it to those who want it more than they want anything else. in the eighth chapter of the book of Proverbs, another dimension is added when Wisdom is personified. Initially, that personification is simply extended imagery of Wisdom calling out to humanity.

"Does not Wisdom call out? Does not understanding raise her voice? She stands on the top of the heights along the way, where the ways meet. She joyfully cries aloud beside the gates leading into the city, at the entrances. 'I call out to you men, my voice to humanity. Let the naive understand discernment, and let the foolish have an understanding heart.'" (Prov. 8:1-5, cf. 9:1-5)

The text then goes on to ascribe to Wisdom personified an auxiliary role in the creation of the world. "'The Everpresent possessed [kanah] me, the beginning [raysheet] of His way, before [kedem] His deeds of old [me'az]. I was poured out from eternity [me'olam], from the beginning [me'rosh], even before [mi'kadmei] the earth. When there were no deeps, I was brought forth, when there were no springs abounding with water. Before the mountains were settled in place, before the hills, I was brought forth, when He had not yet made the earth or its fields or any of the dust of the world.

"I was there when He established the heavens, when He marked out the horizon on the face of the deep [tehom]. When he established the clouds above and fixed securely the fountains of the deep [tehom], when He gave the sea its boundary so the waters would not go beyond His command, and when He marked out the foundations of the earth, then I was the craftsman at His side. I was His delight each day, rejoicing always in His presence, rejoicing in His inhabited world and delighting in humanity." (Prov. 8:22-31)

Kanah, the word in the first verse which I have translated as "possessed," means "to buy or own". Some translate it here as "create," but that seems inconsistent with the normal usage, with the immediate context, and with the way the word is used throughout Proverbs.

For example, in Prov. 4:7, we are told that "Wisdom is the beginning [raysheet]. Possess/buy [kanah] wisdom and with all your possessions [kinyankha], buy [k'nay] understanding." (Prov. 4:7) Throughout Proverbs, Wisdom is not something one creates, but rather something that one seeks to buy, gain, or possess. In the particular section in chapter 8, Wisdom is contrasted with all the things that God did create. There does not seem to be any reason to forsake the normal, linguistic meaning in translating this section.

In the Midrash, this personified Wisdom is equated with the living Torah, which is said to have existed before Creation. Therefore, according to the Midrash, Prov. 8:22-23, "by these six words, [it indicates that] the Torah preceded [the creation of the world]: kedem ['before'], me-'az ['of old'], me-'olam ['from eternity'], me-rosh ['from the beginning'], and mi-kadmei ['from before,' which is a plural form], is two." (Mid. Genesis 1.8, cf. 1.4)

The Midrash equates this "Wisdom" with the Torah, paraphrasing God to say: "It was by the Torah that I created [barati] heaven and earth, as it is said (Prov. 3), 'By Wisdom the Everpresent founded the earth...'" (Mid. Exodus 47.4)

The very first section of the Midrash presents a personified Torah saying. "'I was the tool for work of the Holy One, blessed be He.' In the way of the world, when a king of flesh and blood builds a palace, he does not build it from his own knowledge, but from the knowledge of a construction foreman. And the construction foreman does not build it from his own knowledge, but he has plans and notebooks to know how he should make the rooms and how he should make the construction. In this way, the Holy One, blessed be He, looked to the Torah and created [bara] the world. And the Torah says, 'In the beginning God created [bara]' (Gen. 1:1), but there is no beginning except the Torah, as in the verse, 'The Everpresent possessed [kanani] me as the beginning of His way' (Prov. 8:22)." (Mid. Gen. 1.1)

The presentation of Wisdom as a thinking, speaking, acting being — "the construction foreman" — continues in Proverbs chapter 9. "Wisdom has built her house, She has hewn out her seven pillars. She has surely slaughtered [her meat]; she has mixed her wine; she has also arranged her table. She has sent her young women; she calls out on the highest places of the city: 'Whoever is naive, let him turn in here.' To the one who lacks understanding, she speaks to him..." (Prov. 9:1-4).

And in the Rabbinic understanding, in an extended commentary, the Midrash connects each phrase of these verses to specific actions of God in Creation and in His interaction with Adam and Havah. In effect, the Midrash is equating personified

Wisdom with the Everpresent Himself.

"'Wisdom has built her house': This is the Holy One, blessed be He, as it is written, 'The Everpresent by wisdom founded the earth...'

"'She has hewn out her seven pillars': These are the seven days 'in the Beginning,' as it says (Ex. 20), 'because in six days the Everpresent made heaven and earth...'

"'She has surely slaughtered [her meat]': 'And God said, *Let the earth bring forth [all kinds of living creatures, cattle...]*'

"'She has mixed her wine': 'And God said, *Let the waters be gathered...*'

"'She has also arranged her table.' 'And God said, *Let the earth bring forth grass...*'" (Mid. Lev. 11.1)

[The "She" is used because the word for Wisdom, *chokma*, is grammatically feminine. The grammatical gender of a word does not indicate the gender of what it designates. Many words for animals — e.g. *yonah* (dove, feminine), *chasidah* (stork, feminine), *namer* (leopard, masculine) — designate both the male and the female of the species.]

This personified Wisdom of God, this eternal living Torah, is greater than the Torah which has been reduced to two-dimensional print. Torah is said to be an incompletely developed form of that Wisdom which was alongside God in the beginning. That Wisdom is complete and whole, whereas the written "Torah is the unripened form of the Wisdom from above." (Mid. Genesis 17.5, 44.17) The apocryphal "Wisdom of Solomon" speaks of Wisdom being enthroned next to God. (Apoc. Wisdom 9:4,10)

In rabbinic understanding, the fully ripe form of Wisdom comes to earth with Messiah. "The Torah which a person learns in this world is a passing breath before the Torah of Messiah." (Mid. Lamentations 11.7)

That Wisdom of God comes into the world to redeem and teach (as God did through Moses), to bring the people of Israel into what God promised them (as God did through Joshua), to prepare a place for God to live on the earth (as God did through Betzal'el, Aholiab, and others), and to establish God's kingdom and justice upon the earth (as God has promised to do through Messiah). Wisdom assisted God in creating the world, and Wisdom will assist God in redeeming it.

An interesting picture emerges from the Scriptural passages (and the rabbinic comments on them). The Wisdom of God is presented as an eternal living Torah which assisted God in creating the world. It is therefore distinct, but wholly possessed and appointed by God; it is distinct, but neither independent of nor separable from God. It is not a separate force or power, such as a gnostic demiurge or an additional, lesser god. But the Wisdom of God is one of the ways, the primary way, by which God Himself created the world and does His work in the created world.

# THE SECOND VERSE

וְהָאָרֶץ הָיְתָה תֹהוּ וָבֹהוּ וְחֹשֶׁךְ עַל פְּנֵי תְהוֹם
וְרוּחַ אֱלֹהִים מְרַחֶפֶת עַל פְּנֵי הַמָּיִם

And the earth was without order and empty; and Darkness was on the surface of the deep. And the Spirit of God was hovering over the surface of the waters.

# THE SECOND VERSE

## *TOHU vaVOHU*

*v'ha'aretz haita tohu vavohu*
"and the earth was without order and empty..." (Gen. 1:2)

Initially, the earth was not yet ordered and structured; and it was uninhabited. But that initial state was not the goal of what God wanted. It was the starting point of a process.

God created the earth for a purpose. "He did not create it to be *tohu*/empty, but formed it to be inhabited..." (Is. 45:18b) After that initial act of creation, God set the structure of the earth, and then He caused it to produce vegetation. That made it look quite different from its original form, almost unrecognizably so.

Then God created living creatures to swarm in the waters, fly through the sky, and move upon the ground. The earth was no longer empty and uninhabited. It was filled with multiple forms of life, their sounds, smells, and movements.

But God wasn't finished. "Then the Everpresent Lord God formed Adam of dust from the ground [*adamah*], and breathed into his nostrils a breath of life; and Adam became a living soul." (Gen. 2:7) God formed the physical body of Adam from the earth, but his life came from the mouth of God. Then the earth was fully formed and inhabited.

God created the earth to be a place where justice and righteousness flourish, but He knew what was coming. He created humanity in His own image and likeness to live out its identity upon the earth. He gave humanity the opportunity, and the requirement, to be faithful, responsible, and fruitful on the earth. But it didn't play out that way.

And God knew that it wouldn't. "From the beginning of the creation of the world, the Holy One, blessed be He, foresaw the deeds of the righteous and the deeds of the wicked. 'the earth was without order' — this is the deeds of the wicked." (Mid. Genesis 3:8)

In the beginning, God Himself walked on the earth, seeking out humanity. (e.g. Gen. 3:8) But instead of filling the earth with justice and righteousness, people filled it with violence and perversity. (cf. Gen. 6:11-12) "'without order and empty': this refers to Ka'in, who sought to turn the world back to disorder and emptiness." (Mid. Gen. 2.3)

God was patient, but He eventually brought judgment. Time and again, the same tragedy played itself out. In spite of that cycle, humanity never changed, never turned back to God. The nations/*goyim* stubbornly continued in their willful blindness.

So God created Israel to be a light to them, to bring them back to Himself. For that purpose, an infinite God caused His presence to first fill the very finite Tabernacle, and then the Temple. He had prescribed both of these for Israel. (e.g. Ex. 40:34-35; 1K. 8:11) His presence was to be the center of Israel's existence.

But, unfortunately, the history of Israel followed the same futile, self-destructive, self-indulgent pattern that had become the trademark of humanity. "For the house of Israel is the vineyard of the Everpresent Commander of forces, and the men of Judah are the plant of His delight. He expected justice/*mishpat*, but behold, oppression/*mishpakh*! righteousness/*tz'daka*, but behold, a cry/*tz'aka* [for help]!" (Is. 5:7) So He said to Israel, "I saw the earth, and surely it was unformed and empty/*tohu vavohu* and there was no light to the heavens." (Jer. 4:23)

And, unfortunately, the nations/*goyim* did not want to be reconciled and restored to God. They did not want to be told that the path they had chosen for themselves was fatally wrong. So the very fact that Israel was created for their redemption became a source of great hostility toward Israel. A fully inhabited earth became more chaotic than it had been at the very beginning. "All the nations/*goyim* are as nothing before Him, they are considered by Him to be less than emptiness/*tohu*." (Is. 40:16) Humanity created its own form of a world without order.

Even so, God continually promised to redeem Israel from her sins and her enemies. And, as He said to Ezekiel when showing him a restored Temple yet to be established upon the earth, "Son of Adam, this is the place of My throne and the place of the soles of My feet, where I will dwell among the children of Israel forever..." (Ezek. 43:7) God never relinquished His intention to walk and live on the earth. (cf. Ex. 29:45, 1K. 6:13)

He calls Yerushala'im "My city"; He calls Israel "My land"; He calls the descendants of Israel "My people". (e.g. Joel 3:2, Is. 45:13) Yet Zechariah the prophet spoke of a time when the armies of all the nations of the earth would come against Yerushala'im to forcibly remove the Jewish people from half of the city. (cf. Zech. 14:1-2)

"Then the Everpresent Lord will come out and battle against those nations as in the day of battle, the day of war. And in that day, His feet will stand on the Mount of Olives which is across from Yerushala'im to the east... And the Everpresent Lord will be King over all the earth... And it will be that all who remain from all the nations which came against Yerushala'im will then go up from year to year to bow down to the King, the Everpresent Lord of forces, and will make a pilgrimage to keep the festival of Sukkot." (Zech. 14:3-4,9,16) The Lord intends to rule over all the earth from Yerushala'im.

"You heavens above, rain down righteousness; let the clouds shower it down. Let the earth open wide, let salvation spring up, let justice grow with it. I, the Everpresent Lord, have created it." (Is. 45:8) As the earth needs the rain from heaven, so humanity needs God to bring forth salvation and justice. "Truth will sprout from the earth, and justice will look down from heaven." (Ps. 85:12H) Humanity was not designed to live separately from God.

Though Israel has failed to be what God created it to be, He has promised to redeem and restore a remnant. (e.g. Is. 11:11) Though the nations of the earth have failed to be what God created them to be, God will also redeem and restore a remnant from them. He intends to fulfill His purposes for the earth and the humanity He created upon it. "For even as I live, all the earth will be filled with the glory of the Lord." (Num.14:21, cf. Hab. 2:14)

Technological advances are the present glory of humanity. Technological advances in medicine and agriculture are wonderful; technological advances in the speed and variety of communication are amazing; but one staggering fact becomes increasingly evident. The more humanity progresses in technology, the more violent the earth becomes. The twentieth century was the bloodiest century in human history; the twenty-first century is on a pace to rapidly surpass it.

War is a thriving business, a growth industry. Humanity is more barbaric and arrogant than it has ever been, with technologically advanced and enhanced means of pursuing what is in their hearts. Humanity has become the most deadly specie on the planet, defiling and destroying both itself and the earth it inhabits. Humanity has made the earth a desolate place.

As one of the most beautiful aspects of all that God created, He created humanity so that we could have children, so that we could be fruitful and fill the earth. It was intended to be a blessing: a unique unformed child develops and is born. The infant becomes a toddler, and the toddler becomes a bright-eyed, inquisitive, loving little person. That little person develops in personality, skill, and understanding, bringing joy to his or her parents. Or, at least, that was the purpose.

Because "Children are an inheritance from the Everpresent, and the fruit of the womb is a reward." (Ps. 127:3) And that is followed by greater blessing: "May you see your children's children; peace be upon Yerushala'im." (Ps. 128:6) "And the lovingkindness of the Everpresent is from everlasting to everlasting on those who fear Him, and His righteousness to children's children." (Ps. 103:17)

Unfortunately, in a world where humanity seeks to establish its own order, it doesn't always work out that way. Humanity was almost unformed when Adam and Havah made their choice to go their own way. After that, their firstborn murdered his brother, and the tragedy continued from there.

The richest, wisest man upon the earth tried to understand the meaningless futility that life had become. "Then I turned to look at all the deeds which my hands had done and on the work which I had labored to do. And it was all surely futility and a striving spirit, and there was no profit under the sun. ...And I hated all my work which I had labored under the sun that I must leave to a man who will come after me. And who knows if he will be a wise man or a fool, but he will rule over all my work which I had labored, in which I was wise under the sun. This also is futility." (Eccl. 2:11,18-19)

When the earth was without order or inhabitant, who knew what it would become? God knew, but He let humanity make its choices. When a child in the womb is being formed, who knows what its life will be? God knows, but He lets each of us make our choices. And those choices have consequences beyond the span of our own lives.

God commanded, "Let there be light," but people have chosen darkness instead. There is a pattern in God's judgments: He gives people what they choose, but not in the same way they have chosen it. "Know this, the darkness will cover the earth, and thick darkness the people..." (Is. 60:2a) "That day is a day of wrath, a day of trouble and distress, a day of devastation and desolation, a day of darkness and gloominess, a day of clouds and thick darkness." (Zeph. 1:15)

That day will not be pleasant, but it will serve its purpose. The great darkness will indicate a coming dawn. "Then the trees of the forest will rejoice before the Everpresent Lord for He is coming to judge the earth." (1Ch. 16:33) The earth will be restored, "Because, watch, I create new heavens and a new earth. And the first will not be remembered nor come upon the heart." (Is. 65:17)

## *Choshekh* / DARKNESS

"and **darkness** was on the surface of the deep..." (Gen. 1:2)

Darkness existed in the world before God spoke light into it. Darkness is part of Creation. It is not simply the absence of light; it is something in and of itself, something which God created. It existed in a particular location — "on the surface of the deep" — but not in every location.

God said, "I form the light and create darkness..." (Is. 45:7) Darkness was created. Light was formed in this world, not created, because light already existed as a characteristic of God Himself. (e.g. Ps. 27:1, Ps. 89:15, Is. 60:19-20)

"And God saw the Light, that it was good, so God separated the Light from the Darkness." (Gen. 1:4) God saw that the Light was good, and that is the reason that He separated the Light from the Darkness. The Darkness was different from the Light; the Light was good in itself, the Darkness, though created for a good purpose, was not. God made a separation between them.

Humans need an external source of light to enable us to see. God doesn't. King David prayed, "If I say, 'Surely the darkness will bruise me [*yeshufayni*],' the night will be light around me. Even the darkness is not dark to You; the night shines like the day, as the light, so is the darkness." (Ps. 139:11-12)

No one can hide from God in the darkness. God still sees everything. He sees everything that is done in the darkness just as clearly as He sees everything that is done in the light.

David used a particular word [*yeshufayni*] to indicate the harm he feared from the darkness. The same word is used to indicate the conflict between the Serpent and Havah, the mother of humanity. In God's judgment, He said to the Serpent, "And I will put hostility between you and the woman, and between your seed and her seed. He will bruise [*yeshufaykha*] your head, And you will bruise [*t'shufaynu*] His heel." (Gen. 3:15)

The Serpent had deceived Havah, and she had chosen to believe him rather than believe God. The result was the source of all human catastrophes. In His judgment, God was saying that there would be a future conflict between a particular descendant of the Serpent and a particular descendant of the woman. In that conflict, though the descendant of Havah would be injured, he would overcome the descendant of the Serpent.

People are sometimes deceived about what is good and what is evil, what is light and what is darkness. But God warns: "Woe to those who say of evil that it is good, and of good that it is evil; who present darkness as light and light as darkness; who present what is bitter as sweet and what is sweet as bitter. Woe to those who are wise in their own eyes and discerning in their own estimation." (Is. 5:20-21)

Before God redeemed us from Egypt, He brought plagues of judgment upon the Egyptians and their gods. The last plague before the death of the firstborn was a thick darkness. God told Moses, "'Stretch out your hand toward the heavens, and there will be darkness over the land of Egypt, and the darkness will be felt.' So Moses stretched out his hand toward the heavens, and there was deep darkness in all the land of Egypt three days. No one could see anyone else or rise from where he was for three days. But for all the children of Israel, there was light in the places where they lived." (Ex. 10:21-23)

The darkness was much more than the absence of light. It was a force that could be felt. The New JPS translation says, "a darkness which can be touched." That darkness also covered a deep abyss, one which was open before Pharaoh.

God says that a similar darkness will cover all the earth at the end of this age. As all the world comes against Israel, God will say to Yerushala'im, "Arise, shine, because your light has come, and the glory of the Everpresent Lord is risen upon you. Know that the darkness will cover the earth, and deep darkness the people; but the Everpresent Lord will arise upon you and His glory will be seen upon you." (Is. 60:1-2)

It will be the culmination of the conflict between light and darkness in this age. The Midrash says: "'God sets an end to darkness...' [Job 28:3] A time was set for the world to spend in deep darkness, a certain number of years.... For all the time that the Evil Inclination exists in the world, deep darkness and the shadow of death are in the world.... When the Evil Inclination is uprooted from the world, there will be neither deep darkness nor the shadow of death in the world." (Mid. Gen. 89.1)

After Pharaoh let Israel go, he changed his mind, took his army and chariots, and pursued after the people. So God sent His angel and a pillar of cloud which "came between the camp of Egypt and the camp of Israel. And it was a cloud and darkness [to Egypt] and illuminated the night [to Israel]. So neither one went near the other the whole night." (Ex. 14:20)

God can see through darkness, but humans can't. So for us, darkness sometimes brings with it the fear of the unknown. We don't know what it hides.

God promised Abram that He would give the land of Canaan to his descendants. Abram asked for some kind of confirmation. God told him to offer certain sacrifices, "Then when the sun was going down, a deep sleep fell upon Abram; and great fear and great darkness fell upon him!" (Gen. 15:12) The Midrash says that the darkness represented the nations that would attack the land of Israel in the future. (Mid. Gen. 44.17)

In describing the fear and helplessness which Israel would experience in exile for our sins, the Everpresent said, "And you will feel your way at noonday, as a blind man feels his way in deep darkness; you will not prosper in your ways; you will be only oppressed and robbed continually, and there will be no savior." (Dt. 28:29)

Sometimes, because of the darkness which we see and feel, we don't see God; we don't know where He is. But God wants us to know that He is still there, even when we are overcome by fear and darkness.

On the day that God spoke the Ten Commandments, "Then all the people saw the lightning and the smoke of the mountain, and heard the thunder and the sound of the shofar. When the people saw, they trembled and stood far off.... Then the people stood afar off, but Moses drew near to the deep darkness where God was." (Ex. 20:15,18H, cf. Dt. 4:11) Sometimes one needs great courage to come near to God.

# *Tehom* / THE DEEP

"the surface of the **deep**..." (Gen. 1:2)

There are many things about Creation that the Scriptures do not tell us. They do, however, tell us the things that God wants us to know. What is recorded, as well as what is not recorded, intentionally tells us something about God.

For example, "darkness" and "the deep/*tehom*" are the first specific entities mentioned in the account of the creation of the earth, but the text does not tell us when or how either came into existence. The Septuagint uses *abussos* for *tehom*, often transliterated into English as "abyss". This early existence of darkness and the abyss indicates that God did not design the earth to be a playground or a vacation resort. Even in its primitive form, the earth contained something hidden, something ominous. What is hidden in the abyss? What is its purpose?

God created a world with darkness over an abyss. What is it that He wanted? And why did He want it? Certainly it underlines the seriousness of His purpose.

Similar questions arise when we look at the signs that God gave Moses to perform before Israel and before Pharaoh. (Ex. 4:1-9) Without taking all the time that would be needed to speak of what these signs say about God, humanity, and the world in which we live, it is still important to be aware of their significance.

God's first sign was to change the rod of Moses into a serpent, which God then commanded Moses to grab by its tail. That rod was the indispensable implement of the shepherd, and Moses later used it to perform miracles. It was called "the rod of God," (e.g., Ex. 4:20). That rod of God, the symbol of His authority, turned into a deadly serpent which later swallowed up the serpents of Pharaoh's magicians.

God's second sign was for Moses to put his hand under his cloak, over his heart, to bring it out and find it to be afflicted with a plague that made him unclean; and then to restore its health when Moses again placed it over his heart and brought it out again. This speaks of the deadly evil of the human heart and the uncleanness of the works of our hands, a filth which can only be cleansed, and an evil which can only be healed, by God.

The third sign was to take water from the Nile and pour it out on the land where it would become blood. The Egyptians relied upon the Nile for their crops, their livestock, and themselves; it was the lifeblood of the land of Egypt. it was also the river in which they drowned every baby boy born to the Hebrew people.

The river, the center of Egyptian life, was supposed to kill Moses and Israel, but Pharaoh's daughter took him out of it, and he grew up on the land of Egypt. After Pharaoh's rejection of the signs, all the Nile would be turned to blood.

These are the signs — a serpent, a plague, and blood — that signify God's power and authority. In them, God signifies many things about Himself, about humanity, and about redemption. These are not innocuous symbols. They demonstrated what God was going to do to Egypt and they demonstrate what He Is going to do at the end of this age to all who afflict His people.

All of this is foreshadowed in the Darkness over the Abyss. For the redemption of Israel, "He rebuked the Red Sea, and it dried up; so He led them through the **depths** [*tehomot*], as through the wilderness." (Ps. 106:9)

For the destruction of Egypt, "He has thrown Pharaoh's chariots and his army into the sea; his chosen captains also are drowned in the Red Sea. The **depths** [*tehomot*] have covered them; they sank to the bottom as a stone." (Ex.15:4-5) Some survive the depths, some are destroyed in them.

Though we live on the surface of the earth, there is much more to the earth than the surface. There are depths greater than we know. Job asked, "Then where is Wisdom found? and where is the place of understanding? People do not know its value, and it is not found in the land of the living. The **deeps** say, 'It is not in me,' and the sea says, 'It is not with me." (Job 28:12-14)

Wisdom existed before the darkness or the abyss: "I was poured out from eternity, from the beginning, even before the earth. When there were no **deeps**, I was brought forth, when there were no springs abounding with water. Before the mountains were settled in place, before the hills, I was brought forth, before He had yet made the earth or its fields or any of the dust of the world. I was there when He set the heavens in place, when He marked out the horizon on the face of the **deep**. When he established the clouds above and fixed securely the fountains of the **deep**, when He gave the sea its boundary so the waters would not go beyond His command, and when He marked out the foundations of the earth, then I was the craftsman at His side." (Prov. 8:23-29)

People often live superficial lives, relating only to the surfaces of things, each other, and God. "...humanity looks at the appearance, but the Everpresent looks at the heart." (1Sam. 16:7) God sees people, and all things, the way they really are, not simply the way they appear on the surface.

That, unfortunately, is why the deeps are often connected with judgment. "In the six hundredth year of the life of Noah, in the second month, on the seventeenth day of the month, on that day all the fountains of the great **deep** were broken up, and the windows of heaven were opened." (Gen. 7:11, cf. 8:2) Only 8 people survived. When God created the deep, He knew what would happen in the time of Noah.

When Israel was in exile, Tyre boasted against Yerushala'im, expecting to pillage it. "In response, the Everpresent Lord said, 'When I make you a dried up city, like the uninhabited cities, when I bring up the **deep** upon you, and the great waters cover you, then I will bring you down with those who go down to the Pit, to the people of old, and I will make you dwell in the lowest part of the earth, in places desolate from of old, with those who go down to the Pit, so that you will not be inhabited; and I will set My beauty in the land of the living." (Ezek. 26:19-20) When God created the deep, He knew what judgment He would bring upon Tyre.

God created Israel as a means of calling the nations to turn from their evil so that they would not suffer the judgment they have earned. It is not an easy or welcome task, and so we have not always wanted to do it. God told Jonah to go to Ninevah and proclaim an imminent destruction. Jonah, as is well known, did not want to go. He ran away, but God used a storm and a large fish to get Jonah where He wanted him.

Afterwards, Jonah recounted his experience: "I am cast out from Your presence; yet I will look again toward Your holy temple. The waters surrounded me, even to my soul. The **deep** encompassed me. Reeds ensnared my head. I went down to the base of the mountains. The earth with its bars closed behind me forever, but You, my Everpresent God, have brought up my life from destruction." (Jonah 2:6-7H)

An individual, or a nation, can sink very deep. As Jonah found out, if we surrender to God and His purposes, there's a way back up. The psalmist cried out to God: "You, who have shown me many and grievous troubles, restore me back to life, and bring me back from the **depths** of the earth." (Ps. 71:20)

But *tehom* can be more than a place of trouble and despair. It can be a good place to hear God. We tend to see the world, including our own lives, superficially, without thinking about what lies beneath. But God created us for much more than that, and He calls us to much more than that, though we can be so distracted with what is superficial that we do not hear. Sometimes, of course, we do not hear because we do not listen.

"**Deep** calls out to **deep** [*tehom el tehom*] at the sound of Your waterfalls; all Your breakers and waves have gone over me." (Ps. 42:8H) When we are beaten and crushed, the superficial loses its attraction. When we desperately need to hear from God, deep within us there is a place where we can hear.

Moses had no one else to turn to. Neither did Joseph, or Abraham, or Jeremiah. In the darkest of days, God told Jeremiah to tell Israel: "You will seek Me and you will find Me when you search for Me with all your heart." (Jer. 29:13) We may find ourselves in the depths, but God can find us there too.

*Tehom* can signify something other than despair; it can be connected to deep blessings. As his life neared its end, Jacob blessed his sons. For Joseph, he prayed: "By the God of your father who will help you, and by the Almighty who will bless you with blessings of heaven above, blessings of the **deep** that lies beneath, blessings of the breasts and of the womb." (Gen. 49:25) Joseph was promised blessings in the heights, and blessings in the depths.

As the life of Moses neared its end, he also blessed the tribes of Israel. "And of Joseph he said: 'His land is blessed by the Everpresent with the desirable things of heaven, with the dew, and with the **deep** that lies underneath." (Deut. 33:13) What lies on the surface is more accessible, but what is most valuable may lie deep beneath it.

Moses told our fathers that "the Everpresent Lord your God is bringing you into a good land, a land of brooks of water, of springs, and **depths** that flow out of the valley and the hill." (Dt. 8:7) Water that comes from the depths is cleaner and fresher than what flows on the surface, and more reliable.

In the beginning, God set darkness over the surface of the deep. "You laid the foundations of the earth on its fixed places, so that it would not ever be moved. You covered it with the **deep** as a garment when the waters stood above the mountains." (Ps. 104:5-6) God first covered the earth with the deep, and after that He made the dry land appear. Underneath the deep lay the tops of the highest mountains.

God's purposes are neither shallow nor unknowable. "Your lovingkindness is in the heavens, O Everpresent, Your faithfulness is unto the clouds. Your righteousness is like the great mountains. Your judgments are a great **deep**. O Everpresent, You save man and animal." (Ps. 36:6-7H)

God's purposes are neither shallow nor futile. The good things He has promised, even those that seem impossible, will appear when the waters subside. The chariots of Pharaoh drew near for vengeance, and the waters of the sea blocked all escape for our ancestors, but God's purpose still towered over them.

It will be the same in the end. "Therefore the redeemed of the Everpresent will return, and come to Zion with shouts of joy and everlasting joy upon their heads. Joy and gladness will overtake them; sorrow and groaning will flee away." (Is. 51:11)

# GOD CREATED EVIL

We live in a world filled with evil. If God is both good and almighty, why is there evil in the world? This question is difficult, not only because we do not have an answer that is completely satisfying, but also because the fragments of the answer that we do have are painful and somewhat troubling.

When we ask, "Why do good people suffer?" or "Why is there so much tragedy in life?" we are asking the preliminary questions. We cannot satisfactorily answer these questions, certainly not completely.

The root question, however, is more difficult. It is not, "Why does God allow evil?" because God does not simply allow evil. "I form the light and create darkness, I make peace and create evil. I, the Everpresent, do all these things." (Is. 45:7) The root question, the one behind all the others is: "Why did God create evil?"

The Scriptures do not offer us a dualistic way of escape. There is no eternally existent evil principle. The answer to this question must be found in who God is, in the relationship He desires with humanity, and in His purposes for Creation. The answer is integrally connected to His having created, in the beginning, darkness over an abyss.

Before I begin to examine these things, I want to mention an evening I spent some years ago with three Holocaust survivors in Belarus. One man, who was a young teenager when the Holocaust began, asked me some questions. Perhaps they were, in a sense, rhetorical questions, but they were the questions that shadowed his whole life, and he wanted answers. He was not engaged in idle philosophical speculation. In different ways, he was simply, painfully asking, "Why the Holocaust?"

I'm sure that the question reverberated continually in the core of his being. Perhaps he was asking me because he knew that I believe in God and I say that I know Him. 'If you know God, ask Him about this...' Perhaps he wasn't asking me at all, but just letting some of his pain out into the world.

I did respond, however. In essence, I said, "I don't know, but I think there are some answers. The first answer is, 'There is no answer.' Once we settle that, we can talk about the other answers." On that evening, that was good enough to enable us to begin to talk.

I do know God. Sometimes I feel that I don't know Him very well, but I do know Him. Sometimes I don't understand why He lets certain painful things happen, but I don't doubt His goodness or His wisdom. Sometimes I don't understand why I do some of the things I do, and I have come to doubt my own goodness and wisdom. I have given my life into His hands, because I trust Him, even though that doesn't make life easier.

God does not need to justify Himself to me, nor does He need me to justify Him to others. But God has been so good and merciful to me, and I owe Him everything. If I did not try to speak on His behalf, I feel that I would be betraying the One who has always been faithful to me, the One who has always loved me.

There are some things that are beyond us, but that doesn't mean we can't think, talk, and care about them. If we don't ask and wrestle with these questions, I think we imprison ourselves in an artificially small world. With that understanding, let's look at some of the other answers. We will probably still need that first answer when we are finished, but the other answers may also be helpful.

### It was very good?

God made the Garden of Eden. At the end of the third day, God created the fruit-bearing trees, "every tree that appears desirable and is good to eat." (Gen. 2:9) "And God saw that it was good." (Gen.1:12b) In the middle of the garden, God had placed the tree of the knowledge of good and evil, which was soon to bear ripe fruit. (Gen. 2:9,17) Since the knowledge of good and evil was available, evil must have already existed. Why then did God see that "it was good"?

On the sixth day, God made "all the creatures that move along the ground according to their kinds. And God saw that it was good." (Gen. 1:25b) How could that be? The Serpent which would soon deceive Havah was moving in the garden.

Then, on that same sixth day, God created Adam and placed him in the garden. "God saw all that He had made, and behold, it was very good." (Gen.1:31a) How could that be? God knew that the Serpent would tempt Havah. God knew that Adam and Havah would yield to the temptation, disobey Him, and eat of the fruit of the knowledge of good and evil. He knew what the terrible consequences of that disobedience would be, down to the present day and beyond. God knew that the Holocaust would be in that act of disobedience. And yet, somehow, all that God had made "was very good."

"I form the light [*yotser ohr*] and create darkness [*boray choshekh*], I make peace [*oseh shalom*] and create evil [*boray rah*]. I, the Everpresent, do all these things." (Is. 45:7) The text does not say that God created light or peace. They existed before Creation, since they are aspects of who God is.

God tells us that He created darkness. That means there is a darkness that is not simply the absence of light. It is something in and of itself. It is the opposite of light. God created it.

When God tells us that He created evil [*ra*], He uses the same word that He used to describe the tree from which Adam and Havah ate and what they would come to know from eating its fruit. (Gen. 3:22) That means that there is something that is not simply the absence of good. It is something in and of itself, the opposite of good. God created it.

Darkness and evil are the opposite of what God is. They are unlike God, and yet God created them. They do not have His power, but they have a power that He gave them.

Why did God create something that is the opposite of what He is and the opposite of what He desires? Why did He then put the tree of the knowledge of good and evil in the garden, where Adam and Havah were tempted by it? If there had to be such a tree, why didn't He make it inaccessible to Adam and Havah? Any why did He put the Serpent in the Garden as an *agent provocateur*?

Evil is evil, it is not good. But the question is, 'In the ultimate plan and purpose of God for humanity, can it be good that there is evil?' Can the existence of evil accomplish something good? Can it accomplish something essential in the hearts of humanity?

I understand that these may sound like meaningless, even foolish, philosphical questions. Maybe they are that for some people, but they are not that for me. Evil is not an abstraction. It is something very concrete.

Evil is cruelty, degradation, abuse, and contempt. Evil is suffering, pain, and the crushing of human bodies, dreams, hopes, and lives. But the questions are not meaningless or foolish. They are simply an inadequate attempt to express what may be the most painful puzzle of human existence. They are the beginning of an attempt to wrestle with that painful puzzle.

We can say, and partially understand, that God created humanity with the ability to choose, and that such an ability has greater meaning when people are able to make bad choices as well as good choices. We can say, and partially understand, that love and obedience have greater meaning when one can choose not to love and not to obey; and certainly, for us, such a possibility, by providing a sharp contrast, makes them appear greater. We can understand that God's judgment will eventually come, but as fixed and unavoidable as that judgment may be, it doesn't undo the bitter trail of destruction that evil leaves behind.

God did command Adam and Havah not to eat from the tree; and perhaps that was, and is, His way of making evil inaccessible to humanity. They only needed to accept God as who He is. Had they done that, they would have obeyed Him, and evil would not have taken over the world. Instead, they decided to go their own way.

Couldn't God have made Adam so that he would have had the ability to choose evil, but would, in actuality, always have chosen good? (Couldn't God have made me, my children, my neighbor, or my enemy, so that I, or they, or he, or she wouldn't choose evil?) Yes, I suppose He could have, but that would mean that Adam would not really have had the ability or the freedom to make moral choices. That would mean that Adam could not accept or embrace evil. It would also mean that Adam could not consciously choose to reject or shun evil. Adam would have had to be less than what God created him to be. He would have been more like the animals, and less like God. Adam would have had only the illusion of freedom, not the reality.

Even so, it would still be a better world if there were no evil in it. You think so, I think so too, and God does not disagree. But that is not the same as saying that God should not have created evil. Without doubt, Adam should not have chosen evil. His descendants should not choose evil today, but that is not the same as saying that the choice, i.e. the freedom, should not be possible. I wish the choice of evil were not available, but it is. And God, who is good, has His reasons for it.

Should we then say that God, after all, is the one most at fault? Should we say that God is the one who sinned most of all? That is what Adam said: "the woman **You** gave to be with me, she gave me of the tree, and I ate." (Gen.3:12) I.e., 'If **You** hadn't created the woman as my companion, if **You** hadn't enabled her to disobey, and if **You** hadn't given her the ability and inclination to persuade me, then I wouldn't have done it. **It's Your fault.**'

That is also what Havah said: "The Serpent deceived me, and I ate." (Gen.3:13) I.e., 'If **You** hadn't created the Serpent, if **You** hadn't given it the ability and inclination to deceive, and if **You** hadn't put it in the garden, and if **You** hadn't created me with the ability to believe a lie, then I wouldn't have done it. **It's Your fault.**'

Certainly there is some truth in what Adam and Havah said. If God hadn't created them with certain abilities, if God hadn't created the Serpent with certain abilities, if God hadn't made the encounter possible, then none of it would have happened.

But if God were to respond to these charges in a similarly human way, He could have said to the Man and the Woman: "I love you. I created you with the ability to choose, which is an inestimably precious freedom. I created you in My own image and likeness. I wanted you to be like Me. Without that freedom, you could not be like Me.

"I told you what you should do, and I commanded you to choose what is good. You can't say that you didn't know. You did know. I told you. All you had to do was believe Me and do what was right. Nevertheless, you chose to believe that I was lying, and you chose to seek what is evil. And now you come and blame Me? You blame Me because I gave you the ability to choose? You blame Me because what I told you was true? You blame Me because you're unwilling to accept responsibility for what you did wrong?

"I did not create the Serpent with the irresistable inclination to deceive. I created the Serpent with the ability to choose to deceive. He made that choice, and he will suffer the consequences for that choice.

"I did not create you with the irresistable inclination to do what is wrong. I created you with the ability to choose to do what is wrong. You are free to make your choices, and you will reap the consequences of the choices you make.

"I know the way this world works; I made it. Your freedom will work if you use it in relationship with Me, in accordance with what is true and good. If you don't use it that way, if you use your freedom to deny your own guilt, or to hide from it; if you use your freedom to pretend that you are holier, wiser, and more loving than I, then you are going to have a mighty tough road ahead. Believe Me, I know."

And the toughest part of that road will be at the end, "Because God will bring every action into judgment, upon every hidden thing, whether it is good, or whether it is evil." (Eccl. 12:14) Every person will be called before the Judge of all the earth to give account for every single thing that he or she has done. God will judge according to His standard of right and wrong, and according to His purposes.

Before God brought Israel out of the wilderness into the land, He set before us the same choice He had set before Adam. Moses told our fathers: "See, I set before you today Life and Good, Death and Evil, in that I command you today to love the Everpresent Lord your God, to walk in His ways, and to keep His commandments, statutes and judgments. Then you will live and increase, and the Everpresent Lord your God will bless you in the land you are entering to possess. But if your heart turns away and you will not listen, and you are drawn away to bow down to other gods and serve them, I declare to you today that you will certainly be destroyed. You will not live long in the land you are crossing the Jordan to enter and possess. Today I call heaven and earth as witnesses against you that I have set before you the Life and the Death, the Blessing and the Curse. Now choose life, so that you and your descendants live to love the Everpresent Lord your God, listen to His voice, and cling to Him. For He is your life, and your length of days to live on the ground which the Everpresent Lord swore to give to your fathers, to Abraham, to Isaac, and to Jacob." (Dt. 30:15-20)

Moses makes it clear: "to love the Everpresent Lord your God, to walk in His ways, and to keep His commandments, statutes and judgment" **IS** "Life and Good." "But if your heart turns away and you will not listen, and you are drawn away to bow down to other gods and serve them," that is "Death and Evil". People are always making their own standards of good and evil, and feel justified in doing so. They are always creating their own highest authority, i.e. their own gods, bowing down to them and serving them. But these are the things God calls "Evil"; these are the things that lead to "Death".

Is it God's fault that we knew what was right, but made a conscious choice to do what was wrong? Is it God's fault that we don't believe Him when He says that choosing evil will have bad consequences? Is it God's fault that we choose to serve our own desires instead of serving Him? As the Everpresent said to a generation long ago: "Why do you argue against Me? You have all rebelled against Me." (Jer. 2:29)

We also should note that anything and everything that God created is less than God. It is not God. It can be like God in some ways, it can even be like God in many ways — made in His image and in His likeness — but it cannot be God, and it cannot be equal to God. God IS. He has always been and He always will be; and what He is will not change. What He creates can be "good," it can even be "very good," but, compared to the

Creator, it will always be less than His goodness. Whatever is not God, by that fact alone, will always be deficient when compared to God. It is part of humility, and sensibility, to recognize that we are subservient to God.

## To Learn to Fight

God brought a new generation from the wilderness into the land of Israel, and began to destroy the nations which were there because of their centuries of unrelenting violence, immorality and idolatry. But after Joshua died, the people turned away from God and became like all the peoples of the earth.

Then the Everpresent said, "'Because this people has transgressed My covenant which I commanded their fathers, and have not listened to My voice, I also will no longer drive out from before them any of the nations which Joshua left when he died; so that through them I may test Israel, whether they will keep the way of the Everpresent to walk in it, as their fathers kept it, or not.' ...These are the nations which the Everpresent left, to test Israel by them ...so that the generations of the children of Israel might know, to teach them war, those who did not know these things before.'" (Judg. 2:20b-22; 3:1-2)

War is an evil. It is cruel, deadly, and heart-rending. It is not what God wanted for Israel, or for anyone. But because we turned away from Him, we turned away from what is good. He gave us what we chose, only we found it to be the evil that God knew it was. He gave us what we chose, so that we might learn something good from it.

God wants us to know how to fight, not with each other, but for each other. This is one of His core purposes for humanity: that we be committed to fighting against what is evil. The existence of evil enables us to learn what the holy character of God is; it enables us to choose to pay the price to embrace and develop that character in ourselves.

"The fear of the Everpresent is to hate evil. I hate pride and arrogance, evil behavior and a perverse mouth." (Prov. 8:13) "Let those who love the Everpresent hate evil. He guards the lives of His godly ones; He delivers them from the hand of the wicked." (Ps. 97:10) "Hate evil and love good; maintain justice in the gate." (Amos 5:15a)

Nevertheless, if there were no evil, we wouldn't need to learn to hate it, we wouldn't need to fight against it. Life would be a lot easier then. It would be easier and simpler. It would be idyllic, but we would be less than God created us to be.

In Belarus, the man who had been a young teenager when the Holocaust began, who had escaped from the ever-tightening noose around the ghetto to become a partisan fighter in the forest, asked, "But what about the children? What about the innocent children who were slaughtered? How could God allow that?"

This man knew more about fighting evil than I do. He knew more about destroyed innocence and pain. But it was an unanswerable question that demands an answer. I said simply, "The children died in the gas chambers, and everywhere else, because someone threw them in, and no one else took them out."

Reductionist absurdity? Maybe. No, probably. Immoral evasion of facing up to God's complicity and guilt in the suffering and death of a million defenseless little children? I don't think so.

'But who could have stopped it? and how? Many tried. Many good people tried, and they were killed too. Evil people committed themselves to destroying everything good. It was a tidal wave. There was no way to stop it. But God, God could have prevented it from happening.'

Yes, God could have prevented it from happening, but He didn't. We know that. And that tells us something very important about God that He wants us to know. God lets the innocent suffer. Not just in the Holocaust and the rest of Jewish history, but throughout the Scriptures and throughout the history of the world. God lets the innocent, and the righteous, suffer.

That doesn't mean that He wants the innocent and the righteous to suffer. And it doesn't mean that He can't prevent that suffering. It just means that because of who He is and because of what He wants from humanity, He doesn't prevent evil from destroying what is good. He wants us to prevent evil from doing that, or, at least, to give our lives in trying.

Maybe our own responsibilities are more and greater than we want to know. As Alyosha Karamazov said, "little heart of mine, my joy, believe me, every one is really responsible to all men for all men and for everything. I don't know how to explain it to you, but I feel it is so."[1]

You cannot change what happened yesterday, but there are innocent children suffering and dying today. If you are concerned about the children, or the poor, or the oppressed, or anyone, you can choose to do something today. You can choose to spend your time, your talents, your money, and your life to help them today. You can decide that the purpose of your life is to help others, no matter what it costs you.

'But if we are responsible to give our lives for one another, isn't God, who created all people, much more responsible to do the same? If He is good, then how could He create beings who would do what the Nazis did to little children? If He loves the little children, it is inconceivable that He would not prevent such evil from being done to them. God is all powerful, but He did not prevent that evil, and every day there is more evil that He does not prevent. How can we believe in the goodness of an all-powerful God who both created evil and does not prevent its spread across the earth?'

But maybe God did give His life in the camps. Maybe He did lose His life caring for people. If you don't know God, don't be so sure that He didn't die six million times, and more.

Does the murder of the children stand as an indictment of God, or as an indictment of humanity? It was people who murdered them; it was human neighbors who looked away and did nothing; it was indifferent and self-serving leaders and masses who didn't care.

God created something that is the opposite of what He is, and God created humanity with the ability to choose that something. Humanity could, and humanity still can, choose God, who is good, or His opposite, which is evil. Humanity can choose to resist evil today, or choose not to.

The animals God created are not capable of making these kinds of heart choices. God did not make them so they could. To a certain degree, a dog can know, and even love, its master. So can a horse, or many other kinds of animals. Sometimes they will sacrifice their lives for one another or for their human family. But God designed humanity to have a much greater relationship with Him.

People can consciously choose to love and serve God at a staggeringly high level. People can choose to walk with God and be like Him. And people can choose the opposite. If we couldn't choose the opposite, our relationship with God would become a somewhat greater version of His relationship with the animals. That was not God's purpose in making humanity in His own image and likeness.

Adam was made in the image and likeness of God, but there is clearly a difference between the creature and the Creator. The Creator exists before time and outside of space. He exists unchanging, independent of all creation. Nothing that He created, including Evil, can change His nature or character. It does not tempt Him. Adam, the creature, exists within time and space. Evil exists within the same dimensions. We can be tempted by evil, and our nature and character can be changed by it.

But people do not have to choose evil. As God said to Adam's son Ka'in, when Ka'in brought an unacceptable gift: "Why are you angry? Why is your face downcast? If you do what is good, isn't there acceptance? But if you do not do what is good, Sin is crouching at the door. It desires to have you, but you must master it." (Gen. 4:6-7)

To paraphrase what God said: 'It is up to you. Sin is waiting to swallow you up. You must master it. Do not let it master you.' There is no other alternative.

It was then that Ka'in decided to kill his brother, Abel, simply because Abel's gift, a sacrifice from his flock, had been acceptable to God. The existence of Abel was a continual, unwanted reminder that it was possible for Ka'in to do what was good. Ka'in wanted to do what he wanted to do, and he didn't want to be criticized for it.

He chose not to humble himself to seek to do good. That narrowed his choices considerably. Even as God did not stop Adam and Havah from disobeying Him and choosing the evil of rebellion instead, so God did not stop their son Ka'in from killing their other son, Abel.

Why didn't God stop Ka'in? Why did He create the evil that made murder possible? Why did He allow it to fill Ka'in's heart?

"Then the Everpresent said to Ka'in, 'Where is your brother Abel?'

"'I don't know,' he replied. 'Am I my brother's guardian?'" (Gen. 4:9)

Ka'in was saying, "I don't know, and I don't care," but he was saying much more than that. There is a diabolical genius in Ka'in's reply. In saying, "Am I **the** *shomer* — the protector and guardian — of my brother?" he was rejecting any responsibility at all towards any other human being. Ka'in thought he could define himself apart from a relationship with his brother and apart from a relationship with God. He thought he could define himself any way he wanted to. When he said, "Am I my brother's guardian?" he was pinpointing the issue exactly. His answer to that question was, "No." He said it because he was rejecting what God had created him to be.

But even more than that, he was accusing God. God, after all, must surely be the one primarily responsible for guarding His Creation. In another passage, written many years later, the priests were commanded to put this blessing upon the people of Israel: "The Everpresent Lord bless you and guard you [*yishmerekha*]..." (Num. 6:24) The Scriptures also tell us that God, "the *Shomer* of Israel, neither slumbers nor sleeps." (Ps. 121:4)

God created Adam and his family so that they would care for, protect, and guard one another. "The Everpresent said, 'What have you done? The sound [or "voice"] of your brother's blood cries out to Me from the ground.'" (Gen. 4:10) Adam hid when he heard the voice of the Lord. Ka'in killed Abel to silence Abel's voice. But there is no place to hide, and no way to destroy the evidence of the evil we do. It ascends to heaven.

In the phrase, "your brother's blood," the plural is used, i.e. "bloods". The Rabbis understood this to mean that Ka'in was guilty not only of murdering Abel, but also of murdering all his descendants. "Whoever destroys a single soul, Scripture imputes [guilt] to him as though he had destroyed an entire world. And whoever preserves a single soul, Scripture ascribes [merit] to him as though he had preserved an entire world." (Tal. Sanhedrin 37a)

One man, Ka'in, killed one-fourth of the world's population, his brother, and everyone who would have been descended from him. This was the greatest slaughter that humanity has ever committed against itself.

Yes, preserving, or saving, an entire world is a great good, but if there were nothing that could destroy that world, saving it would not be necessary. Is it necessary that such a great good be possible only because a great evil is? The answer lies in the character of humanity: how great is our capacity for good?

"We who lived in concentration camps can remember the men who walked through the huts comforting others, giving away their last piece of bread. They may have been few in numbers, but they offer sufficient proof that everything can be taken from a man but one thing: the last of the human freedoms — to determine one's attitude in any given set of circumstances — to choose one's own way."[2]

How big were these acts of kindness? How great was their impact? If we think that they were obscure, insignificant deeds, lasting only for a moment until the whip came down again or until the giver or recipient of the kindness was crushed in the gears of the Nazi machine, we have missed what life is all about.

Maybe kindness doesn't eliminate cruelty, but it overcomes it. Maybe compassion doesn't undo the works of cruelty, but it still triumphs. Who can know the weight of a world of suffering? Who can calculate the value of self-sacrificing love? I can't, but God can.

God created life, and He defines it. These deeds, and those who performed them, were somehow greater than the Holocaust itself. They were bigger than the most sickening display of Man's inhumanity to Man. These few passing shadows of goodness defeated Evil with a few kind words and a tiny hard crust of barely edible bread. (cf. Ps. 144:4)

'But what did they accomplish? They didn't stop the slaughter. They didn't end the suffering. The world didn't notice, and didn't care.'

Wait a minute, my friend. What is worth accomplishing? What is worth being? What would you like to accomplish or achieve with your life? Each of these who showed kindness, even at the expense of his or her own life, achieved a great victory. The evil surrounded them, but it didn't possess them. It didn't control them. They turned a place of slaughter into holy ground. They embraced the image and likeness of God within them and within those all but unrecognizable, emaciated and tormented human beings around them. By choice, they were citizens of the Kingdom of God.

We should remember also that there were rescuers during the Holocaust. The Nazis and their accomplices were children of Ka'in, and they committed crimes against humanity, crimes against the very nature of being human. But there were others who recognized and accepted the nature of being human. They, though not Jewish, risked their lives, and in many cases lost their lives, seeking to save Jewish people. They were children of God, living in His image and in His likeness. And in making that choice, they highlighted the guilt of those who chose to do nothing. To be human, by God's design, is to be the guardian of one's brother and sister, all of them.

In the Scriptures, God does not create a religion, He creates life. He does not give a name to what it is to know and serve Him. But if we were to help Him out, if we were to pick an appropriate name, it would be difficult, at least content-wise, to find anything better than "The Brother's Guardian Society."

That is why the Scriptures say, "Above all, set a guardpost to protect your heart, because life goes forth from it." (Prov. 4:23) To accept the responsibility of being the *shomer* for your own heart means that you choose to let in the good and keep out the bad. If you do that, it will soon entail the responsibility of being the *shomer* for your brother and sister.

The ability to choose is an awesome and terrible thing, but that is how and why God made humanity. God does not remove the possibility of our choosing evil. He does promise, however, that He will judge us and reward us as our choices deserve.

If there were no evil, would it matter whether or not we obeyed God? We could say, as the Scriptures do, that disobeying God is in itself evil, but if it didn't cause any harm, if it didn't cause pain or some kind of damage to ourselves or someone else, what would be so bad about disobeying God? But that is precisely what all evil is: disobeying God. All things exist for His purposes. And the fact that I, or you, don't know the damage that my, or your, self-serving actions cause does not mean that there is no damage.

To sum up the Ten Commandments: 'If you make something more important to you than God is, that is evil. If you make your own image and likeness of who God is, rejecting the image of Himself which He has placed in humanity, that is evil. If you act as if these false images are to be obeyed, that is evil. If you invoke the Name of the Lord upon what is false and empty, that is evil.

'If you do not work and rest as He has commanded, that is evil. If you do not honor your father and your mother, that is evil. If you murder, whether by action or by word, that is evil. If you seek sexual pleasure from one who does not belong to you, that is evil.

'If you take for yourself something that belongs to another, that is evil. If you desire for yourself what belongs to your neighbor, or those who belong to your neighbor, that is evil.'

It is true that people don't all agree that all those things are evil. And they don't all agree on what is good. But that doesn't affect the distinctions that God has made. "Woe to those who say of evil that it is good, and of good that it is evil; who present darkness as light and light as darkness; who present what is bitter as sweet and what is sweet as bitter. Woe to those who are wise in their own eyes and discerning in their own estimation."

(Is. 5:20-21)

God will destroy Evil, after it has accomplished the purpose for which He created it. God will deliver those who are His, and now we have the opportunity to show ourselves to be His. "I will ransom them from the power of She'ol; I will redeem them from death." (Hos. 13:14a)

But in the meantime, "He has told you, Adam, what is good and what the Everpresent seeks from you: that you do justice, love mercy, and walk humbly with your God." (Micah 6:8)

## To Choose Life

'Yet even if we grant that God has a good purpose in creating evil, it still does not seem right that God left Adam and Havah alone to face the Serpent, knowing that the Serpent was cunning enough to seduce them to do evil.'

But God did not simply leave them alone in the garden and say, "You're on your own." Adam and Havah had been given what they needed in order to resist the temptation. God spent time with them and instructed them in what they were created to do. How do we know that? After Adam and Havah rebelled, they tried to cover their nakedness. From whom? From the animals? From the Serpent? From each other? No, from God. (cf. Gen.3:10) They knew that God would come by, and God would see.

"Then the man and his wife heard the *kol* ["voice" or "sound"] of the Lord God as He was walking in the garden in the cool of the day, and they hid from the Lord God among the trees of the garden." (Gen. 3:8) Adam and Havah heard a sound or a voice, and they knew that it was God walking in the garden. That means they had heard the sound or voice before, and they recognized it for what it was. They knew it was God walking in the garden.

That means that God had walked in the garden before; they had heard His voice before. God had wanted to spend time with them. After all, He loved them, and He had put them in charge of the garden. "And the Everpresent Lord God took the man, and put him into the garden of Eden to cultivate it and to keep it." (Gen. 2:15) God lifted him up and put him in the garden.

God did not leave Adam and Havah on their own. He sought them out. He brought every individual animal to Adam to name. (Gen. 2:19) Perhaps He had also come to show them all the beauty of creation, and to teach them how to properly take care of the earth and all its creatures.

Instead of accepting that responsibility, they had chosen to disobey. They wanted something for themselves that God hadn't given to them. And then, rather than face up to their actions, they hid when they heard God coming to them.

In the wilderness, our fathers made a choice that was much the same. God had been close to our fathers. God had cared for them, and in so doing, had cared for us.

God reminded Israel as we stood at the base of Mt. Sinai. "You yourselves have seen what I did to Egypt, and how I carried you on eagles' wings and brought you to Myself. Now if you obey Me fully and keep My covenant, then out of all nations you will be My treasured possession. Although the whole earth is Mine, you will be for Me a kingdom of priests and a holy nation." (Ex. 19:4-6b)

God showed us special care, power, and closeness. "Has any other people heard the voice of God speaking out of fire, as you have, and lived?" (Dt. 4:33)

But the people did not want to be that close to God, "and they said to Moses, 'Speak to us yourself and we will listen. But do not have God speak to us or we will die.' Moses said to the people, 'Do not be afraid. God has come to test you, so that the fear of God will be with you to keep you from sinning.'" (Ex. 20:16-17H)

The fear of God, which is the beginning of wisdom, will keep a person far from sin. The love of God will bring us close to Him. God uses physical circumstances to enable us to learn the great reality of our continual dependence upon Him. Not only did He create us and the world, He sustains us and the world.

"He humbled you, causing you to hunger and then feeding you with manna, which neither you nor your fathers had known, to teach you that it is not by bread alone that humanity [*haAdam*] will live, but humanity [*haAdam*] will live by all that comes from the mouth of the Everpresent." (Dt. 8:3) Adam and Havah had heard the voice of the Everpresent before, but they didn't want to hear it again. Our fathers had heard the voice of the Everpresent, but they didn't want to hear it again. Yet we are to live by everything that comes from the mouth of the Everpresent Lord.

Adam and Havah tried to hide from God. Our fathers turned away from Him. Jonah tried to flee from His presence.

David asked, "Where can I go from Your Spirit? Where can I flee from Your presence? If I go up to the heavens, You are there; if I make my bed in the She'ol, You are there. If I rise on the wings of the dawn, if I settle on the far side of the sea, even there Your hand will guide me, Your right hand will hold me fast. If I say, 'Surely the darkness will hide me and the light become night around me,' even the darkness will not be dark to You; the night will shine like the day, for darkness is as light to You." (Ps. 139:7-12)

Why do we want to escape from God? God is light, but men choose darkness. God is life, but men choose death. God is good, but men choose evil.

'Yes, and men are responsible for their own choices. But nevertheless, it is still true that God is the one who made those choices possible. God is the one who created humanity. God is the one who knew the choices humanity would make. Couldn't God have lessened the harm, the consequences, and the penalty of doing evil?'

In other words, couldn't God have made it less important whether we do good or not? Certainly it is less important in our own eyes than it is in His. Maybe God could have, but we should ask the opposite question: couldn't God have made doing good more important in Adam's eyes? in our eyes? in the eyes of every person?

Who made us so hardheaded and hardhearted? Who made us so stiffnecked? Not God. We ourselves, by the choices we make, are responsible for that.

God says that if we spend time with Him, if we learn to follow

His example, we will be different. What is important to God will be important to us.

The Talmud encourages people "to walk after the attributes of the Holy One, blessed be He. As He clothes the naked, for it is written: 'And the Lord God made for Adam and for his wife coats of skin, and clothed them,' so you should also clothe the naked. The Holy One, blessed be He, visited the sick, for it is written: 'And the Lord appeared unto him [Abraham] by the oaks of Mamre,' so you should also visit the sick. The Holy One, blessed be He, comforted mourners, for it is written: 'And it came to pass after the death of Abraham, that God blessed Isaac his son,' so you should also comfort mourners. The Holy one, blessed be He, buried the dead, for it is written: 'And He buried him [Moses] in the valley,' so you should also bury the dead." (Tal. Sotah 14a)

What is God like in His relationship with humanity? "The Everpresent Lord is good to all. He has compassion on all He has made." (Ps. 145:9) He is good even to those who reject Him. He provides blessings even for those who hate Him. He wants us to share this aspect of His nature.

"If your enemy is hungry, give him food to eat; if he is thirsty, give him water to drink. In doing this, you will heap burning coals on his head, and the Everpresent Lord will reward you." (Prov. 25:21-22) Your enemy is human, treat him that way, for his sake and for yours.

Will that work? Will it change your enemy? Sometimes it will, but usually it won't. Nevertheless, it will help make you the person God created you to be.

There is more to consider. God does not simply observe the suffering of humanity, He Himself is afflicted by it. We already know that God has feelings. The things that people do and the things that are done to people have an impact upon Him.

"For He said, 'Surely they are My people, children who will not be false.' So He was their savior. In all their affliction He was afflicted, and the angel of His presence saved them. In His love and in His mercy He redeemed them, and He bore them, and carried them all the days of old. But they rebelled and grieved

His holy Spirit. Therefore He was turned to be their enemy, and He fought against them." (Is. 63:8-10)

God is afflicted when Israel is afflicted. He feels every single pain. His Spirit grieves when people rebel against Him.

As God's representatives, the prophets illustrate His pain. Jeremiah said, "I am broken upon the brokenness of the daughter of my people. I mourn, and horror grips me. ...Who will make my head water and my eyes a fountain of tears? Then I would weep day and night for the slain of the daughter of my people." (Jer. 8:21,23H)

The Rabbis spoke of a very difficult to grasp reality: God suffers when His people suffer. "So far I only know that He shares in the affliction of the community. How about the affliction of the individual? Scripture says: 'He shall call upon Me, and I will answer him; I will be with him in trouble' (Ps. 91:15).

"...Likewise you find that whithersoever Israel was exiled, the Shekhinah went into exile with them. When they went into exile to Egypt, the Shekhinah went into exile with them, as it is said; 'I exiled Myself unto the house of your fathers when they were in Egypt' (1 Sam. 2:27). When they were exiled to Babylon, the Shekhinah went into exile with them, as it is said: 'For your sake I ordered Myself to go to Babylon' (Is. 43:14)."³

The Shekhinah is the visible presence of God that led Israel out of Egypt, and then dwelt above the ark of the covenant in both the Tabernacle and the Temple. It is the glory of God come into this world and made visible.

In the section quoted above from Isaiah 63, God tells us that His holy Spirit is grieved when Israel rebels against Him. Affliction comes to Israel because of that rebellion, but God also shares in that affliction because He loves His people. When Israel repents, God is eager to remove the affliction and, by so doing, stop His own suffering. "When they put away the foreign gods from their midst, and served the Everpresent Lord, then His soul was grieved with the misery of Israel." (Judg. 10:16)

When the nations plunder and persecute Israel, God feels pain as though someone had poked Him in the eye. "For this is what the Everpresent Commander of forces says: 'After His glory, He has sent me to the nations which plundered you, because the one who hits you hits the apple of His eye." (Zech. 2:12)

The Rabbis say that Moses said: "As Israel is in trouble, even I will be with them in trouble. And everyone who puts himself in the trouble of the community will merit to see the consolation of the community." (Tal. Ta'anith 11a) If that was true of Jeremiah and Moses, faithful servants of God, how much more so is it true of God Himself.

God does bring judgment, terrible judgment, but it is not what He desires to do. "For He does not willingly bring affliction or grief to the children of men." (Lam. 3:33) "'As I live,' declares the Everpresent Lord, 'I have no pleasure in the death of the wicked; but that the wicked turn from his way and live. Return, return from your evil ways, for why will you die, O house of Israel?" (Ezek. 33:11)

God has no pleasure in the death of anyone, with one exception.[4] God brought judgment on Pharaoh and Egypt, but it did not give Him pleasure. In rabbinic tradition, at the Red Sea, "The ministering angels spoke of singing songs, but the Holy One, blessed be He, said, 'The work of My hands is being drowned in the sea, and you are speaking of songs?'" (Tal. Megillah 10b)

A father suffers pain when his children suffer pain, even if their pain is the result of their own negligence or disobedience. The God of Israel knows that pain very well.

God knows the disappointment and the hurt of having children walk away — more than that, of having His children spit in His face and blame Him for everything, though He never failed them. "When Israel was a youth, I loved him, and called My son out of Egypt. As they called them, so they went from them; they sacrificed to the Baalim, and burned incense to carved idols. I taught Ephraim to walk, taking them by their arms; but they did not know that I healed them. I drew them with human cords, with bands of love; and I was to them like those who lift the yoke from their jaws, and I stretched out food to them." (Hosea 11:1-4)

God Created Evil

"Yet you say, 'The way of the Lord is not just.' Now listen, O house of Israel: Is My way unjust? Is it not your ways that are unjust?" (Ezek. 18:25; cf. 18:29; 33:17,20)

God knows the agony of a broken marriage, of a spouse turning to adultery and degradation, even though He was always a loving and well-providing husband. That's the message of the whole book of Hosea. God used the life of Hosea to demonstrate His own pain.

"When the Lord began to speak through Hosea, the Lord said to him, 'Go, take to yourself an immoral wife and children of immorality, because the land has surely committed immorality in departing from the Lord. ... 'My heart is turned inside Me, all My compassion is kindled.'" (Hos. 1:2, 11:8)

Was that fair to Hosea? From our perspective, definitely not. But God was giving Hosea the opportunity to know Him and be like Him. God was letting Hosea share in His own life, His own pain. That is a great honor and privilege.

Would Hosea have preferred to decline the honor and privilege and have had a good family life instead? Probably. But God's perspective is much broader in time and space than ours, and His mercy endures forever. In the ages to come, will Hosea still feel the same way about what his life was. I don't think so. Some things that fifty years ago I thought were good, I now know to be bad; some things that I thought were bad, I now know to be good. The life of Hosea the prophet illustrates God's faithful love for Israel.

God is not an impersonal force. He is a living, caring, feeling being, who created Israel and all humanity that we might share and return His love. We know our own pain, and it can swallow us up, but do we know God's pain from what seven billion people do to themselves and to each other every day?

How deep is His pain? It is piercing. As we read in Zechariah 12:10, "And I will pour out on the house of David and the inhabitants of Jerusalem a spirit of grace and supplication. They will look on Me, whom they have thrust through, and they will mourn for him as one mourns for an only child, and grieve bitterly for him as one grieves for a firstborn son."

The Rabbis say, "There is peace for the one who explains that the cause [of the mourning] is the slaying of Messiah the son of Joseph, since that agrees with what is written (Zech. 12): 'And they will look upon Me whom they have thrust through, and they will mourn for him as the mourning for the only son.'" (Tal. Sukkah 52a)

Messiah is the anointed of God, representing Him in a special way, even more than the prophets. When Messiah is thrust through, God is thrust through. It is in this capacity of being God's representative that Messiah suffers in a special way. The Rabbis say that all Israel will mourn for him in deep bitterness, having somehow been responsible for his death. There will be a day when we will see how much we have hurt God. We will see how much God suffered because of His love for us.

So why does God endure suffering? The nature of genuine love includes a willingness to suffer for others. Because God loves, He suffers. Because God loves us, He suffers with us and because of us.

The nature of God and His love for us are such that He Himself is willing to be afflicted for us. He is more than willing, He designed the world so that He would be afflicted with us and for us. I wouldn't have designed it that way, but there is something about love that cannot be demonstrated without paying a price.

Somehow, in God's design, suffering, pain, and evil exist to enable us to imitate God. They exist to enable us to choose what is painfully right over what is pleasurably wrong. They exist to enable our hearts to break, even as His does.

## To Know Him

When God appeared to Moses on the mountain, He revealed His eternal nature to Moses in what the Rabbis call "The Thirteen Attributes". "Then the Everpresent came down in the cloud and stood there with him and proclaimed His name, the Everpresent. And He passed in front of Moses, proclaiming, 'The Everpresent, the Everpresent, God, merciful and gracious, slow to anger, abounding in lovingkindness and truth, maintaining love to thousands, and forgiving iniquity, rebellion and sin. Yet He does not leave the guilty unpunished; visiting the iniquity of the fathers upon the children and their children to the third and fourth generation.'" (Ex. 34:5-7)

God came down to Moses, and revealed His loving, righteous nature. All God's attributes are good. They are what Good is.

But how could we know these attributes of God and His goodness if there were no evil? How could we know His mercy or His grace if there were no need for them? How could we know His patient endurance of what angers Him if nothing did? How could we know His faithfulness and forgiveness if there were no sin or unfaithfulness? I may not think that all the pain and suffering in the world is thereby justified, but I cannot imagine an alternative way, if there were no evil, for humanity to know and embrace these attributes of God.

God is not untouched or unmoved by the pain and suffering. We may know the pain of sickness or natural disaster destroying what is most precious to us, but we do not know God's pain over the destruction that Adam's disobedience loosed in the world.

"And the Everpresent God commanded the man [ha'Adam], 'Of every tree of the garden, you may eat. But from the tree of the knowledge of good and evil, you must not eat from it, because in the day you eat of it you will surely die.'" (Gen. 2:16-17)

But Adam did eat from the tree of the knowledge of good and evil, and he didn't die that day. We know that he didn't die, but we also know that death entered into the world on that day. "The Everpresent Lord God made garments of skin for Adam and his wife and clothed them." (Gen. 3:21)

Nothing that they could make for themselves was sufficient to deal with what they had done. Animals were put to death, and their skins were used to cover Adam and Havah. Imagine walking around in the skins of animals who were killed because you sinned. What would you feel? What would you understand?

From God's point of view, death is more than a solitary event; death is a condition. In that same garden, there was also a tree of life. After Adam and Havah rebelled, God had to exclude them from the garden, and separate them from the tree of life so that they would not taste its fruit. Their changed condition made that necessary.

King Saul said to his son Jonathan, "As long as the son of Jesse lives on this earth, neither you nor your kingdom will be established. Now send and bring him to me, for he is a son of death!" (1Sam. 20:31) When Nathan the prophet presented King David's own sin to him in a parable, "David burned with anger against the man and said to Nathan, 'As surely as the Everpresent lives, the man who did this is a son of death!'" (2Sam. 12:5)

What did King Saul and King David mean by "a son of death"? They meant someone whose death was at that moment fixed with certainty. They meant someone whose death was imminent, someone for whom death was inescapable.

Adam and Havah did not die on the day that they disobeyed God, but from that day on, death awaited them. The momentary event of their own death was in the future, but the condition of death became present everywhere. It became inescapable. The stench of death began to rest upon the earth. From that day on, death owned them.

How does the event of death come? It comes from sickness, from infirmity, from accident, from disaster, from hatred, from war, from a multitude of evils. Death has its ways, and its servants.

In choosing not to listen to God, Adam brought deafness into the world. In choosing not to see what God had shown him, Adam brought blindness into the world. In hardening his heart and feeding his forbidden lusts, Adam brought disease and uncleanness into the world. In choosing to take what was not theirs, they loosed coveting and theft into the world.

Adam did not think he was choosing all those things. He did not understand the ramifications of the plague of evil he invited, he did not comprehend the magnitude of his decision, but none of that changed anything. He could have chosen to believe and obey God because God is God, i.e. THE Authority. That was the right thing to do. But he chose not to do that.

In choosing to disobey, Adam and Havah chose death, what brings it, and what it brings. "They have sown the wind and they will reap the whirlwind." (Hosea 8:7a) The Serpent's assurance to the contrary was a lie. On that day, they were changed, and the world was changed. All of their descendants, whether righteous or unrighteous, have had to face the whirlwind. No one, no matter how righteous, is completely protected and free from the harmful effects of their actions.

"In the land of Uz there lived a man whose name was Job. This man was blameless and upright; he feared God and turned away from evil." (Job 1:1) Because Job was blameless and upright, because Job feared God and turned away from evil, he was singled out for horrendous affliction. It was Satan, the Adversary, who attacked Job, but it was God who suggested the attack. "Have you considered My servant Job?" (Job 1:8)

God had blessed Job considerably. "He had seven sons and three daughters, and he owned seven thousand sheep, three thousand camels, five hundred yoke of oxen and five hundred donkeys, and had a large number of servants. He was the greatest man among all the people of the East." (Job 1:2-3)

Then, in one day, without a moment of time to consider and mourn each loss separately, Job lost everything. "A messenger came to Job and said, 'The oxen were plowing and the donkeys were grazing nearby, and the Sabeans attacked and carried them off. They put the servants to the sword, and I am the only one who has escaped to tell you!'

"While he was still speaking, another messenger came and said, 'The fire of God fell from the sky and burned up the sheep and the servants, and I am the only one who has escaped to tell you!'

"While he was still speaking, another messenger came and said, 'The Chaldeans formed three raiding parties and swept down on your camels and carried them off. They put the servants to the sword, and I am the only one who has escaped to tell you!'

"While he was still speaking, yet another messenger came

and said, 'Your sons and daughters were feasting and drinking wine at the oldest brother's house, when suddenly a mighty wind swept in from the desert and struck the four corners of the house. It collapsed on them and they are dead, and I am the only one who has escaped to tell you!'" (Job 1:14-19)

These things did not happen to Job because he was an evil man; they happened to him because he was a good and just man. And as though that weren't enough, God suggested that Satan attack Job further. "And the Everpresent Lord said to Satan, 'Have you considered My servant Job, that there is none like him in the earth, a blameless and an upright man, one who fears God and turns away from evil? And still he holds fast to his integrity, although you moved Me against him, to destroy him without cause.'

"And Satan answered the Everpresent, and said, 'Skin for skin! A man will give all that he has for his life. But put forth Your hand now, and touch his bone and his flesh, and he will curse You to Your face.'...

"So Satan went out from the presence of the Everpresent and afflicted Job with painful sores from the sole of his foot to the top of his head." (Job 2:3-5,7)

Satan was wrong, and not only in the case of Job. The act of sacrificing one's life for others is a normative part of the human experience. Every culture exalts and honors those who have chosen to give their lives for the good of another, for the good of their family, for the good of their people, their country, or their cause. If there were a culture that did not, it would not exist for long. No one would fight to preserve it.

But then, three of Job's friends came to comfort him, but their comfort turned into an attack, only adding to his pain. Job was in agony, wanting to know why God had done this to him. He cried out for the opportunity to confront God and argue his case face to Face, because God was distant, untouched by his suffering, inaccessible and unapproachable.

God finally did appear to Job, and answered his questions, but the answers were not at all what Job expected. God gave Job a different kind of understanding, and a different kind of wisdom.

The Lord said to Job, "Where were you when I laid the foundation of the earth? Tell me, if you understand. ... Surely you know, for you were already born! You have lived so many years! ... Who endowed the heart with wisdom or gave understanding to the mind? ... Who has a claim against Me that I must pay? everything under heaven belongs to Me." (Job 38:4,21,36; 41:11)

I would have expected God to comfort Job, to assure Job of His love, maybe even, somehow, to apologize a little. But that is not at all what God did. To the contrary, His response to Job is a very powerful expression of His own sovereignty. God does not defend Himself, nor does He answer Job's questions. He simply makes Himself known to Job as the Almighty Creator.

I would have expected Job, in his last gasp, to challenge God: 'After what You've put me through, that's Your response?' But far from being outraged, Job understood and accepted God's response. In fact, far from condemning God when he saw Him face to Face, Job apologized to God. "Surely I spoke of things I did not understand, things too wonderful for me and I did not know. ... I had heard of You with the hearing of the ear, but now my eyes have seen You. Therefore I despise myself and repent in dust and ashes." (Job 42:3,5-6)

If ever there was a man who had a case against God, it was Job. Job was humbly doing what was right. He was living in holiness and caring for others. God was the one who instigated all the calamity. God was the one who suggested to Satan that he afflict Job. What possible defense could God have? But when Job saw the Lord, he said, "I despise myself and repent in dust and ashes."

Then the Everpresent turned in anger to Job's friends, the ones who had attacked him in his misery. "So now take seven bulls and seven rams and go to My servant Job and offer up a burnt offering for yourselves. And Job, My servant, will pray for you, and I will accept his prayer and not do to you according to your folly. You have not spoken of Me what is right, as My servant Job has." (Job 42:8)

Now wait a minute. Twice God speaks of Job as "My servant," by which He means, "Job is working for Me." And God says that Job has spoken of Him what is right. That doesn't make any sense. If Job has spoken of God what is right, and if Job is working for God, why did God get so upset with Job? Why did God instigate all this evil against Job? And then, on top of that, God says that Job must pray for his friends — his "comforters who bring misery" — so that they can be forgiven?!

That is too much. Job should explode. He shouldn't let God talk His way out of this and blame everyone else. God didn't let Adam and Havah get away with what they did.

There are a lot of people who go around thinking that they never do anything wrong, always blaming everybody else. But you know what? In God's case, it's true. He never does do anything wrong. By definition.

And you know what else? Job didn't murmur a word of complaint, even though his wife had told him to "Curse God and die." Accusing God was the farthest thing from his mind. The closer we get to God, the smaller we become in our own eyes.

Truly, fortunately or not, God is greater than we can understand. "'For My thoughts are not your thoughts, neither are your ways My ways,' declares the Everpresent. 'As the heavens are higher than the earth, so are My ways higher than your ways and My thoughts than your thoughts.'" (Is. 55:8-9)

When Isaiah saw the Lord, he melted. "'Woe to me!' I cried. 'I am destroyed! For I am a man of unclean lips, and I live among a people of unclean lips, and my eyes have seen the King, the Everpresent Commander of forces.'" (Is. 6:5)

You think you have a case against God? You think you're going to call Him to account for what He has done wrong? I assure you that on the day when you stand before Him, you will not be able to charge Him with any guilt or wrongdoing. I assure you that on the day when you stand before Him, your mouth will be shut and your eyes will be downcast in shame, even as it was with Job and Isaiah.

I would even suggest that when we judge or condemn God, it is a sign of how wrong we are. It is a sign that we are just like

Adam and Havah. Why is it that we, finite and guilty, on the basis of our own diluted and distorted sense of right and wrong, feel competent to judge God, the One who imparted to us the distinction between right and wrong?

Whether I like it or not, there are tests in life. Job was tested to determine and demonstrate whether or not he was committed to God only because of the benefits he received. Job's answer to the test was, "Though He slay me, yet I will trust in Him; but I will maintain my own ways before Him." (Job 13:15)

The prophet Habakkuk faced the same test and responded like this: "Although the fig tree does not blossom, there is no fruit on the vines, the produce of the olive fails, the fields yield no food, the flock be cut off from the fold, and there be no cattle in the stalls, yet I will rejoice in the Lord, I will joy in the God of my salvation." (Hab. 3:17-18) I.e., 'No matter what happens or doesn't happen, I will trust in God.'

We don't make God nervous with our questions. We don't make Him insecure with our doubts. We don't embarrass Him with our knowledge of the evils committed upon the earth. God is willing to explain to us what we are able to understand, if we are willing to listen, and He is also able to demonstrate that He is beyond our understanding.

But "Woe to the one who quarrels with his Maker, the one who is but a potsherd among the potsherds on the ground. Does the clay say to the potter, 'What are you making?' Does your work say, 'He has no hands'?

"This is what the Everpresent says, the Holy One of Israel and his Maker: 'Do you interrogate Me about things to come? Do you give Me orders about My children and the work of My hands? It is I who made the earth and I created Adam upon it. My own hands stretched out the heavens. I commanded their forces." (Is. 45:11-12H)

Here on the earth, almost everyone quarrels with their Maker. We're all so smart, so righteous, and so good. In the heavens, however, "Your Word, O Everpresent Lord, is eternal. It stands firm in the heavens." (Ps. 119:89) There is no contradiction, no equivocation. When we enter a realm where nothing obscures our vision of who God is, then His word will be the same for us. It is like the air of the birds, the sea of the fish, and the ground of the worm. It is the breath of those who breathe. And it is settled.

Job found out that there was nothing to say, except to repent. It is not just that God is bigger and stronger than we are and so He doesn't have to answer. God is also wiser, kinder, and more compassionate. God is wisdom. He is kindness and compassion. Whatever we truly know of these things, it is only because He made us in His own image and likeness.

God chose and appointed Joseph above his brothers. In response, Joseph's brothers sought to kill him, but settled on selling him into slavery. In slavery, Joseph served his master faithfully and well. His master began to raise him up. Then his master's wife tried to seduce Joseph. When Joseph refused, she accused him of the very thing he refused to do. His master threw him into prison. Even there, he continued to be faithful and conscientious, though he was forgotten and abandoned.

Then God raised him up out of prison and made him the second most powerful man in a great empire. Eventually his brothers came down to Egypt for food, and Joseph had the opportunity for revenge. He didn't take it. He saved them and their families from the famine.

When Jacob died, Joseph's brothers came to him and pleaded for forgiveness and mercy in their father's name. Joseph wept because of their mistrust of his goodness. He had learned something invaluable through his suffering. "You meant it to me for evil, but God intended it for good to do as it is this day, to save a multitude of people." (Gen. 50:20)

What they had done, following in the steps of Ka'in, was evil. No question about it, it was evil. But in the hand of God, it was used for good, and Joseph had come to understand that. Joseph could see that God had been working His good purpose through all the evil that his brothers had done, and through all the evil that they had caused. The evil played an indispensable role in God's purposes of testing and redemption.

Joseph was not a philosopher or theorist. He was not someone somehow shielded from everything negative. His own brothers had sought to kill him. They sold him into slavery. He spent years in prison in the Egypt of the pharaohs.

But God says, "Vengeance and retribution are Mine." (Dt. 32:35) God will avenge the afflicted and oppressed. When a person accepts that, he or she can be set free from the burden of hatred, or the burden of despair.

Naomi, her husband Elimelech, and their two sons left Bethlehem to stay in Moab during a famine in Israel. Elimelech died there; her sons married, but then each of them died too. She came back to Israel as a broken, bitter woman. One of her daughters-in-law, a young woman named Ruth, came with her.

"So the two of them went on until they came to Bethlehem. When they arrived in Bethlehem, the whole town was stirred because of them, and the women exclaimed, 'Can this be Naomi?'

"'Don't call me Naomi,' she told them. 'Call me Mara, because the Almighty has dealt bitterly with me. I went away full, but the Everpresent has brought me back **empty**. Why call me Naomi, when the Everpresent has afflicted me, and the Almighty has done evil to me.'" (Ruth 1:19-21)

"Naomi" means "pleasant," as in Ps. 133:1-3; "Mara" means "bitter," as in Ex. 15:23-26. It is easy to understand why Naomi felt the way she did. She felt that God had brought all this evil upon her. But Naomi was overlooking something when she said, "the Everpresent brought me back **empty**." She could see what had been taken away from her, but she could not see what God had given to her.

Ruth was an unusual woman. Naomi had told her several times to stay in Moab, because there was no point in following a hopeless, bitter, old woman, especially when God was the one who had caused her bitterness. "The hand of the Everpresent has gone out against me." (Ruth 1:13)

But Ruth replied, "Don't urge me to leave you or to turn back from you. Where you go I will go, and where you stay I will stay. Your people will be my people and your God my God. Where you die I will die, and there I will be buried. May the Everpresent deal with me, be it ever so severely, if anything but death separates you and me." (Ruth 1:16-17)

Naomi said, "the hand of the Everpresent has gone out against me," but Ruth replied, "your God will be my God." Ruth saw something Naomi couldn't see. Ruth was a young woman whose husband had just died. But despite the pain and death, Ruth could see the hand of the Everpresent upon Naomi, and upon Israel, for blessing. Ruth could see that it was better to die with Israel and Israel's God than to live in comfort in Moab.

As the poorest of the poor, Ruth gathered what was left over from the harvest in the fields of a man named Boaz. Boaz turned out to be a kinsman redeemer of Naomi — someone who had the responsibility to care for her well-being. When he decided to redeem Ruth and Naomi, he gave Ruth a large quantity of barley, saying, "Don't go back to your mother-in-law **empty**." (Ruth 3:17) Through Boaz, God was saying to Naomi, "You think I brought you back empty, but I brought you back full."

Boaz and Ruth married and had a son. "The women said to Naomi, 'Praise be to the Everpresent, who this day has not left you without a kinsman-redeemer. May he become famous throughout Israel! He will renew your life and sustain you in your old age. For your daughter-in-law, who loves you and who is better to you than seven sons, has given him birth.'"

"Then Naomi took the child, laid him in her lap and nursed him. The women living there said, 'A son has been born to Naomi.' And they named him Obed. He was the father of Jesse, the father of David." (Ruth 4:14-17)

Naomi probably didn't live to see the birth of Obed's son Jesse. Certainly she didn't live to see the birth of Obed's grandson David or to see him become God's anointed king over all Israel. But if she had, would she have said it was worth it? I don't know how to calculate such things, and probably Naomi didn't either, but God does. We don't see a relationship between the suffering and the kingship, but God does.

Many evils come crashing down upon the righteous like huge waves upon the rocks of the shore. The waves keep up their relentless attack, an attack which no rock, no matter how big or how strong, can withstand. Nor can any man, no matter how good or how brave, especially when God does not answer, and it seems that the battering forces have been sent by Him.

"Everpresent Lord, God of my salvation, I have cried out day and night before You. Let my prayer come before You; Incline Your ear to my cry, because my soul is full of troubles, and my life draws near to She'ol. ...

"You have laid me in the lowest pit, in darkness, in the depths. Your wrath lies heavy upon me, and You have afflicted me with all Your waves. ...

"Your fierce wrath has gone over me; Your terrors have cut me off. They surround me all day like water; they completely engulf me." (Ps. 88:2-3,7-8,17-18H)

The sea, despite its charms, has many dangers — pounding waves, powerful undertows, and violent storms. When Job's life was in ruins, his family almost totally destroyed, God asked him, "Who covered the sea with doors, when it burst forth from the womb and went out... When I enforced My statutes on it and set bars and doors; when I said, 'This far you may come, but no farther, and here your proud waves must stop!'" (Job 38:8,10-11) Personally, I would have fixed a more restrictive limit to Evil, but my ways are not like God's ways. They are much lower.

God knows the end from the beginning, and He is always working for redemption. The author of Psalm 119, the longest chapter in the Bible, praised God because, "Before I was afflicted I went astray, but now I keep Your word. ...It is good for me to be afflicted so that I might learn Your statutes. ...I know, O Everpresent Lord, that Your judgments are righteous, and in faithfulness You have afflicted me." (Ps. 119:67,71,75) I don't fully embrace such praises, but I believe they are truthful.

Our history is filled with a lot of pain, but, somehow, the end will be quite different. "Therefore the redeemed of the Lord will return, and come with singing to Zion; and everlasting joy will be upon their head. They will obtain gladness and joy; and sorrow and mourning will flee away." (Is. 51:11)

King David was the great-grandson of Ruth, who came back to Israel with a bitter, hopeless Naomi. It is written of one of Ruth's descendants through David: "The Spirit of the Lord will rest upon him..." (Is. 11:2) This descendant is the Messiah (e.g. Tal. Sanhedrin 93b), and he will declare, "The spirit of the Lord God is upon me; because the Lord has anointed me to announce good news to the humble; He has sent me to bind up the broken hearted, to proclaim liberty to the captives, and the opening of the prison to those who are bound; to proclaim an acceptable year of the Lord, and the day of vengeance of our God; to comfort all who mourn; to provide for the mourners of Zion — to give to them glory instead of ashes, the oil of joy instead of mourning, and a garment of praise instead of a faint spirit. They will be called trees of righteousness, a planting of the Everpresent Lord, to glorify Him." (Is. 61:3) There will be redemption, deliverance, and new life for those who mourn, for those who have lost everything.

Towards the end of our evening together, I hesitated, knowing that our discussion of evil was not theoretical, but vital. Then I shared with these Holocaust survivors a song I had written some years before.

Where was God on that day
When my people knelt to pray
And the soldiers with their guns
Came and shot them, every one?
Where was God? Where was God?

Adam, Adam, where are you?
Have you done what I told you to?
Do you think I cannot see
The secret sin you hide from Me?
Where are you? Where are you?

Where was God through the years
When we feasted on our tears
And the heart within our breast
Was torn and trampled without rest?
Where was God? Where was God?

Tell Me Ka'in, surely you know
Where your brother had to go.
With your fists you struck him down
His blood cries to Me from the ground.
Where were you? Where were you?

Where was God my whole life through?
Pain and sorrow were all I knew
Every time I tried to rise,
The darkness came down from the skies.
Where was God? Where was God?

Tell Me child, where have you gone?
I've waited for you oh so long.
I called and called you without cease
You never came to Me for peace.
Where were you? Where were you?

As we said goodnight, the man who had been a young teenager in a world that was destroyed by evil, losing everything and everyone, said, "Maybe tonight we have learned something." Maybe we have.

**Footnotes**

1. Fyodor Dostoevsky, The Brothers Karamazov, ed. by Manuel Komroff, Signet Books, NY, 1958, P. 264

2. Viktor Frankl, Man's Search for Meaning: An Introduction to Logotherapy, trans. by I. Lasch, Pocket Books, NY, 1971, P. 104

3. Mekhilta d'Rabbi Ishmael, Massekhet d'Pisha, parashah 14, cited in Norman J. Cohen, "Shekhinta ba-Galuta: A Midrashic Response to Destruction and Persecution," JSJ, Dec. 1982, P.151

4. "Yet it pleased the Lord to crush him, to make him weak, if he would present his soul as a guilt offering..." (Is. 53:10) It pleased the Lord to make him weak [he'heli] as Samson was made weak [haliti]. (cf. Judges 16:11,17) This Servant of the Lord is put to death as a guilt offering, to bring forgiveness. That is the only death that pleases God.

# TESTED BY GOD

In the wilderness, Israel was commanded to "love the Lord your God with all your heart, and with all your soul, and with all your might." (Dt. 6:5) That means we are commanded to choose to make Him and His desires more important than anything and everything else, including our own desires.

God commanded us to love our neighbor and the stranger who comes into our lives, in the same way that we love ourselves. (Lev. 19:18, 34) That means I am to choose to make their needs and pains as important to me as my own. This is commanded, not suggested, behavior.

God will judge the decisions that each person makes in response to His commands. Every soul will be weighed in the balances, evaluated by God's standard of weights and measures: God's values which He has placed within each heart. God has designed life so that the thoughts and intents of every person's heart will be revealed. (e.g. Gen. 6:5, 1Sam. 16:7)

God did not design life to be easy; He designed it to be a means of testing, to reveal and demonstrate what is in each heart. The purpose of testing something is to know and show whether it can be used for a particular purpose.

We can see this illustrated when David prepared to go into battle against Goliath. Though still young, David was angered by Goliath taunting Israel. David's brothers told him that he couldn't fight Goliath. King Saul told him the same, but David was undeterred.

"So Saul armed David with his armor, and he put a helmet of bronze on his head... And David fastened his sword upon his armor, and he tried to walk, because he had not tested them. And David said to Saul, 'I cannot go in these, because I have not tested them.' And David took them off." (1Sam. 17:38-39)

Saul's armor and helmet had protected Saul in battle, but it would have been fatal for David to go into battle and rely upon them. David approached Goliath without them. When Goliath taunted him, David responded, "You come to me with a sword, and with a spear, and with a javelin; but I come to you in the Name of the Commander of forces, the God of the armies of Israel, whom you have defied." (1Sam. 17:45)

David had not tested Saul's armor in battle, so he declined to rely on it as his strength and shield. He had tested God before and had found Him to be faithful. God had tested David before and found him to be "a man after His own heart." (1Sam. 13:14)

In the battle against Goliath, David relied upon God and God relied upon David. God tests people so that they can choose to rely upon Him.

### "There He tested them"

**1)** "And when they came to Marah, they could not drink of the waters of Marah, because they were bitter; therefore its name was called Marah. And the people murmured against Moses, saying, 'What are we to drink?' And he cried to the Everpresent Lord, and the Everpresent Lord showed him a tree. When he threw it into the waters, the waters became sweet. There He set before them a statute and an ordinance, and **there He tested them**, and said, 'If you will diligently listen to the voice of the Lord your God, and will do that which is right in His sight, and will give ear to His commandments, and keep all His statutes, I will put none of these diseases upon you, which I have brought upon the Egyptians; for I am the Lord who heals you.'" (Ex. 15:23-26)

God had been leading the people through wilderness for three days, and they were thirsty, naturally enough. He led them to a place where the water was bitter and undrinkable — it doesn't seem right. They complained against Moses, naturally enough, and he cried out to God.

The solution to the physical problem was simple, but far from obvious. A particular tree, thrown into the waters, took away the bitterness of the waters and turned them into sweet water. The people had complained against Moses, but they hadn't called upon God. God showed the solution to Moses, because Moses cried out to Him.

God had led the people into the situation. He was testing

them in order to show whether or not they trusted Him. They didn't. He set before them a principle on which He operates: 'if you'll listen and obey, and do what is right, then you will not suffer what the Egyptians suffered. I will heal you.' The opposite is implied: if you won't listen, trust, and obey, then you will suffer as the Egyptians did. It was a test, and there was a lesson to be learned.

**2)** A short time later, as God continued to lead them, the people were hungry, and they complained against Moses again. "'Would to God we had died by the hand of the Lord in the land of Egypt, when we sat by the meat pots, and when we did eat bread to the full; for you have brought us forth into this wilderness, to kill this whole assembly with hunger.' Then the Everpresent Lord said to Moses, 'Behold, I will rain bread from heaven for you; and the people will go out and gather a certain portion every day, **that I may test them**, whether they will walk in My Torah, or not.'" (Ex. 16:3-4)

The people viewed God as their enemy: they thought He had brought them out of Egypt to kill them. The people valued food more than freedom, but God said, "I am the Everpresent Lord, your God, who brought you out of the land of Egypt, that you should not be their slaves; and I have broken the bars of your yoke, and made you walk upright." (Lev. 26:13) Freedom is a responsibility that not everyone wants.

God provided food for them in a way that would show His faithfulness. Each day they would need Him to provide, and each day He would provide. But they didn't want to need Him. They didn't begin to see God as their friend, and, therefore, did not embrace the way He set before them.

Sometimes people complain that God is far off. In those days, they complained that He was too near. He came down to them. "And all the people observed the sounds of thunder, and the bolts of lightning, and the sound of the shofar, and the mountain smoking. And when the people saw it, they were shaken, and stood far away. And they said to Moses, 'You speak with us, and we will hear; but do not let God speak with us, lest we die.'

And Moses said to the people, 'Do not be afraid, because **God has come in order to test you**, and in order that His fear will be before your faces, that you sin not." (Ex. 20:15-17H)

The people feared God, but not in a way that prevented them from sinning. They feared God because they wanted to be far away from Him. They wanted to hold on to their own ways. But God hadn't come near to kill them; He had come near to give them life.

They were tested by the closeness of the presence of God. Sometimes people complain, "God is too far off." Sometimes they complain, "He's too close." Our reactions to God reveal who we are, not who He is. God is not the one being tested here; we are.

**3)** While still in the wilderness, we were warned: "Everything that I command you, that you are to observe to do. You are not to add to it, nor diminish from it, because there will arise among you a prophet, or a dreamer of dreams, and gives you a sign or a wonder — and the sign or the wonder which he spoke to you happens — to say, 'Let us go after other gods, which you have not known, and let us serve them.' You are not to listen to the words of that prophet, or that dreamer of dreams; for **the Lord your God is testing you**, to know whether you love the Lord your God with all your heart and with all your soul." (Dt. 13:1-4H)

This means that there will be people who falsely claim to speak for God, to have heard from God, and to be serving God. Some of these people will "confirm" their claims by a sign or wonder. There will be others, such as the prophets God sent, who will truthfully claim to speak for God, to have heard from Him, and to be serving Him.

God told the people to be careful to do what He has said to do and not be deceived by those people who claim that their own teachings are from Him, or by those who say that what God has commanded is no longer relevant. There will be voices that encourage people to turn away from Him and go a different way. The Serpent was that voice in the Garden, telling the first recorded lie. In the Garden, our parents believed the Serpent because they wanted to be independent of God.

Since then, there have been countless numbers of such voices. Many people, past and present, follow at least one of them. Why doesn't God silence the voices, the temptations, and the lies? **"The Lord your God is testing you**, to know whether you love the Lord your God with all your heart and with all your soul."

God is not testing to find out which people are the best analysts or smartest logicians. Apparently, God has provided to everyone everything that is necessary to not be deceived. The command — and the responsibility to discern who is speaking the truth and who is lying — is in the singular, i.e. it is addressed to each individual.

Deception takes place, a person is drawn astray, when that person does not love God with all his or her heart and soul. God created us with desires, and those desires are not bad in themselves. We go in the wrong direction, however, when we give more importance to any of those desires, even life, than we do to the One who created us. And when a person wants something other than what God provides, then that person will believe a lie.

**4)** Joshua led the people into the land, fighting the battles that God set before him. The generation that followed Joshua was not as faithful. "And the anger of the Everpresent Lord burned against Israel; and He said, 'Because this nation has transgressed My covenant which I commanded their fathers, and have not listened to My voice, I also will no longer drive out from before them a man of the nations which Joshua left when he died; so that **through them I may test Israel**, whether or not they will keep the ways of the Lord to walk in them as their fathers kept them.' ...He only did this for the generations of the sons of Israel to know — to teach them war — especially those who did not know it before." (Judg. 2:20-22,3:2 cf. 3:1,4)

War is more than a military endeavor; it is a test of will that demands perseverance. The generation that came after Joshua did not persevere in their commitment to God. Perhaps they grew weary of the constant struggle, or lost sight of what was worth fighting for, or were distracted by the pleasures of life. In any case, they didn't hold on to God's purpose in their lives.

Maybe they thought that life would be easier if it weren't an endless battle. So they stopped fighting. But their enemies remained, and God was no longer willing to drive out those enemies.

Life did not become easier, it became harder. The people were oppressed until they cried out to God. Then He raised up a deliverer; but when things got better, the people soon turned away again. The pattern kept repeating itself, but no one seemed to learn anything. "In those days there was no king in Israel; every man did what was right in his own eyes." (Judg. 21:25)

Everyone acted as though there were no authority over them. In actuality, there was a king in Israel in those days, but the people refused to recognize His authority. The time of the judges ended when the people demanded a human king. And God said, "They have rejected Me from being king over them." (1Sam. 8:7)

[The generation in the wilderness had done the same. "And they said to each other, 'Let's appoint a head, and let's return to Egypt.'" (Num. 14:4) But the Everpresent Lord is our head. (e.g. 1Ch. 29:11)]

As long as Israel refused to walk in His ways, God also refused to drive out the nations, the very nations He had already condemned to destruction. Instead of continual war, those generations had continual oppression, broken every so often by a short-lived deliverance. God used those oppressing nations to test Israel, to reveal what was in each heart.

There are many things that we would rather learn than war. But there are things we need to learn: "Patience, fortitude, perseverance .... all those qualities we learn about only when tested. Knowledge we might gladly live without, I suppose."[1] We choose whether or not we will listen to God's voice, whether or not we will walk in His ways. He chooses what we need to learn and how we are to be tested.

**5)** "...And Hezekiah prospered in all his works. And in the matter of the mediators of the princes of Babylon, who had been sent to him to inquire about the wonder that was done in the land, **God withdrew from him to test him**, to know everything in his heart." (2Chr. 32:30-31, cf. 2Kings 20:12-19)

To understand what God was doing, we need to remember that Hezekiah was a good king, "And he did what was right in the eyes of the Lord, like all that David his father had done." (2Chr. 29:2) He repaired and cleansed the Temple, publicly called the priests and people to come back to God, revitalized their lives, and personally provided the necessary sacrifices for atonement and thanksgiving.

He called all the people to observe Passover, and provided a thousand bulls and seven thousand sheep for it. "And in every work that he began in the service of the house of God, and in the Torah, and in the commandments, to seek his God, he did it with all his heart, and prospered." (2Chr. 31:21)

Then the king of Assyria came and warred against the land. Hezekiah and Isaiah the prophet cried out to God, and God supernaturally destroyed the Assyrian army and delivered the land. Later, Hezekiah became deathly ill, but God healed him. Hezekiah was faithful to God, and God was faithful to Hezekiah.

But Hezekiah, being human, was not without flaws. After God healed him, he became proud and ignored God. He did soon humble himself, and God forgave him, but it was evidence that there was a problem in his heart.

That problem, pride, surfaced again when the ambassadors came from Babylon. God didn't prevent Hezekiah from becoming proud; that was Hezekiah's responsibility. In fact, God left Hezekiah alone so that his heart would be revealed.

It's difficult to truly grasp, but God does command us to love Him with **all** our heart — not only when we sense His presence, but also when we feel that He is far away. He doesn't want us to overlook the evil in our hearts, even if it's just a little thing that hasn't made its public appearance yet.

Instead of crushing Hezekiah's pride, God let it come out. He didn't do this so that He could point a finger at Hezekiah and condemn him. He did it so that Hezekiah could know what was in his own heart and deal with it. "Above all, guard your heart diligently; for out of it goes forth life." (Prov. 4:23) God left him alone so that he would learn not to trust in himself.

Some people think that kings and great or important people — whatever the field of their greatness or importance — should be judged by a different standard than that applied to ordinary people. 'Ordinary people, little people, can't really understand how far above them the great ones are.'

In writing to a bishop who held this view, Lord Acton said, "I cannot accept your canon that we are to judge Pope and King unlike other men, with a favourable presumption that they did no wrong. If there is any presumption it is the other way, against the holders of power, increasing as the power increases. Historic responsibility has to make up for the want of legal responsibility. Power tends to corrupt, and absolute power corrupts absolutely. Great men are almost always bad men... "[2]

What made Alexander the Great, Peter the Great, Frederick the Great, et al. "great"? They enforced their own desires on many other people; they killed many, stole their land, and oppressed the survivors. For God, however, the greater the power an individual has, the greater is the responsibility and accountability.

Life is a test, revealing what we do with what we have in the circumstances we find ourselves. Abraham was tested. So were Isaac and Jacob. So were Joseph, Moses, Pharaoh, Job, Saul, David, Jeremiah, Nebuchadnezzar, and everyone else we read about in the Scriptures.

Some people are tested by scarcity, and some people are tested by abundance. Which was the more difficult test for David: being hunted by King Saul or being king himself with the leisure time to gaze at Bathsheba? Some people are tested by storms, and some are tested by smooth sailing. While Daniel was being tested in the palace, Ezekiel was being tested in the dust.

Some are tested by failure, and others by success, by ability or inability. Some are tested by imprisonment, or by freedom. Some are tested because of the sins of others, while some are tested because of their own sins. Some are tested by lies, and others are tested by Truth. Everyone is tested, for "The Everpresent has made all things for Himself, even the wicked for the day of evil." (Prov. 16:4)

God designed life to reveal what is in our hearts. We can acknowledge what is there, and take steps to nurture the good and cut off the bad, or we can choose to do the opposite. Everyone is tested by the necessity of making choices.

### The Testing of Abraham

"And it came to pass after these things, that **God tested Abraham**, and said to him, 'Abraham,' and he said, 'Behold, here I am.' And He said, 'Take now your son, your only son, Isaac, whom you love, and go to the land of Moriah; and offer him there for a burnt offering upon one of the mountains which I will tell you.'" (Gen. 22:1-2)

This is one of the most troubling and controversial passages in the Bible. How could a good God demand that a human father sacrifice his own son? To find the answer, we need to look at some relevant aspects of the context.

**1) The practice of killing one's own children was widespread in the ancient world.**

For those who place a very high value on human life, the killing of any innocent person is an evil; the killing of a child is especially evil; and to kill one's own child is unspeakably so. But not everyone in the world, then or now, places such a high value on human life, or upon the life of a child.

"Infanticide is a practice present-day westerners regard as a cruel and inhuman custom, resorted to by only a few desperate and primitive people living in harsh environments. We tend to think of it as an exceptional practice, to be found only among such peoples as the Eskimos and Australian Aborigines, who are far removed in both culture and geographical distance from us and our civilized ancestors. The truth is quite different.

Infanticide has been practiced on every continent and by people on every level of cultural complexity, from hunter gatherers to high civilizations, including our own ancestors. Rather than being an exception, then, it has been the rule."[3]

It was practiced in Britain, in Rome, in Greece, among the Germanic tribes, in Russia, in India, in China, and in Japan. Killing children was just as much a part of "high" civilizations as it was of "barbaric" communities. "High culture" is a human evaluation, not God's. "High culture" is not synonymous with "respect for life".

"We tend to think that primitive peoples who practice infanticide show a lack of love, even cruelty, towards children. However, killing a newborn is often explained as a caring act, done to save the life of an older sibling who is too young to be weaned but is already a member of the social group and cherished as such... The killing is made easier by cultural belief that a child is not fully human until accepted as a member of the social group. ...The Peruvian Amahuaca, for instance, do not consider children fully human until they are about three years old."[4] Such children are fully human biologically, but the parent or the culture decrees that, in the chosen value system, they are less than human.

It was a common practice, protected and encouraged by law, among Romans, Greeks, and others throughout the world to abandon their own unwanted children to die. It was the primary method of limiting population growth. If a parent didn't want a particular child — because of its poor health, its female gender, its light or dark skin color, its racial impurity, its mixed caste parentage, the economic burden it would place on the family or community, because it was a twin, or for some other reason — the child was killed.

The Egyptian Pharaoh instituted a policy of infanticide for political reasons. He believed that killing every boy born to the Hebrews would make his rule more secure. He was wrong. Instead, it insured that God would totally destroy his kingdom. One of those baby boys, Moses, was protected and raised by Pharaoh's daughter. The God of Israel later sent Moses to

Pharaoh with His message and His authority.

Laws are the product of beliefs and values. Law — whether tribal, national, or international — is designed to enforce a behavioral code upon a society. It dictates what behavior will be rewarded, what behavior will be allowed, and what behavior will be punished.

**2) The practice of sacrificing children was widespread in the ancient world.**

Most of the children who were killed in the ancient world were not sacrificed to a particular god, but some were. Even older children who were cherished by their parents were sometimes sacrificed throughout the ancient world, on every continent. Children were sacrificed to a god to gain that god's favor or to appease that god's wrath.

During ancient times, it was not unusual for parents to sacrifice their children to a god. Some incidents of this are recorded in the Scriptures. At a time when Israel was warring against Moab, the king of Moab "took his first-born son who would have reigned in his place, and offered him up as a burnt offering upon the wall. And there was great wrath against Israel; and they departed from him, and returned to their own land." (2K. 3:27) The king sacrificed his son to induce the gods of Moab to support him in battle.

Despite prohibitions in Torah, there were times when some in Israel sacrificed their children. King Ahaz "made his son pass through the fire, like the abominations of the nations, whom the Everpresent Lord cast out from before the people of Israel." (2K. 16:3) So did King Manasseh. (2K. 21:6)

King Josiah, whose heart was towards God, destroyed the places the people had made for sacrificing their children to Molech. (2K. 23:10) And in the days before the exile into Babylon was complete, God rebuked both the leaders and the people because "They built the high places of Baal, which are in the valley of Ben-Hinnom, to cause their sons and their daughters to pass through the fire to Molech; which I did not command them, nor did it come into My mind, that they should do this abomination to cause Judah to sin." (Jer. 32:35; cf. 2K.

17:17; Ezek. 16:21, 20:26,31)

### 3) God commanded Abraham to not sacrifice Isaac.

God was testing Abraham, and knew how Abraham would respond. Abraham did not know that he was being tested, he only knew that God was faithful. The same God who had miraculously caused Sarah to conceive Isaac — the same God who had promised "I will establish my covenant with him for an everlasting covenant and with his seed after him" (Gen.17:19) and "in Isaac your seed will be called." (Gen. 21:12) — that same God was now asking him to sacrifice Isaac.

It was sixty years since God had first called Abraham to follow Him, sixty years of walking with God and learning to know Him. Abraham knew, as Rashi observed three thousand years later: "'I am the Everpresent.' ...'I am faithful to give back a good reward to those who walk before Me. ...I am faithful to punish. ...I am faithful to establish the truth of My words. ...I am the One who is faithful in My promise.'" (Rashi on Ex. 6:2,3,6)

Abraham believed that God was faithful to do what He had promised. And, therefore, as we read in the Mldrash: "'So Abraham took the wood of the burnt offering and put it on Isaac his son...' [Gen. 22:6] like one who carries his stake [*tzelav*] on his shoulder." (Mid. Genesis 56:3)

The entire incident is not a demonstration of how cruel God is, but rather how faithful He is; and it is a demonstration that He expects the same faithfulness from those who are called by Him. He gives everything, and He expects everything.

In response to Abraham's obedience, God then commanded him not to sacrifice Isaac. "'Do not lay your hand on the youth, and do not do anything to him; because now I know that you fear God, since you did not withhold your son, your only son from Me.' And Abraham lifted up his eyes and looked, and behold behind him there was a ram caught in a thicket by his horns; and Abraham went and took the ram, and offered it up for a burnt offering in place of his son." (Gen. 22:12-13)

As they were walking up the mountain, Abraham had told Isaac, "My son, God will provide Himself [*yireh lo*] a lamb for a burnt offering." (Gen. 22:8) That day, God provided a ram [*ayeel*] instead of a lamb [*seh*]. "And Abraham called the name of that place *Adonai-Yireh*; as it is said to this day, 'In the Mount of the Lord it will be seen [provided].'" (Gen. 22:14)

God knew that He did not intend for Abraham to sacrifice Isaac, but He was testing and demonstrating Abraham's trust in Him. It is a sacrifice that God did not require of Abraham, and does not require of his descendants. God knew from the beginning that He Himself was going to provide the sacrifice in the place of Isaac. It was a purposeful, not an arbitrary, test.

In the text, the reason for the sacrifice is the testing of Abraham, but in the Yom Kippur liturgy, appeal is made to God for the forgiveness of our sins because of "the ashes of Isaac," as though he had been presented as a burnt offering. (cf. Tal. Berachot 62b) This was another reason why the nations sacrificed their children: to obtain forgiveness from their gods.

Micah the prophet voiced an acknowledgment of humanity's inadequacy before God. "With what shall I come before the Lord, and bow myself before God on high? Shall I come before him with burnt offerings, with one year old calves? Will the Lord be pleased with thousands of rams, or with ten thousands of rivers of oil? Shall I give my firstborn for my transgression, the fruit of my body for the sin of my soul?" (Micah 6:6-7)

When God told Abraham to put down the knife, He answered that question. In the *akedah*, the binding of Isaac, the God of Israel made it clear that He does not want us to sacrifice our children, not even in an effor to try to obtain forgiveness. He makes that clear throughout the Scriptures.

**4) God destroyed the tribes of Canaan because they sacrificed their children.**

Moses told Israel of the reasons that God was destroying all the tribes of Canaan. He warned Israel not to commit these same abominations, or God would destroy them, too. In the list of warnings was, "You shall not give any of your descendants to pass through the fire to Molech... For in all these things the nations are defiled which I cast out before you. And the land is defiled; therefore I am punishing its iniquity upon it, and the land itself vomits out her inhabitants." (Lev. 18:21,24-25)

After God completely destroyed Sodom and Gomorrah, He waited four more centuries before He utterly destroyed all the tribes of Canaan. He told Abraham, "the iniquity of the Amorites is not yet complete." (Gen. 15:16) The other cities, towns, and tribes had the clear warning of the fire and brimstone from heaven that destroyed Sodom and Gomorrah, but they didn't change their ways. God waited patiently, but each generation was worse than the one before, until finally their iniquity was thorough — their hearts, their minds, their hands, and their feet. There was no desire for, and therefore no possibility of, turning back.

Much earlier, God had sent the flood that destroyed all the earth, because people had perverted their way and had filled the earth with *hamas*, i.e. violence. When God spoke to Ezekiel about the fate of a rebellious people, He said, "Son of Adam, when a land sins against Me by unfaithfulness upon unfaithfulness, then I will stretch out My hand upon it, and will break its staff of bread, and will send famine upon it [or wild beasts, or a sword, or pestilence], and will cut off man and beast from it. Even if these three men, Noah, Daniel, and Job, were in it, they would only deliver their own souls by their righteousness. ..." (Ezek. 14:13-14,15-20)

Because Noah is listed along with Daniel and Job, who interceded for others, we can surmise that he interceded for his generation. There are those who believe that he spoke to his generation to turn them back from their ways (e.g. Mid. Tanhuma Noah 5), but they mocked him, even as Lot was not taken seriously when he warned of coming judgment.

Though not specifically mentioned in Tanakh, it is a logical inference because everyone could see that Noah was building a very large boat, one which could not be launched. Undoubtedly, people asked him, "Why?" And, undoubtedly, he responded that God was going to flood the whole earth, and the boat he was building was the only way to be saved. The fact that no one joined Noah and his family in building or boarding the ark is prima facie evidence that no one believed it would happen.

And God said, "My Spirit will not always strive with man..."

213

(Gen. 6:3) God sought to turn people back from the destruction that awaited them, but they kept their hearts far from Him, and would not listen. There is a point of no return that an individual, a people, or a world can pass.

**5) God commanded Israel not to sacrifice their children.**

"Do not defile yourselves in any of these things... You shall not give any of your descendants to pass through the fire to Molech... You are to keep My ordinance, so that you do not commit any one of these abominable customs, which were committed before you, so that you do not defile yourselves in it; I am the Everpresent Lord your God." (Lev. 18:24, 21,30 cf. Dt. 18:10) Torah prohibits sacrificing a child, the Writings show that people disregarded the prohibition, and the Prophets proclaimed warnings and condemnations for that disregard.

In general, however, the Jewish people obeyed the prohibition. "The Roman historian Tacitus deemed it a contemptible prejudice of the Jews that 'it is a crime among them to kill any child!'"[5]

The Rabbis echoed God's "prejudice". "Jewish law makes no distinction whatever between infants and adults in their claim to life. It expressly construes the verse 'And he that smites any human life [mortally] shall surely be put to death' (Lev. 24:17) to include the murder of minors."[6] There is no pretension that children aren't fully human.

"...The whole notion of assessing human life by some arbitrary differential — instead of deeming its worth as beyond measure, unique, and transcending any utilitarian quantification or qualification — is utterly repugnant to Judaism. It is an affront to the cardinal teaching that every human being is created 'in the Divine image.'"[7]

Wherever the Scriptures of Israel were embraced, the killing of children ceased to be an accepted societal practice or duty. It became, instead, a terrible crime. Search the great civilizations, the barbaric tribes, and everyone in between, it is the Bible — including the story of the *akedah* — that is the primary source for a respect for life. That respect for life didn't come from some great philosophy or rational process; it came from the Scriptures

God gave to Israel.

Likewise, where those Scriptures are rejected, the ancient barbaric practices are again embraced. Children are again killed because they are "not fully human," or because of their poor health, female gender, light or dark skin color, racial or caste impurity, economic burden, or some other reason.

**Footnotes**

1. Mon frère me l'a ecrit.

2. Letter to Bishop Mandell Creighton, April 5, 1887 published in Historical Essays and Studies, edited by J. N. Figgis and R. V. Laurence, Macmillan, London, 1907, P. 504

3. Williamson, Laila (1978). "Infanticide: An Anthropological Analysis," Pp. 61–75 In Kohl, Marvin, Infanticide and the Value of Life, NY: Prometheus Books. 1978, P.61

4. Ibid., Pp. 63,64

5. The Pentateuch and Haftorahs, ed. and commentary by R. Joseph Hertz, Soncino Press, London, 1956, P. 54

6. Immanual Jakobovits, "Jewish Views on Infanticide," In Kohl, Marvin, Infanticide and the Value of Life, op. cit., pp23-31, P. 24, fn5. "Sanhedrin 84b; See Rashi on Ex. 21:12; and Lev. 24:17"

7. Ibid., Pp.28-29

## *Ruakh Elohim* / THE SPIRIT OF GOD

With our developed understanding of the world, the mention of "the Spirit of God" is somewhat perplexing. God does not have a physical body; He is spiritual. (He is therefore not subject to the laws which He established to govern the physical world.) But since God IS a spirit, what is the meaning of "the Spirit of God"? How can a spirit have a spirit?

To ask the question is to highlight our own lack of understanding of the relationship between spiritual and physical entities. We know that all of physical existence was created by what is not physical; the physical didn't exist until it was created. But we don't really understand what non-physical entities are, or what the nature is of the realm in which they exist.

What is a spirit? It's a simple question. But I don't know any answer that tells me what I need to know, or at least what I want to know.

So if I want to understand what "the Spirit of God" is, I don't really have much to build on. I know what non-physical concepts are, or at least I have some idea. I even have some idea of what an idea is, albeit not a clear one.

Does the Spirit of God have dimensions? Being the Spirit of God, it must be unlimited. Can the Spirit of God be in more than one place at the same time? or is it everywhere at the same time, only emphatically some places at some times?

The text says, "When You send forth Your *Ruakh*, they [God's works] are created; and You renew the face of the earth." (Ps. 104:30) But, since God is everywhere, what does it mean that He sends forth His *Ruakh*? Theren't isn't any place where God is not already there. And if God is there, His Spirit must be there also. So how can He send forth His Spirit to some place?

I think, however, that this is the wrong way to try to understand "the Spirit of God". If I begin with my own finite understanding, there is no way to grasp and define the infinite. If, on the other hand, I look at the text as a whole, rather than looking to my own categories, some of the perplexity disappears. I don't have to fully comprehend the nature of God in order to reach a simple understanding of what it is that He is saying. The text tells us what God wants us to know about Himself.

In this case, He wants us to know that He has a spirit. About 90 times, Tanakh speaks about "the Spirit of the Lord," or "the Spirit of God," or "the holy Spirit," or "My Spirit," or some similar phrase. Regardless of anyone's theological constructions, the second verse of the Bible tells us explicitly that God has a Spirit. If we search all the passages that speak of the Spirit of God, we get a better understanding of what the Spirit of God does and is.

The second explicit mention of the Spirit of God occurs in Gen. 6:3, before God sent the flood upon the earth. "Then the Everpresent said, "My Spirit will not strive in the man forever, in that he is also flesh. So his days will be a hundred and twenty years." (Gen. 6:3) God told Noah, "And I, know that I am bringing the flood of waters over the earth, to destroy from under the heavens all flesh in which there is a spirit/breath of life. Everything that is on the earth will die." (Gen. 6:17, cf. Gen. 7:15,22) Within a man, there is "a spirit/breath of life," but "he is also flesh".

This brings us to a little complication in understanding "the Spirit of God". The Hebrew word *ruakh*, as well as the Greek word *pneuma*, can be correctly translated into English as "spirit," "breath," or "wind", depending upon the context and, to some extent, the inclination of the translator. There is also another Hebrew word, *neshamah*, that is translated as "breath".

For the land animals, God said, "Let the earth bring forth all kinds of living creatures..." (Gen. 1:24) The creation of humanity was different. "The Everpresent God formed the man from the dust of the ground and breathed into his nostrils the breath/*neshamah* of life, and the man became a living soul." (Gen. 2:7)

Many gnerations later, Job said, "As long as my breath/*neshamah* is in me, and the Spirit/breath/*ruakh* of God in my nostrils, my lips will not speak unrighteousness, and my tongue will not moan deceit." (Job 27:3-4) Job comes close to equating his own breath with the Spirit/breath of God.

Elihu responded to Job, "Surely a spirit/*ruakh* is in a man, the breath/*neshamah* of the Almighty causes him to understand. ...The Spirit/*ruakh* of God has made me; the breath/*neshamah* of the Almighty gives me life." (Job 32:8, 33:4) Elihu continued: "If He set His heart on it, and He gathered to Himself His Spirit/*ruakh* and His breath/*neshamah*, all flesh would die as one, and humanity would return to the dust." (Job 34:14-15) The Spirit of God and the breath of God are closely related but they are distinguished one from the other.

"When You hide Your face, they are troubled; when You take away their spirit/breath/*ruakh*, they die and return to their dust. When You send Your Spirit/*ruakh*, they are created, and You renew the face of the earth." (Ps. 104:29-30) After death, "Then the dust returns to the ground as what it was, and the spirit/breath//*ruakh* returns to God who gave it." (Eccl. 12:7)

It seems that these verses are speaking of the spirit of a person, rather than the spirit of God. But what is the spirit of a person? It would seem to be what the person truly is, the essence of the person, or what gives life to him or her.

Yet it would be strange to speak of the Spirit of God as the essence of God. There are no extraneous, non-essential components of God. Likewise, we can't speak of the Spirit of God as some driving force within God. What God is, He is in all ways, everywhere, at all times.

And somehow, by God's choice, the existence of those He has created depends upon His Spirit. In his commentary on the Chumash (Gen. 1:2), R. Joseph Hertz said, "Matter in itself is lifeless. The Spirit of God quickens it and transforms it into material for a living world."

These passages make it difficult to distinguish precisely between the Spirit/*ruakh* of God and the breath/*neshamah* of God. Both were involved in Creation. God breathed life into Adam, and humanity has been breathing ever since. God is the One "who created the heavens and stretched them out, who spread out the earth and all that comes out of it, who gives breath/*neshamah* to its people, and spirit/*ruakh* to those who walk on it." (Is. 42:5)

But the Scriptures say things about the Spirit of God that

cannot easily be attributed to breath (or wind). "You gave your good Spirit to make them discerning. You did not withhold Your manna from their mouths, and You gave them water for their thirst." (Neh. 9:20) "For many years You were forbearing with them. You warned them by Your Spirit through Your prophets. But they did not open their ears, so You gave them into the hand of the peoples of the lands." (Neh. 9:30) God's Spirit makes people wise, and His Spirit warns them against the ways in which they should not go.

But people are stubborn, and they don't want to go the way they should. They want to go the way they want to go. "'Woe to the stubborn children,' declares the Everpresent, 'who make counsel, but not from Me, forming a covering, but not by My Spirit, so that they may add sin upon sin." (Is. 30:1)

Sometimes people don't know what they should do; other times they don't care what they should do. "They angered Him by the waters of Meribah, and it was bad for Moses because of them, because they rebelled against His Spirit, and rash words came from his lips." (Ps. 106:32-33)

When people don't rely on God's Spirit, they are relying upon their own spirit. And that is a problem. "And Moses spoke to the descendants of Israel in this way, but they did not listen to Moses because of shortness of spirit, and because of the cruel slavery." (Ex. 6:9) We suffer from "shortness of spirit," i.e. impatience, because we have a short term view of life. God, whether we like it or not, always takes a long term view.

"Then He said, 'Surely they are My people, children who will not lie.' And He became their savior. In all their affliction He too was afflicted, and the angel of His presence [*panav*] saved them. In His love and in His mercy, He redeemed them; He lifted them up and carried them all the days of old. But they rebelled and grieved His holy Spirit. So He turned to be an enemy against them, and He fought against them." (Isa. 63:8-10)

People can rebel against God's Spirit; they can grieve God's Spirit. People can't rebel against, or grieve, a wind or a breath, both of which pass on or pass away. The Spirit of God is different than a passing movement.

David prayed, "Teach me to do Your will, because You are my God. May Your good Spirit lead me in a land of uprightness." (Ps. 143:10) And at the end of his life, David said, "The Spirit of the Everpresent spoke through me, and His word was on my tongue." (2Sam. 23:2) God's Spirit leads people — guides and teaches them — and sometimes God's Spirit speaks through someone in order to guide and teach others.

There's an interesting passage in which Micaiah the prophet describes the spiritual mechanics which will bring about death of the evil king Ahab. "'And the Lord said, *Who will entice Ahab king of Israel, so that he goes up and falls at Ramoth-Gilead?* And one spoke in this way, and another in that way.

"'Then a spirit came out, and stood before the Lord, and said, *I will entice him.*

"'And the Lord said to him, *With what?*

"'And he said, *I will go out, and be a lying spirit in the mouth of all his prophets.*

"'And the Lord said, *You will entice him, and you will also prevail. Go out, and do so.* Now therefore, know that the Lord has put a lying spirit in the mouth of these your prophets, and the Lord has spoken evil against you.'

"Then Zedekiah the son of Kenaanah came near, and struck Micaiah upon the cheek, and said, 'Which is the way the Spirit of the Lord passed from being with me to speak to you?'

"And Micaiah said, 'Behold, you will see on that day when you go into an inner chamber to hide yourself.'" (2Ch. 18:19-24)

## Individuals Who Received God's Spirit

Though God gives breath to everyone, He gives His Spirit in a special way to particular individuals, such as David. Sometimes what He imparts is for that individual alone, sometimes it is for the whole community, or the whole world.

God told Moses to have Israel build the Mishkan in the wilderness. For that purpose, He told Moses, "I have chosen Betzalel son of Uri, the son of Hur of the tribe of Judah, and I have filled him with the Spirit of God, with wisdom, understanding, and knowledge in all work." (Ex. 31:2-3, cf. Ex. 35:31) And not only Betzalel, as God told Moses, "And you are to speak to everyone who has a wise heart, each one whom I have filled with the Spirit of wisdom, and they will make the clothes for Aaron to consecrate him to be a priest to Me." (Ex. 28:3)

God puts His Spirit on or in individuals to give them wisdom. God gave Joseph the wisdom to know and interpret Pharaoh's dreams, and to know what to do to preserve Egypt through the coming famine. "So Pharaoh said to his servants, 'Can we find anyone like this man, one in whom is the Spirit of God?" (Gen. 41:38)

David gave to Solomon, "the plans of all that the Spirit had put in his mind for the courts of the house of the Everpresent and all the surrounding rooms, for the treasuries of the house of God and for the treasuries for the holy things." (1Chr. 28:12)

King Belshazzar of Babylon was feasting with his nobles when a hand appeared in the air and wrote upon the plaster wall. The king was troubled and perplexed, but none of his counselors and wise men could interpret the writing on the wall. The queen mother came in and told him, "There is a man in your kingdom in whom is the Spirit of the holy God. And in the days of your father, light and understanding and wisdom — like the wisdom of the gods — were found in him. And King Nebuchadnezzar, your father, made him chief of the magicians, astrologers, Chaldeans, and soothsayers. Your father the king raised him up. ...Now let Daniel be called, and he will declare the interpretation." (Dan. 5:11-12, cf. Dan. 5:14)

God also put His Spirit upon different people He raised up to lead Israel. "Now Joshua son of Nun was filled with the Spirit of wisdom because Moses had laid his hands on him. ..." (Dt. 34:9) In commenting on this verse, the Midrash says, "The Holy One, blessed be He, said: 'In this age a few prophesy, but in the Age to Come all Israel will be made prophets'; as it says, *And afterward it will be that I will pour out My Spirit upon all flesh; and your sons and your daughters will prophesy, your old men...'* [Joel 3:1]." (Mid. Num. 15.25)

Throughout the time of the Judges, God put His Spirit upon those He raised up to deliver Israel. "And when the descendants of Israel cried to the Everpresent, the Everpresent raised up a savior to the descendants of Israel, and he saved them, Othniel the son of Kenaz, Caleb's younger brother. And the Spirit of the Everpresent came upon him, and he judged Israel, and went out to war; and the Everpresent delivered Kushan-Rishathaim king of Aram into his hand; and his hand prevailed against Kushan-Rishathaim." (Judg. 3:9-10 ) God's Spirit gave him discernment in civil cases and wisdom in fighting battles.

"Then the Spirit of the Everpresent came upon Gideon,..." (Judg. 6:34)

"Then the Spirit of the Everpresent came upon Yiftah..." (Judg. 11:29)

"The woman gave birth to a boy and named him Samson. He grew and the Everpresent blessed him, and the Spirit of the Everpresent began to stir him ... The Spirit of the Everpresent came upon him in power so that he tore the lion apart with his bare hands as he might have torn a young goat...." (Judg. 13:24-25, 14:6)

God also put His Spirit in or upon individuals to cause them to prophesy — to guide, to encourage, or to rebuke. "And the Spirit of God was upon Azariah son of Oded. And he went out before Asa and said to him, 'Listen to me, Asa and all Judah and Benjamin. The Everpresent is with you when you are with Him. And if you seek Him, He will be found by you, but if you abandon Him, He will abandon you.'" (2Chr. 15:1-2)

"Then the Spirit was clothed with Amasai, chief of the Thirty, and he said ..." (1Chr. 12:19H)

"Then the Spirit of the Everpresent was upon Yahaziel son of Zechariah, the son of Benaiah, the son of Yeiel, the son of Mattaniah, a Levite from the descendant of Asaph, in the midst of the assembly. ..." (2Chr. 20:14) Sometimes the prophet was well-known, sometimes he, or she, was almost unknown.

Sometimes the intended audience — people, priest, or king — listened to the prophet, but usually they didn't. "Then the Spirit of God was clothed with Zechariah son of Yeho'yada the priest. And he stood above the people and said to them, 'This is what God says: *Why do you transgress the commandments of the Everpresent? You will not prosper. Because you have abandoned the Everpresent, He has abandoned you.'* But they conspired against him, and by the commandment of the king they stoned him to death in the courtyard of the house of the Everpresent." (2Chr. 24:20-21)

Saul, before he was established as king over Israel, prophesied. "When they arrived there at Gibeah, a group of prophets came to meet him. The Spirit of God came forcefully upon him, and he prophesied among them." (1Sam. 10:10) Shortly after that, messengers told Saul of the threats of the Ammonites against the town of Yabesh. "When Saul heard these words, the Spirit of God came forcefully upon him, and his anger burned very hot." (1Sam. 11:6) The Spirit of God moved him to prophesy, and the Spirit of God moved him to anger.

But Saul became unfaithful, so God sent Samuel the prophet to anoint David to replace Saul. "So Samuel took the horn of oil and anointed him among his brothers, and the Spirit of the Everpresent came forcefully upon David from that day onward. Then Samuel rose up and went to Ramah." (1Sam. 16:13)

When Saul learned that David had been anointed to replace him as king, he tried to kill David. "So Saul sent men to capture David. But when they saw a company of the prophets prophesying, with Samuel standing there as their leader, the Spirit of God came upon Saul's men and they also prophesied. ...So Saul went there to Naioth in Ramah. But the Spirit of God came even upon him, and he walked along and prophesied until he came to Naioth in Ramah." (1Sam. 19:20,23)

Saul had rebelled against God, and was trying to kill David, whom God had anointed to replace Saul. Yet God sent His Spirit upon Saul, and Saul again prophesied by the Spirit of God. But he didn't change. He stubbornly refused to yield to God. Strangely enough, God sometimes put His Spirit, His holy Spirit, upon individuals who were not holy in their behavior.

Balaam was hired to prophesy against Israel, but God spoke to him and told him not to do it. "When Balaam raised his eyes and saw Israel encamped by its tribes, then the Spirit of God was upon him, and he said... How pleasing are your tents, O

Jacob, your dwelling places, O Israel." (Num. 24:2,5) Balaam could hear from God and speak for God; but he still didn't desire what God desired.

Each prophet spoke as the Spirit of God directed him, or her. They had different personalitities and different experiences. Micah said, "But surely I am filled with power, with the Spirit of the Everpresent, and with justice and might, to declare to Jacob his transgression, and to Israel his sin." (Micah 3:8)

The message of the prophets was often rejected and their lives were often endangered by those angered by the message. God told Zechariah that the people, "refused to listen, set their shoulders in stubborness, and turned their heavy ears away from hearing. They made their hearts as hard as flint and would not listen to the law or to the words that the Everpresent Lord Almighty had sent by His Spirit through the earlier prophets. So there was great wrath from the Everpresent Lord of forces." (Zekh. 7:11-12)

Before Ezekiel had begun to prophesy, God told him: "But the house of Israel will not be willing to listen to you, because they are not willing to listen to Me; because all the house of Israel have a strong forehead and they have a hard heart." (Ezek. 3:7) Of all the prophets, the experiences of Ezekiel, living in the exile in Babylon, were probably the most dramatic and bewildering. His visions were unsettling, and his encounters with God's Spirit were equally startling. Here are some of them.

The same Spirit of God that hovered over the waters "in the beginning" forcefully took hold of Ezekiel. "And the Spirit lifted me up, and took me away, and I went in bitterness, in the heat of my spirit; but the hand of the Everpresent was strong upon me.

"Then the Spirit lifted me up, and I heard behind me a voice like a great earthquake: 'May the glory of the Everpresent be blessed from His place!' There was the sound of the wings of the living creatures kissing each other, and the sound of the wheels beside them, and the sound of a great earthquake. Then the Spirit lifted me up and took me away, and I went in the bitter anger of my spirit, with the hand of the Everpresent strong upon me." (Ezek. 3:12-14)

"Then the Spirit came into me and made me stand on my feet. And He spoke to me and said: 'Go, shut yourself up inside your house.'" (Ezek. 3:24)

"He stretched out the form of a hand and took me by the hair of my head. The Spirit lifted me up between the earth and the heavens and, in visions of God, took me to Yerushala'im, to the door of the inner gate that faces toward the north..." (Ezek. 8:3)

"Then the Spirit of the Everpresent fell upon me, and told me to say: 'This is what the Everpresent says: *This is what you are saying, O house of Israel, but I know what has come up into your spirit.*'" (Ezek. 11:5)

"The Spirit lifted me up and brought me to the exiles in Chaldea in the vision given by the Spirit of God. ..." (Ezek. 11:24)

"The hand of the Everpresent was upon me, and he brought me out by the Spirit of the Everpresent, and set me in the middle of a valley; and it was filled with bones." (Ezek. 37:1)

No one could predict what the Spirit of God was going to do, or what the Spirit of God was going to cause someone to do. As Isaiah said, "Who has directed the Spirit of the Everpresent, or instructed Him as His counselor?" (Is. 40:13) God often tells us what is coming, but in many ways the Spirit of God is still beyond our understanding.

The Spirit of God is an irresistable force, but an irresistable force that anyone can choose to resist and ignore. The Scriptures show us this. There is a day coming, however, when no one, at least no one in Israel, will be able to ignore God's Spirit.

## Upon All Israel

When Moses complained to God about the heavy burden of dealing with all the complaining of the people, God told him to pick seventy elders to assist him. "Then the Everpresent descended in the cloud and spoke to him. And He took from the Spirit that was on him and put the Spirit on the seventy men who were elders. When the Spirit rested on them, they prophesied, and did not cease." (Num. 11:25) ["Cease" follows the Targums and the sense of the whole passage.]

Two of the seventy hadn't come to the assembly, but God put His Spirit upon them as well. When Joshua heard that the two were prophesying in the camp, he asked Moses to make them stop. "And Moses said to him, 'Are you jealous for my sake? If only it were given to all the people of the Everpresent to be prophets, and that the Everpresent would put His Spirit upon them!'" (Num. 11:29)

We have already encountered the Midrashic comment: "In this age a few prophesy, but in the Age to Come all Israel will be made prophets." (Mid. Num.15.25) The passage it speaks about is Joel 3:1-2H: "And afterward, I will pour out My Spirit on all flesh. And your sons and your daughters will prophesy; your old men will dream dreams; your young men will see visions. And in those days, I will pour out My Spirit even on male servants and female servants." (Joel 3:1-2H) It speaks of the time of the end of this age when all the nations gather against Yerushala'im for battle, but God delivers His city and His people.

Some of the other prophets speak of this time as well. It is a time of restoration for Israel. Isaiah prophesied for the God of Israel: "For I will pour water on the thirsty land, and streams on the dry ground; I will pour out My Spirit on your offspring, and My blessing on your descendants." (Is. 44:3)

God spoke often through Ezekiel about this outpouring of His Spirit. "I will give them one heart and will put a new spirit in them. I will remove the heart of stone from their flesh, and give them a heart of flesh, so that they will walk in My statutes and keep My judgments. They will be My people, and I will be their God." (Ezek. 11:19-20)

He repeats much of this promise a little bit later, making it clear that it is His Spirit that He is giving to Israel. "I will give you a new heart and will put a new spirit within you. I will remove the heart of stone from their flesh, and give them a heart of flesh. And I will put My Spirit within you and cause you to walk in My statutes, and you will walk in My judgments, to keep them and do them. And you will live in the land I gave to your fathers; and you will be My people, and I will be your God. I will save you from all your uncleanness. ..." (Ezek. 36:26-29)

"'I will put My Spirit in you and you will live, and I will give you rest in your own land. Then you will know that I, the Everpresent Lord, have spoken, and I have done it,' declares the Everpresent." (Ezek. 37:14) "'And I will no longer hide My face from them, in that I will pour out My Spirit on the house of Israel,' declares the Everpresent Lord." (Ezek. 39:29)

God also spoke of that time through Zechariah: "And I will pour out on the house of David and the inhabitants of Yerushala'im a spirit of grace and entreaty. They will look unto Me, the one whom they have pierced, and they will mourn for him as the mourning for an only son, and grieve bitterly for him as the bitterness for the firstborn." (Zech. 12:10)

Zechariah was describing a time of national mourning and repentance which precedes the final restoration and redemption of Israel. God pours out His Spirit to bring about a change in people. God is merciful.

Because of God's Spirit, the whole world will be changed in the days of Messiah. "And the Spirit of the Everpresent will rest upon him, the spirit of wisdom and understanding, the spirit of counsel and might, the spirit of knowledge of and fear of the Everpresent.... And with righteousness he will judge the poor and decide with equity for the humble of the earth; and he will strike the earth with the rod of his mouth, and with the breath of his lips he will slay the wicked." (Is. 61:1,4, cf. Tal. Sanh. 93b)

The Targum Yonatan gives the second verse of Genesis as: "And the earth was vacancy and desolation, solitary of the sons of men and void of every animal, and darkness was upon the face of the abyss; and the Spirit of Mercies from before the LORD breathed upon the face of the waters." God's Spirit brings mercy into the world.

It's not easy to reduce and summarize what God tells us in Tanakh about His Spirit, the Spirit which hovered over the surface of the waters in the beginning. But if we try to do so, we end up with something like this: The Spirit of God is sent by God into the world to enable people to know Him. The Spirit of God is not other than God, but comes from God to accomplish His purposes in the earth.

## *Mera<u>h</u>efet* / HOVERED OVER

*v'ruakh elohim mera<u>h</u>efet al p'nay hamayim*
"And the Spirit of God hovered over the surface of the waters."

The word *mera<u>h</u>efet*, translated as "hovered," only appears two other times in Tanakh, Jer. 23:9 and Dt. 32:11. The context of each is interesting, especially when we remember that everything is connected before God and His word choices are intentional.

At the time when Jeremiah was prophesying in Yerushala'im, there were false prophets in the city who said that the exile would not reach them, and that those already in exile would soon be brought back. (cf. Jer. 28) It was a pleasant prophecy, one that even Jeremiah wanted to believe, but it was a lie. Even Yerushala'im would go into exile, and most of the people would die in exile.

Yet at the same time that God promised destruction, He also promised restoration. "'Therefore, know that the days are coming,' says the Everpresent, 'and they will no longer say, *As the Lord lives, who brought up the descendants of Israel from the land of Egypt; But, As the Lord lives, who brought up and brought in the seed of the house of Israel from the land of the north and from all the lands where I had driven them.* And they will live in their own land. My heart is broken within me because of the prophets. All my bones tremble/*ra<u>h</u>afu*. I am like a drunken man, like a man overcome by wine, because of the Everpresent and His holy words." (Jer. 23:7-9)

God had Jeremiah prophesy that the people of Judah would be exiled from the land. And, before the exile was complete, God had Jeremiah prophesy that a future restoration would take place. The things Jeremiah prophesied overwhelmed him, and caused his bones to rapidly shake within him.

In 1979 I had an interesting conversation with a Russian Jewish friend, Anatoly, who had managed to emigrate to the

United States. Like many Russian Jews at that time, he was not familiar with the Scriptures, but didn't believe them anyway.

I told him about these verses in Jeremiah which declared that God would deliver the Jewish people from the land of the north and bring them to Israel. I told Anatoly that Russia was the country to the far north of Israel, and that God was going to open the iron doors of the Soviet Union and do exactly what He had promised.

Anatoly responded, "You don't know what it's like. It will never be."

"Maybe I don't know what it's like," I said, "but it will be, because God has said it will be."

"No, it will never be."

Some years later, when the Jewish exodus from the Soviet Union was fully underway, I spoke to Anatoly again. "You remember that conversation we had about the Scriptures and God's promise to bring the Jewish people out of the land of the north, out of the Soviet Union?"

"Yes, I remember."

"And you said it would never be."

"No, I didn't say 'never'."

"Yes, you did. You said it would NEVER be."

"No, I didn't say 'never'."

"Then what did you say?"

"I don't remember."

Ah, but I remember. And more importantly, God remembers exactly what He has said and promised. ("Zechariah" means "the Everpresent remembers".)

And if we look again at the verses in Jeremiah, we see that God promised to bring the Jewish people back to Israel not only from the land of the north, but also "from all the countries where I had driven them." At the same time that the Diaspora was beginning, God was promising that it would one day come to an end. It will be.

The other passage where hovered/*merahefet* appears also speaks of Israel and the nations. "When the Most High divided to the *goyim* their inheritance, when He separated the children of Adam, He set the boundaries of the peoples according to the number of the people of Israel. For the portion of the Everpresent is His people; Jacob is the measured portion of His inheritance. He found him in a desert land, and in a howling, uninhabited/ *tohu* wilderness. He encircled him, caused him to understand, and guarded him as the apple of His eye — as an eagle stirs up its nest, hovers over/*yirahef* its young, spreads out its wings, takes them, and carries them on its pinions." (Dt. 32:8-11)

Because God intends to receive something special from Israel — Jacob is His own particular inheritance — He uses Israel as a measure for setting limits for the nations. "And you, My servant Jacob, do not fear, ' declares the Everpresent. 'Do not be frightened, O Israel, because know that I will save you from afar, and your seed from the land of their captivity. And Jacob will return and will be quiet and peaceful, and no one will terrify him. For I am with you,' declares the Everpresent, 'to save you. Though I make total destruction in all the nations to which I have scattered you, yet I will not totally destroy you. Nevertheless, I will discipline you in judgment, and will not leave you altogether unpunished.'" (Jer. 30:10-11)

The eagle hovers over its young to protect, feed, and instruct them. By creating the eagle, God told us something about Himself. God hovered over Israel in the wilderness. He was never far away. "'I am the God who is near,' declares the Everpresent, 'and not a god far off. Can a person hide himself in secret places so that I will not see him?' says the Everpresent. 'Do I not fill the heavens and the earth?' says the Everpresent." (Jer. 23:23-24)

R. Simeon ben Zoma said, "'It is said, *And the spirit of God hovered over the surface of the waters* — as a dove hovers over her children but does not touch [them].' Then R. Joshua said to his disciples, 'Ben Zoma is still outside [i.e. excommunicated].'" (Tal. Hagigah 15a, cf. Mid. Gen. 2.4) The Talmud says that Ben Zoma was one of only four men to enter the Garden of Eden and receive mystical enlightenment. (Tal. Hagigah 14b) In some way, he departed from rabbinically acceptable belief.

R. Joshua told his disciples that ben Zoma's comment

indicated that his views were still unacceptable. But it is not clear why ben Zoma's comment would indicate that. The Midrash says, "'And the Spirit of God hovered...' This is the spirit of Messiah the King." (Mid. Genesis 2:4, cf. Mid. Gen. Alt. 97.1 and the reference to Messiah and the Spirit in Is. 11:2) And Rashi commented, "The throne of the Glory stands in the air and hovers over the face of the waters ...like a dove which hovers over the nest". (on Gen. 1:2) Rashi connects "the throne of the Glory" with "the Spirit of God".

"The Spirit of God hovered over the surface of the waters." I am not a visual person; I don't naturally visualize what I read or hear. Personally, I am totally incapable of imagining the Spirit of God, which is neither visible nor finite, hovering over anything. Yet I understand that God is communicating something. At the very least, He is communicating that His Spirit was active, not motionless or inert. And He is also communicating that His Spirit was near, not far off.

God created the hummingbird, and it helps illustrate what "hovering" is. The wings of a hummingbird move so rapidly that the hummingbird seems to effortlessly stay in the air in the same place. It actively, and powerfully, hovers in the same place.

The Spirit of God is everywhere, but it can also be in a particular place, as it was when it hovered over the surface of the waters. David prayed, "Where can I go from Your Spirit? Where can I flee from Your presence?" (Ps. 139:7) He understood the Spirit of God to be everywhere, but he also spoke of the Spirit of God being in a particular place. "The Spirit of the Everpresent spoke through me, and His word was on my tongue." (2Sam. 23:2)

Gnostics believe that spirit and physical matter exist in separate realms that do not intersect. But God's Spirit gives life to physical beings, and His Spirit hovered, ever so closely, over the earth. Gnostic spirituality denigrates this world, and focuses on some other one. Biblical spirituality consists of walking in the light of the Everpresent in this world. The holiest, most spiritual task that God gave to Adam was to take care of the Garden. *Derekh eretz*, the way we live on the earth, is what God in

Heaven sees and judges.

We earlier looked at some cases where God put His Spirit upon, or within, certain individuals. There is one more individual mentioned in the Scriptures who is closely connected with the Spirit of God. He is Messiah/*Mashiakh*, i.e. the one anointed with the Spirit of God. We should look briefly at him, especially since we arre told that the Spirit hovered over him.

The Midrash says, "'And the Spirit of God hovered' — This is the spirit of King Messiah, knowing what it says, 'And the Spirit of the Everpresent will rest upon him.' (Is. 11:2). From what merit will that which 'hovered over the surface of the waters' eventually come? In the merit of repentance which is compared to water, as it says, 'Pour out your heart like water.' (Lam. 2:19)." (Mid. Gen. 2.4)

Taking into account the verses which are cited, this passage says three things:

1) the Spirit of God is the spirit of Messiah.

2) As the Spirit of God hovered over the waters in the beginning, so the spirit of Messiah hovers over the repentant.

3) With the repentance of Israel, Messiah will come with the Spirit of God upon him.

The passage in Isaiah which the Midrash uses to equate "the Spirit of God" with "the spirit of King Messiah" is Isaiah 11:1-4: "And a rod will come forth from the stem of Jesse, and a branch will grow from his roots and be fruitful. And the Spirit/*ruakh* of the Everpresent will rest upon him: the spirit/*ruakh* of wisdom and understanding, the spirit/*ruakh* of counsel and might, the spirit/*ruakh* of knowledge and of the fear of the Everpresent. And his delight will be in the fear of the Everpresent, and he will not judge by what his eyes see, nor decide by what his ears hear. But he will judge the poor in righteousness, and decide with equity for the humble of the earth. And he will strike the earth with the rod of his mouth, and he will slay the wicked with the *ruakh* of his lips."

God's Spirit and Wisdom will rest upon Messiah, who is descended from Jesse, the father of David. Messiah will rule as the judges ruled, and with the same wisdom of discernment that

God gave Solomon, the son of David, but without the infidelity. Messiah will bring righteous judgment to the earth.

In this age, where the rich and arrogant rule, the poor and the humble often do not receive justice. "So I returned, and considered all the oppression that is done under the sun. And I saw the tears of the oppressed, and they had no **comforter** — and in the hand of their oppressors there was power — and they had no comforter.... And moreover I saw under the sun that wickedness was there in the place of judgment; and that wickedness was there in the place of righteousness. I said in my heart, 'God will judge the righteous and the wicked, because there is a time there for every purpose and for every work.'" (Eccl. 4:1, 3:16-17)

God will judge the righteous and the wicked in the time when Messiah rules on the earth. The oppresssed will then have a comforter. "'What is the name of King Messiah?' ...R. Yudan said in the name of R. Aibu: 'His name is **Comforter**.'" (Mid. Lamentations 1.51, cf. Tal. Sanhedrin 98b)

There are several other passages in Isaiah that speak about Messiah and the Spirit of God. They are important. In Is. 61:1-3, Messiah speaks prophetically and says: "The Spirit of the Everpresent Lord is upon me, because the Everpresent has anointed me to announce good news to the humble. He has sent me to bind up the broken hearted, to proclaim liberty to the captives, and the freedom of release to those who are imprisoned; to proclaim an acceptable year of the Everpresent, and the day of vengeance of our God; to **comfort** all who mourn; to provide for the mourners of Zion, to give to them a garland instead of ashes, the oil of joy instead of mourning, the cloak of praise instead of a fainting spirit. Then they will be called oaks of righteousness, the planting of the Everpresent, to glorify Him." (Is. 61:1-3)

The Spirit of God comes upon Messiah to put an end to this unjust age and make things right. Messiah will proclaim God's liberty and vengeance, bind up the broken hearted, and bring comfort and joy to those who now mourn and are discouraged. "Every valley will be lifted up, and every mountain and hill will be brought low; and the crooked will be made straight, and the rough places will be a plain. And the glory of the Everpresent will be revealed, and all flesh will see it together, for the mouth of the Everpresent has spoken." (Is. 40:4-5)

The high will be brought down, the low will be raised up. Though the wisdom of *Kohelet*/Ecclesiastes tells us that humanity cannot make the crooked straight (cf. Eccl. 1:15, 7:13), the Wisdom of God tells us that God can, and will. (cf. Is. 42:16, 45:2) Everyone will see the glory of God, "because the earth will be filled with the knowledge of the glory of the Everpresent as the waters cover the sea." (Hab. 2:14, cf. Num.14:19)

God puts His Spirit upon Messiah to establish His Law and His justice in the earth. "Here is My servant, whom I uphold, My chosen one, in whom My soul delights. **I put My Spirit upon him**; he will bring forth judgment to the nations. He will not cry out and will not lift up or cause his voice to be heard in the street. A bruised reed he will not break, and the dimly burning wick he will not extinguish. He will bring forth judgment for truth. He will not fail or be discouraged, till he establishes judgment on the earth. And the islands will wait for his Torah." (Is. 42:1-4)

Messiah will establish justice upon the earth. He will rule as King over all the nations. He calls out, "Come near me and listen to this: From the first, I have not spoken in secret. From the time that it was, I am there. And now the Everpresent Lord has sent me, with His Spirit." (Is. 48:16)

Messiah is distinguished by God's Spirit upon him. He is also distinguished here, as in other passages, by his speaking to Israel and all humanity before he has appeared on the earth. Before God sends him with His Spirit, Messiah says that he has been speaking and he has been "there".

This is very difficult to understand, but it is almost clear and obvious when compared to what Ezekiel experienced. Ezekiel first saw strange winged creatures with four faces, six wings, and wheels (Ezek. 1:10-21), with "the likeness of the firmament over their heads". (Ezek. 1:22-23, cf. Gen. 1:6-8) "A voice came from above the firmament that was over their heads," from one having the "likeness of the appearance of Adam" seated on a throne. (Ezek. 1:25-26) This unusual man had a fiery appearance, surrounded by the likeness of the glory of the Everpresent. (Ezek. 1:27-28) Rashi doesn't say, but perhaps he had these passages in mind when he said, "The throne of the Glory stands in the air and hovers over the face of the waters ...". (on Gen. 1:2)

We aren't given the specific identity of this individual seen by Ezekiel, having the "likeness of the appearance of Adam," but it seems that Daniel the prophet also encountered this mysterious being. (cf. Dan. 10:16) Ezekiel described this mysterious man as having a fiery appearance, surrounded by "the likeness of the glory of the Everpresent". Daniel also described him that way. (cf. Dan. 10:5-6)

Ezekiel saw this mysterious being seated on a throne in the firmament, i.e. heaven. Daniel also saw that. "While I gazed, thrones were placed, and the Ancient of Days sat, whose garment was white as snow, and the hair of His head was like pure wool. His throne was like a fiery flame, its wheels like burning fire. ...While I gazed at the night visions, one like a son of man came with the clouds of heaven! He came to the Ancient of Days, and they brought him near before Him. And there he was given dominion, and glory, and a kingdom, that all peoples, nations, and languages should serve him. His dominion is an everlasting dominion, which will not pass away, and his kingdom is one which will not be destroyed." (Dan. 7:9,13-14, cf. Tal. Sanh. 98a)

This is what Daniel saw: A man came to God in heaven and received from Him authority over all the earth, to establish a kingdom which will not end. Isaiah prophesied about this also. "To the increase of the government and to peace there is no end, upon the throne of David, and over his kingdom, to establish it and to order it with judgment and with justice from now and forever. The zeal of the Lord of hosts will do this." (Is. 9:6)

Rabbi Akiba said that the passage in Daniel refers to Messiah, but he was then rebuked by two of his colleagues. (Tal. Hagigah14a) They were offended by Akiba's saying that

Messiah's throne was next to God, as though there could be any other throne next to that of the Almighty.

They were offended by what Akiba said, but they gave no alternative explanation for the text. The question becomes, 'If it is not Messiah who comes to God in heaven and receives authority to be king over all the earth, then who is it?' We don't know of any person equal to or greater than Messiah. The prophets say clearly that Messiah comes to rule as king over all the earth. That's why God puts His Spirit upon Messiah. R. Joshua b. Levi also understood the passage in Daniel to be speaking about Messiah. (cf. Tal. Sanhedrin 98a)

Additionally, 1Chr. 29:23 says, "Then Solomon sat on the throne of the Everpresent Lord as king instead of David his father, and he prospered. And all Israel obeyed him." The throne on which David sat is called "the throne of the Everpresent Lord".

When God redeems Israel, "At that time, they will call Yerushala'im 'the throne of the Lord'. And all the nations will be gathered to it, to the Name of the Lord, to Yerushala'im. And they will no longer walk after the stubbornness of their evil heart." (Jer. 3:17)

## *Al P'nay* / ON THE SURFACE

### The Surface / *P'nay*

"Darkness was on the surface [*al p'nay*] of the deep [*tehom*]... the Spirit of God was on the surface [*al p'nay*] of the waters." (Gen. 1:2) The Hebrew word *p'nay* means "surface, presence, or faces". The context usually indicates sufficiently how it should be translated.

In the second verse of the Bible, *p'nay* speaks of the surface, as distinguished from the depths, of the abyss and of the waters. When something is the same all the way through, then the surface is exactly the same as what is hidden in its depths. Most things, however, are not that way.

The surface of the deep/abyss/*tehom* is only the surface, the visible part. The depths of the abyss are invisible to humanity. God does not tell us what it is that the surface of the abyss conceals.

In general, the depths of the waters of the seas are colder and darker than the surface. They are less affected by the wind and the weather. Things float on the surface; creatures live in the depths.

So when God introduces the concept of "surface," He is telling us that there can be a difference between an outer appearance and an inner depth. He could have made the world so that what you see is exactly what you get. He didn't.

This is clearly the case with some people, and not just in terms of the complexity of their physical bodies. A human being — a being God made in His own image and likeness out of earth, water, and *ruakh* — is not, in any sense, the same all the way through. It is an easy matter for a person to appear on the surface to be one thing, and yet be something quite different deep within. A person's surface appearance can even be the opposite of what s/he really is.

The Scriptures tell us the story of Ḥannah, loved by her husband, but childless. "And she was in bitterness of soul, and prayed to the Everpresent, and wept bitterly.... And it came to

237

pass, as she continued praying before the Everpresent, that Eli observed her mouth. Now Hannah spoke in her heart; only her lips moved, but her voice was not heard.

"Therefore Eli [the priest] thought that she was drunk. And Eli said to her, 'How long will you be drunk? Put away your wine from you.' And Hannah answered and said, 'No, my lord, I am a woman of a sorrowful spirit. I have drunk neither wine nor strong drink, but have poured out my soul before the Everpresent." (1Sam. 1:10,12-15) Eli saw what Hannah looked like, but completely misinterpreted who she was.

God saw who she really was, and He responded to that reality. He caused her to conceive and give birth to a son. God had chosen Hannah to be the mother of Samuel, who became a man of God, a prophet, and a judge.

Towards the end of Samuel's life, the people of Israel asked him to give them a king to rule over them. That was treason, because there was already a king ruling over Israel, the Almighty Himself. But the people wanted to be like all the other nations. (cf. 1Sam. 8:5) The other nations, and their kings, were unrighteous. Why did the people want to put distance between themselves and God?

"And the Everpresent said to Samuel, 'Listen to the voice of the people in all that they say to you, because it is not you they have rejected, but they have rejected Me from being king over them." (1Sam. 8:7)

God gave them Saul, who was big and strong, to be their king. Saul reigned two years, but he never humbled himself to serve the One who made him king, the one who is infinite and almighty. Saul was never willing to face the truth about himself, always having reasons to justify what he did wrong. (Unfortunately, this is a widespread characteristic of government leaders.) So God rejected Saul, the king he had given to Israel.

Then God told Samuel that He had chosen one of Jesse's eight sons to replace Saul. Samuel went and looked at the first son of Jesse, who was big and handsome. So Samuel thought this must be the one that God has chosen. "But the Everpresent said to Samuel, 'Do not look at his appearance or at his great height, because I have rejected him, for I do not see as man sees. For man sees with the eyes, but the Everpresent sees to the heart.'" (1Sam. 16:7)

Sometimes, what we see with our eyes is sufficient for our purposes; it tells us all we need to know. Sometimes, we can add in our understanding and reading of interpersonal dynamics to get a fuller picture. But sometimes, no matter what we understand or know, what we see is not sufficient. What we see is sometimes quite different than what really is, because we haven't seen the depths of the heart of another.

David gave a poignant description of a friend who betrayed him: "The words of his mouth were smoother than butter, but war was in his heart. His words were softer than oil, yet they were drawn swords." (Ps. 55:22, cf. Jer. 9:8) Peace and love on the outside, but violence and destruction within.

Daniel prophesied of a future confrontation where, "Both these kings' hearts will be towards evil, and they will speak lies at the same table. But it will not succeed, for the end is yet to be at the time appointed." (Dan.11:27) It's not unusual for kings or heads of state to lie to each other; it's normal. People find it essential in warfare of all kinds.

Deception, manipulation, and seduction are not solely the domain of government leaders. Unfortunately, these things are a normal part of every aspect of human life. It's also easier for people to relate to one another surface to surface, i.e. superficially, hiding what is beneath the surface. Sometimes we even hide from ourselves what we truly are within.

Our own hearts deceive us. "The heart is deceitful above all things, and it is incurable; who can know it?" (Jer. 17:9) Because of that, "The one who trusts in his own heart is a fool; but the one who walks in wisdom, will be delivered." (Prov. 28:26)

The world is filled with pretense. The Midrash says, "There are ten portions of pretension in the world, nine in Yerushala'im and one in all [the rest of] the world." (Mid. Esther 1.17) In the very place where God most wants integrity, there He finds pretense. It began with Adam and Havah; it continues with their children.

God seeks and requires a deep relationship, heart to heart. A superficial relationship with God is no relationship at all. "Therefore the Everpresent said, 'Since surely this people draws near to Me with their mouth and honors Me with their lips, but they have removed their heart far from Me and their fear of Me is taught as a commandment of men. Therefore... the wisdom of their wise men will perish, and the understanding of their prudent men will be hidden." (Is. 29:13-14) We can outsmart ourselves; we can outsmart others; but we can never outsmart God. And yet people continue to try.

### P'nay Elohim/The Presence of God

"And they heard the voice of the Lord God walking in the garden in the cool of the day. And Adam and his wife hid themselves from the presence [mi'p'nay] of the Lord God among the trees of the garden." (Gen. 3:8)

For Adam and Havah, an infinite God had come down to a particular place. He had come down to be with them. But, because of their guilt and shame, they did not want to face Him. So they hid themselves from the presence [p'nay] of God.

Their attempt to hide from God was futile. By hiding themselves, they made it so that they could not see God, but they could not make it so that He could not see them. They were like little children who cover their own eyes, and think that, therefore, they can't be seen.

But God is always observing everything everywhere. His observation is an inseparable part of the nature of reality, all reality. There is nothing that exists at any time or any place that is not present before Him.

As God said in the days of Jeremiah, "'Can anyone hide himself in secret places so that I will not see him?' said the Everpresent. 'Do I not fill heaven and earth?' says the Everpresent." (Jer. 23:24) The presence of God is everywhere, but people shut their eyes to His presence. They think that because they can't see God, He can't see them.

If we truly understood that nothing, not even a thought, can be hidden from God, we might live differently. At some point in his life, King David understood it. "Where can I go from Your Spirit? Where can I flee from Your presence [*mi'panekha*]? If I ascend up to heaven, You are there! If I lay down in Sheol, behold, You are there! If I take the wings of the dawn, and dwell in the uttermost parts of the sea, even there Your hand will lead me, and Your right hand will hold me. If I say, 'Surely the darkness will cover me, the light will be night about me.' Even the darkness is not dark for You; but the night shines like the day; darkness is as light with You." (Ps. 139:7-12)

There is no way to escape from God's presence. "The eyes of the Everpresent are in every place, keeping watch on the evil and the good." (Prov. 15:3) The eyes of the Everpresent observe every action, always. And they do not see only the surface; they see all the way through to the core.

That is good news for those who seek to do what is good. "Because the Everpresent, His eyes run to and fro in all the earth, to strengthen those whose hearts are blameless towards Him...." (2Ch. 16:9) In a world that is rushing to get far away from God, an individual needs added strength from the Everpresent to continue in the right direction.

This is, however, bad news for those whose hearts are focused on themselves. "For the wicked are like the troubled sea, when it cannot rest, whose waters cast up mire and dirt. 'There will be no peace,' says my God, 'for the wicked.'" (Is. 57:20-21)

Moses called heaven and earth as witnesses to hear that God would surely bring judgment on those who turned away from Him. There will again, as always, be no place to hide. "Because a fire is kindled in My anger, and will burn to the lowest part of Sheol..." (Dt. 32:22)

God delivered us from Egypt, but Moses knew by experience that such deliverance had not caused the people to look to God. To the contrary, if the people had had their way, they would have turned back into slavery. Only God's continuing presence prevented them from doing that. (e.g. Num. 14)

Moses said to God, "Now therefore, I beg You, if I have found grace in Your eyes, please show me now Your way, that I may know You, that I may find grace in Your eyes; and consider that this nation is Your people. And He [God] said, 'My presence [*panai*] will go with you, and I will give you rest. And he [Moses] said to Him, 'If Your presence [*panekha*] does not go with us, do not bring us up from here." (Ex. 33:14-15)

God's presence is tangible, and powerful. After the generation that refused to trust God had died in the wilderness, Moses reminded the new generation before they were to enter the land: "Yet because He loved your fathers, therefore He chose of their seed after them, and brought you out, with His presence [*b'panav*], with His mighty power, out of Egypt." (Dt. 4:37) God's presence brought us out of Egypt.

God's presence is almost personified in the Scriptures. His presence delivers, and His presence saves. "In all their affliction He was afflicted, and the angel of His presence [*panav*] saved them; in His love and in His compassion He redeemed them; and He bore them, and carried them all the days of old." (Is. 63:9)

In the Septuagint, this is presented as: "Out of all their affliction, it was not an envoy, nor a messenger, but the Lord Himself who saved them. Because He loved them and spared them, He Himself redeemed them, and took them up, and raised them up all the days of old." (Is. 63:9LXX)

"God's presence" represents God Himself. "The mountains tremble before Him, and the hills melt, and the earth heaves at His presence (*mi'panav*) — even the world and all who dwell in it." (Nahum 1:5)

To be cast away from God's presence means to be utterly forsaken. God patiently waits for people to turn back to Him. "And the Everpresent was gracious to them, and had compassion on them, and turned towards them, because of His covenant with Abraham, Isaac, and Jacob, and would not destroy them, nor yet cast them away from His presence (*panav*)." (2Kings 13:23)

But there comes a time when God stops waiting, when people are determined to walk in the stubbornness of their own hearts. (e.g. Dt. 29:18) Then God gives them up to what they have chosen, though they think they have chosen something different. "For through the anger of the Lord it [the exile] came to pass in Yerushala'im and Judah, until He had cast them out from His presence (*panav*)..." (2Kings 24:20)

God entreats, and God warns, but God will do all that He has promised, both the good and the bad. "Therefore, behold, I, myself, will utterly forget you, and I will forsake you and the city that I gave you and your fathers, and cast you out of My presence (*panav*)." (Jer. 23:39)

Some people make a list of all the great places they want to go, or the beautiful places where they want to live, or the pleasures they want to experience. Personally, I've already been in a lot of those places, and done a lot of those things, but the greatest and most beautiful place is the presence of God. The highest and most intense pleasure is to be in the presence of God, that is, if your heart is towards Him. As David sang, "You will show me the path of life. In Your presence (*panekha*) is fullness of joy; at Your right hand there are pleasures for evermore." (Ps. 16:11)

That is why we are encouraged to come near to Him. That is why we need to get our hearts right. "Let us come forward into His presence (*b'panav*) with thanksgiving, and make a joyful noise to Him with songs of praise." (Ps. 95:2)

God doesn't think the way we think, and He doesn't do things the way we do things, but there is no one who loves us more. There is no one who cares for us more. "Serve the Everpresent in joy; come before His presence (*panav*) with shouts of exultation." (Ps. 100:2)

### The Face of God

One of the meanings of *p'nay* is "face". Actually, since the word is in the plural form, the meaning is "faces". But except for creatures like cherubim (e.g. Ezek. 1:5-10), living beings only have one physical face. So when "faces" is the contextual meaning of *p'nay*, it is usually translated into English as the singular "face".

God said to Moses, "'You are not able to see My **face**. because no man will see Me and live.' And the Everpresent said, 'Look, there is a place by Me, and you will be standing upon the rock. And it will be, while My glory passes by, that I will put you in a crevice of the rock, and will cover you with My hand while I pass by. Then I will take away My hand, and you will see My back; but My **face** will not be seen.'" (Ex. 33:20-23)

God tells us that He has a face. As we have seen, God tells us that He has eyes (e.g. 2Chr. 7:15), and He tells us that He has ears (e.g. 2Kings 19:28). He tells us that He has a mouth (e.g. Is. 45:23) and a nose (e.g. Is. 65:5). Whatever it means, God wants us to know that He has a face.

Again, this is not anthropomorphic language. The Scriptures do not begin with humanity; they begin with God. The Scriptures describe humanity in terms of God; the creation of Adam and Havah was a theomorphic act. God created humanity in such a way that we bear His image and likeness. The human face — with its mouth, and eyes, and nose — was created to represent something about God.

Jacob said that he saw God "face to Face," *panim al panim.* (Gen. 32:30) God said that He spoke mouth to mouth with Moses, *peh el peh.*, and that Moses "sees the appearance of the Lord." (Num. 12:8, cf. Ex. 33:11, Dt. 34:10) Moses told the people that the Lord spoke with them face with Face, *panim b'panim.* (Dt. 5:4) I have no idea what this means in a physical sense, but I understand it to mean communication that is direct and very close.

God commanded the priests to bless the people of Israel with this blessing: "The Lord bless you, and keep you. The Lord make His **face** shine upon you, and be gracious to you. The Lord lift up His **face** upon you, and give you peace."(Num. 6:24-26)

The face of the Lord can shine. Apparently it shone upon Moses when Moses was in His presence forty day and forty nights on the mountain. Because when Moses came down from the mountain, the skin of his own face shone. (cf. Ex. 34:28-35)

David prayed, "Let Your **face** shine upon Your servant; save me in Your loving kindness." (Ps. 31:17H) Maybe David didn't expect his own face to shine the way that of Moses did, but he knew that if God's face were to shine upon him, he would be saved. He was hoping to find grace in God's eyes.

Esther went before King Ahashuerus hoping to find grace in his eyes, to plead with him to prevent the destruction of the Jewish people. She was reluctant to go, as she told Mordechai: "All the king's servants and the people of the king's provinces know that there is one law for any man or woman who comes to the king into the inner court, who has not been called — to put him to death unless the king extends to him the golden scepter. Then he will live, but I have not been called to come to the king these thirty days." (Est. 4:11)

Esther knew the law, but she went to the court of the king, risking her life to try to save her people. "And it was so, when the king saw Esther the queen standing in the court, that she found grace [*hayn*] in his eyes; and the king held out to Esther the golden scepter that was in his hand. So Esther drew near, and touched the top of the scepter." (Est. 5:2)

Finding grace in the eyes of the king meant that Esther would not be punished for her approach. She could have been, but the king was gracious to her.

In the days of Noah, God decreed judgment on all humanity for their ungodly and anti-godly behavior. "But Noah found grace in the eyes of the Everpresent." (Gen. 6:8) Noah was a just man, but "even Noah, however, survived only because he found grace..." (Mid. Gen. 28.8-29.1) God's face shone upon Noah, and He spared him and his family from the coming destruction.

In the Psalms, we read the repeated entreaty:

"Restore us, O God, and let Your **face** shine; and we will be saved....

"Restore us, O God of hosts, and let Your **face** shine; and we will be saved....

"Restore us, O Lord God of hosts, let Your **face** shine; and we will be saved." (Ps. 80:4, 8, 20H)

For God can also hide His face from a person or from a people. Moses knew that. As the new generation was about to enter the land of Israel, God told Moses that he would die soon.

## THE SECOND VERSE

"Then the Everpresent said to Moses, 'Know that you will sleep with your fathers, and this people will rise up and be a harlot after the foreign gods of the land, where they go among them, and will forsake Me and break My covenant which I have made with them. Then My anger will burn against them in that day, and I will forsake them and hide My **face** [*panai*] from them. Then they will be devoured, and many evils and troubles will find them; and they will say in that day, Did not these evils find us because our God is not in our midst? And I will surely hide My **face** [*panai*] in that day because of all the evils which they will have done, because they are turned [*panah*] to other gods.'" (Dt. 31:16-18, cf. Dt. 32:20; Job 13:24; Ps. 13:1)

How many times in our history has it seemed as if God had turned His face away from us? How many times has it seemed that He had forsaken us? As the psalmist prayed: "Awake, why do You sleep, O Lord? Arise, do not cast us off for ever. Why do You hide Your **face**, and forget our affliction and our oppression? For our soul is bowed down to the dust; our belly sticks to the earth. Arise for our help, and redeem us for the sake of Your loving kindness." (Ps. 44:24-27H)

When God hides His face from us, the world is a very dark place. Darkness not only covers the earth, it rules over the earth. And the abyss seems open and threatening before us. But we have to remember that God says that He hides His face from us because of the evil which we do in turning our faces away from Him.

In arrogance and pride of power, King David committed adultery with Bathsheba and then killed her husband. When he was confronted with the evil of his sins, he was broken. He humbled himself and began to entreat God.

David pleaded, "Hide Your **face** [*panekha*] from my sins, and blot out all my iniquities. Create in me a clean heart, O God; and renew a steadfast spirit inside me. Do not cast me away from Your presence [*panekha*]; and do not take Your Holy Spirit from me." (Ps. 51:11-13H) In other words: 'Don't hide Your face from me; hide Your face from my sins.'

Elsewhere, David asked the same: "...Your **face**, O Lord,

I will seek! Do not hide Your **face** from me; do not put Your servant away in anger. You have been my help; do not abandon me, nor forsake me, O God of my salvation." (Ps. 27:8-9)

Because of God's grace, He did not condemn David as the Law prescribed. Because of God's grace, He does not automatically condemn me, or you, as the Law prescribes. "If you, Everpresent Lord, were to keep iniquities, who could stand? But the forgiveness is with You, so that You may be feared." (Ps. 130:3-4)

Sometimes people think that God forgives everything, and so it doesn't matter much what they choose to do. But God doesn't forgive everything. No one has ever earned or merited God's forgiveness. If He chooses not to forgive, if He chooses to turn His face away from me, rather than from my sins, then I am hopelessly lost. The choice to forgive or not is God's. That should impress upon me the consequences that lack of forgiveness will bring. That should cause me to fear Him, not to disregard His commands.

This is true for nations as well as for individuals. "...And when He hides His **face**, then who can see Him? whether a nation or a man, it is the same?" (Job 34:29)

Tanakh is filled with God's promises of judgment upon the nations and upon Israel. It is also filled with God's promises of restoration. Often both promises are found together, but not always. One promise is that God will hide His face from His people; the other is that He will no longer hide His face.

"'And the nations will know that the house of Israel went into exile for their iniquity; in that they acted unfaithfully against Me. Therefore I hid My **face** from them and gave them into the hand of their enemies. So they all fell by the sword. I treated them according to their uncleanness and according to their transgressions, and I am hiding My **face** from them.' Therefore this is what the Everpresent Lord says: 'Now I will bring back the exile of Jacob, and be merciful to all the house of Israel, and will be zealous for My Holy Name. ...Then they will know that I am the Lord their God, who caused them to be exiled to the nations; but I have gathered them to their land, and left none of them there any more. And I will no longer hide My **face** from them in that I pour out My Spirit upon the house of Israel,' says the Everpresent Lord." (Ezek. 39:23-25,28-29)

It seems that even when God turns His face away, His heart is still towards Israel. No matter how things may appear upon the surface, God is always desiring repentance and reconciliation. In the wilderness, God pronounced judgment upon Israel, but He was waiting for Moses to intercede.

God pronounced judgment upon Nineveh, but Jonah, unlike Abraham and Moses, did not step up to intercede. He wanted the people of Nineveh to receive the destruction they had earned for themselves. That's not what God wanted.

We err when we judge God by surface appearances. God is just, and so He will bring judgment. But He wants something better for both Israel and the nations. "And I searched among them for a man who would build up the wall and stand in the breach before Me [*l'panai*] for the land, so that I would not destroy it; but I found none." (Ezek. 22:30) God is still searching for someone who will stand before His face and intercede for the rebuilding of the wall, to keep out destruction.

"Yet there is none who calls upon Your Name, who stirs up himself to take hold of You; for You have hidden Your **face** from us, and have consumed us, because of our iniquities." (Is. 64:6H) Abraham interceded for Sodom and Gomorrah. Moses interceded for Israel. Job interceded for his friends.

They sought God's mercy and grace for others. Abraham didn't pretend that the people of Sodom and Gomorrah were not guilty; Moses didn't pretend that Israel wasn't guilty. They simply asked God to find a way to save them from the destruction they deserved.

## *P'nay haMayim /*

# THE SURFACE OF THE WATERS

In the beginning, "The Spirit of God hovered over the surface of the waters." Why? The Spirit of God gives life, and water is essential for life on the earth. There are aspects of water, its surface and its depths, which illustrate aspects of life.

The surface of the waters is subject to tension which causes it to have shape, making it act as though it were a very flexible solid rather than the infinitely divisible liquid that it is. It takes energy to maintain the surface. Minimizing the surface area of a quantity of water minimizes the amount of energy that must be expended; i.e. it minimizes the surface tension. That's the reason drops of water tend towards a spherical shape, minimizing, but never eliminating, the surface tension. At the same time, the surface tension is not great enough to give a fixed shape to a quantity of water.

Surface tension is what enables long-legged water striders to walk on water. Surface tension enables some objects that are denser than water to float, whereas by weight alone they should sink into the liquid. And surface tension causes thrown stones to skip, given sufficient velocity, the right shape, and the right angle of striking the water.

Given the role that water plays in bodily fluids, cells, and processes, its surface tension is biologically important. Too little or too much tension can have harmful effects on the living organism. In such cases, what happens on the surface affects the life that takes place within.

Because water is a liquid, the push of atmospheric pressure and the pull of gravity cause it to flow to the lowest reachable location. When no further flow is possible, the surface of the water is basically flat, i.e. equidistant from the spherical earth's center of gravity. That is the meaning of "Water seeks its own level." The surface of the water is adjusted: what is high is brought down, and what is low is filled up.

But the earth's oceans, which now contain about 96% of all the water on the planet, are not flat. Geological activity and tides caused by the pull of the moon continually move the waters. And waves, primarily caused by wind, endlessly change the surface of the waters. Navigators, surfers, and public safety personnel keep their eyes on the wind and the waves. The surface of the waters can inspire fear, as well as excitement, reflection, and tranquillity.

"Those who go down to the sea in ships, who do business on great waters; these see the works of the Everpresent Lord and His wonders in the deep. For He speaks, and raises the stormy wind/*ruakh*, which lifts up its waves." (Ps. 107:23-25) There is uncertainty and possibly danger upon those waves.

The moods of the waters illustrate the swirling currents of human life on the earth. "'I **create** fruit of the lips: peace, peace for him who is far off and for him who is near,' says the Lord, 'and I will heal him. But the wicked are like the troubled sea, when it cannot rest, whose waters cast up mire and dirt. There will be no peace,' says my God, 'for the wicked.'" (Is. 57:19-21)

Whether an individual is near or far off, God invites each one to turn to Him. Whether a people is near, i.e. Israel, or far off, i.e. the nations, God offers peace and healing. But for those who stubbornly continue in their own direction, there will be turbulence and war. One way or another, the words that come through their lips will bear fruit.

The actions of the peoples are compared to the sounds and upheavals of the waters and the waves. "He stills the noise of the seas, the roaring of their waves, and the tumult of the peoples" (Ps. 65:8H) Even as God silences and sets limits for the waves of the sea, so He does the same for the nations.

Babylon had exalted itself against Israel, conquering the land and bringing the people into exile. God had allowed it. More than that, He brought it as judgment upon His people because of their sin. But the leaders of Babylon drew the wrong conclusion, thinking that Israel was helpless. "For Israel has not been widowed, nor Judah of his God, of the Lord of forces; though their land was filled with sin against the Holy One of

Israel." (Jer. 51:5

God promised to silence the proud waves. "'Though Babylon should mount up to heaven, and though she should fortify the height of her strength, yet destroyers will come to her from Me,' says the Lord. ...Because the Lord has ruined Babylon, and stilled her mighty voice; their waves roar like great waters, the noise of their voice is raised. ...for the Lord God of recompenses will surely pay back." (Jer. 51:53, 55, 56)

Tyre also exalted itself against a downtrodden Israel. "Son of Adam, because Tyre has said against Yerushala'im, 'Aha, she, who was the gates of the people, is broken; she has turned to me; I will be made full, now that she is laid waste.'

"Therefore this is what the Lord God says: 'Behold, I am against you, O Tyre, and I will cause many nations to come up against you, as the sea causes its waves to come up. And they will destroy the walls of Tyre, and break down her towers; I will also scrape her dust from her, and make her like a bare rock.'" (Ezek. 26:2-4)

The *ruakh* will raise up powerful waves, which will completely destroy Tyre. Instead of bringing life, the waters will bring destruction and death.

Even in the midst of violent storms, God still calls indivduals and nations to turn to Him. "Deep calls to deep at the noise of Your waterfalls; all Your waves and Your billows have gone over me." (Ps. 42:8H, cf. Jonah 2:4H) The time when one is helpless can be the time that one finds Strength.

Some sink in the waters. Others float on the surface. A very few walk with God. "He alone spreads out the heavens, and treads on the waves of the sea." (Job 9:8)

No matter how forcefully the wind blows, God walks on the waters. In His design, the surface of the waters is shaped by tension, and covered by waves. But whether the surface is placid or tempestuous, the Spirit of God is hovering over the surface of the waters. God is never far away from those who call on Him.

## *haMayim* / THE WATERS

Today, about 71% of the earth is covered with water. That's a lot of water. In the beginning, all the earth was covered with water. "Then God said, 'Let the waters under the heaven be gathered together to one place, and let the dry land appear.' And it was so." (Gen. 1:9)

God designed an amazing distribution system to water the dry land. Actually, He designed two different systems, the first was very simple. "And it was before any plant of the field was in the earth, and before any herb of the field grew; for the Lord God had not caused it to rain upon the earth, and there was not a man to work the ground. And a mist went up from the earth, and watered the whole face of the ground." (Gen. 2:5-6)

That was the simple system, and all the earth was well-watered by it. But with the appearance of Adam, designed to work the ground from which he had been made, the need changed a little. "And the Lord God took the man, and put him into the garden of Eden to work it and to watch over it." (Gen. 2:15) To cultivate certain plants, there was a need for an uneven distribution of water — some places needing more water, some places needing less.

The second distribution system was more complex, put into operation after the flood. The sun, from 93 million miles away, warms the waters so that some turns into vapor and rises into the air. Then, in a complex system, the air holding the vapor moves great distances over the water and over the land. And then, with the right combinations of humidity, altitude, and temperature, the water vapor again condenses and falls upon the earth as rain, hail, snow, or some combination of them.

The water which falls on the land seeps into the soil, nurturing plants, and filling streams, rivers, and lakes. "The wind goes toward the south, and turns around to the north; it whirls around continually, and the wind returns again according to its circuits. All the rivers run into the sea; yet the sea is not full; to the place from where the rivers come, there they return again." (Eccl. 1:6-7)

The water in the seas is salt water. That salt will kill the land plants it encounters, and is not good for people either. Salt water doesn't satisfy thirst, it increases it. People who drink only salt water will soon die of dehydration, if something else doesn't kill them first.

But when salt water turns to vapor, the salt is left behind. Rain, hail, and snow bring fresh water to the earth, except when they pass through poisoned air. Then they bring back to earth some of the acid and pollution which we have sent into the air.

But the system itself was designed to provide a continual supply of fresh water, the water of life, for the earth. There are no monthly bills for desalinating and purifying the salt water, no transportation charges for the thousands of miles the water is carried. And there are no pollutants from the energy expended. It is, truly, an amazing system.

## A Short, Personal History of Water

When a person is born, that little baby, causing all kinds of emotions and reactions in others, is 90% water. The percentage decreases over time. About 60% of the adult human body is water. That, I suppose, is why we become less cuddly as we age. The human skeleton, by the way, is only 20% water.

70% of the human brain is water. For better or for worse, we all have water on and in the brain. What an amazing controller, computer, and pilot it is, one which God has made mostly from water.

90% of the lungs is water. We may not be able to breathe under water on our own, but it is mostly water that enables us to breathe. Our lungs bring in air and distribute it to keep the body alive. Photosynthesis — turning sunlight into energy — is amazing, but so is using water to bring in oxygen to keep the human body alive. And it's a built-in feature; we don't have to think with our watery brains in order to get it done.

All the chemical reactions within us take place in water. Our body water functions as a huge transportation medium for heat, chemicals, and bio-electrical impulses. It enables the body to excrete potentially toxic chemicals. These are all amazing feats of engineering which make life as we know it possible.

As the Spirit of God hovered over the surface of the waters in the beginning, God knew the role that water would play in the bodies, lives, and deaths of people throughout the ages. And there was tension on the surface of that water.

God knew that the water would both nourish life and destroy it. He knew that it would bring serenity to some people, and violence to others. He knew that it would carry some ships bringing life-sustaining supplies, and some that carried death-dealing, plague-spreading armies. He knew that it would be both a barrier and a conduit.

All of this was known to God in the beginning as His Spirit hovered over the surface of the waters. He knew that the earth would again, during the flood, be completely covered with water, but with a water that extinguished life. God knew the role that water would play in bringing judgment upon the living. When "the fountains of the great deep were broken up, and the windows of heaven were opened, ...all in whose nostrils was the breath of life, of all that was in the dry land, died." (Gen. 7:22) How appropriate that surface tension is a normal, necessary aspect of the water of life.

### A Symbol for Life/Blood

Water is sometimes used in the Scriptures to represent the transient life which we and other creatures currently have. As the wise woman of Tekoa told King David: "For we will surely die, and are like water spilled upon the ground which cannot be gathered up again...." (2Sam. 14:14) David, later said, "I am poured out like water, and all My bones are out of joint. My heart is like wax; it has melted within me." (Ps. 22:15H)

Concerning animals which are to be eaten, Israel is commanded, "You are not to eat the blood; you are to pour it on the ground like water." (Dt. 12:16) Since the life of the flesh is in the blood (Lev. 17:10-12), this is equivalent to pouring out the life first.

When the Philistines controlled Bethlehem, David expressed his longing for the water of his home town: "'Who will enable me to drink of the water of the well of Bethlehem, which is by the gate!'

"So the three mighty men broke through the camp of the Philistines, drew water from the well of Bethlehem that was by the gate, took it, and brought it to David. Nevertheless he would not drink it, but poured it out to the Everpresent. Then he said, 'Far be it from me, O Everpresent, that I should do this! This is the blood of the men who went at the risk of their lives.' Therefore he would not drink it...." (2Sam. 23:15-17)

Their lives, his life, and our lives are precious to God, but they are only a drop in the vast oceans of life which cover the earth. God is life, an inexhaustible, everpresent fountain of living water. He gives life, and that is a gift that makes all others possible.

The days of our lives, however, are a finite quantity, one which will soon be expended. I have today to work with, or at least part of it; I don't know whether or not I will have tomorrow. Life is an opportunity in which God wants us to succeed. As the wise woman of Tekoa continued in speaking to King David: "... neither does God take away life; but devises means, that none of us be banished." (2Sam. 14:14)

God wants us to succeed, but He defines success in life differently than most people do. "Blessed is the man who trusts in the Lord, and whose confidence is the Lord. For he will be like a tree planted by the waters, which sends out its roots by the river, and will not see when heat comes, but its leaf will be green; and will not be anxious in the year of drought, and will not cease producing fruit." (Jer. 17:7-8)

In the psalms, the righteous person is described in the same way. "He will be like a tree planted by the rivers of water, that brings forth its fruit in its season; its leaf also will not wither; and whatever he does will prosper." (Ps. 1:3)

Those who choose life "take refuge under the shadow of Your wings. They will be fully satisfied from the abundance of Your house; and You will make them drink of the river of Your pleasures. For with You is a fountain of life; in Your light we will see light." (Ps. 36:8-10H)

God Himself is the fountain of life. And He defines failure in life in fairly simple terms: "For My people have committed two evils; they have forsaken Me, the fountain of living waters, and dug cisterns for themselves, broken cisterns, that can hold no water." (Jer. 2:13)

God is a pure fountain, a vast river, a tumultuous ocean covering all the earth, but people deceive themselves into thinking they can control and direct Him for their own purposes. How absurd! How many and how vain are all the broken cisterns that people have built throughout the ages. Why not surrender to the Truth instead?

"There is a river, whose streams make glad the city of God, the holiest dwelling place of the most High." (Ps. 46:5H) The Midrash connects this with Zechariah 14:8: "And it will be on that day, that waters of life will go out from Yerushala'im..." The text in Zechariah continues: "And the Lord will be king over all the earth; on that day the Lord will be one, and His Name one." (Zech. 14:9)

God sent a heavenly being to show Ezekiel things that would happen in the future. One of the things that Ezekiel was shown was water flowing out from under the threshold of the Temple. "And he measured another thousand; and it was a stream that I could not pass over; for the water had risen, water to swim in, a stream that could not be passed over. And he said to me, 'Son of Adam, have you seen this?'

"Then he brought me, and caused me to go to the shore of the stream. And when I had returned, behold, at the shore of the stream were very many trees on one side and on the other. And he said to me, 'These waters flow out towards the eastern region, and go down to the Arabah, and go to the sea. And when they enter the sea, the waters will be healed. And it will be that every thing that lives, which moves, wherever the streams will come, will live. And there will be very many fish, because these waters come there; for they will be healed; and every thing will live where the stream comes.

"...And by the stream, upon its shore, on this side and on that side, there will be all the trees for food, whose leaf will not wither, nor will its fruit fail. And its fruit will continue each month, because the waters for them flow from the Temple [*haMikdash*]; and their fruit will be for food, and their leaves for healing." (Ezek. 47:5-9,12)

The water flows from the Temple in Yerushala'im, bringing healing and life to the Dead Sea. The trees that will flourish on both sides of the river, the Jordan River are characterized in the same way as the righteous in Psalm 1:3.

The Jordan River was not named after the country of Jordan, for there was no such country before 1946. That country, initially called "Transjordan," was founded within the territory which was mandated as a national homeland for the Jewish people — in the land which was on the east side of the Jordan. The country was named after the river.

In the Scriptures, we are told the story of Na'aman, a Syrian general who came to Elisha the prophet to be healed. Elisha, without coming out of his house to greet the general, told him to immerse himself seven times in the nearby Jordan river.

Na'aman, in his pride, was enraged. "Are not Amana and Pharpar, rivers of Damascus, better than all the waters of Israel? May I not wash in them, and be clean? And he turned and went away in a rage." (2Kings 5:12) The Syrian general recognized, but despised, the Jordan river as "the waters of Israel."

But Na'aman's servant encouraged him to humble himself and do as the prophet said. He did, and after the seventh time, he came up out of the waters healed. Through this cleansing, he had learned an important lesson. "Behold, now I know that there is no God in all the earth, but in Israel..." (2Kings 5:12,15)

The God of all the earth has chosen to identify Himself as the God of Israel. In the waters which He has given to Israel, there is healing for all the nations, if they will humble themselves before Him, wherever they are.

## A Symbol for Cleansing

Because water can cleanse us, it is sometimes used in the

Scriptures to represent cleansing from the filth of our sins, which God provides through atonement and forgiveness. King David prayed, "Be gracious to me, O God, according to Your loving kindness; according to the multitude of Your mercies blot out my transgressions. Wash me thoroughly from my iniquity, and cleanse me from my sin. ...Purge me with hyssop, and I will be clean; wash me, and I will be whiter than snow." (Ps. 51:3-4,9H)

The Scriptures speak of many things that make a person unclean. In some cases, it is an external uncleanness which lasts only for a day or a week after the appropriate sacrifice is offered or the prescribed steps are taken. Examples of this type of uncleanness are an internal flow of blood, the discharge of body fluids, or contact with a dead body. (e.g. Lev. 5:2-3, 11:32,36) This type of uncleanness comes through the varying circumstances of ordinary life, from things that happen to us.

Cleansing from the contagious disease *tzara'at* — which most translators render as "leprosy" though it is clearly not what we know today as leprosy — is much more difficult. Someone who has this disease must be excluded from the community. (cf. Num. 5:2-3) The person cannot be cleansed by normal means, but must first be healed. If, however, a person is healed of the disease, then there is a procedure for verifying the healing and then for cleansing the person to allow re-entry into the community.

But there are also things that do not happen to us, but we choose to do to ourselves. Sexual immorality (e.g. Lev. 18:20ff), pursuit of evil spirits (e.g. Lev. 19:31), worship of idols (e.g. Ezek. 23:30), arrogant unclean contact with what is holy (e.g. Lev. 7:21), and mistreatment of others all make us unclean within. Unclean thoughts, words, actions, and motives cannot be cleansed by performing some prescribed process.

We must turn away from these things and turn back to God. The closer we come to God, the more we become aware of our uncleanness. As Isaiah the prophet said when God appeared to him: "Woe is me! for I am undone; because I am a man of unclean lips, and I dwell in the midst of a people of unclean lips; for my eyes have seen the King, the Lord of forces." (Is. 6:5)

Isaiah knew that "We are all as an unclean thing, and all our righteous actions are as filthy rags; and we all fade as a leaf; and our iniquities, like the wind, have taken us away." (Is. 64:5H) We need something stronger than water to make us clean.

Job said, "Who can bring the clean from the unclean? No one!" (Job 14:4) His friends agreed. "What is man, that he could be clean? And one born of a woman, that he could be righteous? ...How then can a man be justified with God? Or how can one be clean who is born of a woman?" (Job 15:14, 25:4)

God knows what is, what will be, and what might have been. We don't. God has given to every person a free will, the ability to make choices. Choices have consequences. That is why God brings all men to judgment for the choices they make. (cf. Eccl. 12:14)

God provided the sacrificial system to atone for our sins, because He knew we would need it. The calendar God gave us focuses on the holy days and the sacrifices that go with them. Most of our recorded Biblical history is about sin, sacrifice, and forgiveness. 71% of the earth is covered with water; perhaps a similar percentage of God's relationship with humanity concerns cleansing. It's fortunate that some dry land appears every so often.

At the dedication of the Temple, the place where the priests would offer the sacrifices, Solomon prayed for Israel: "If they sin against You, for there is no man who does not sin... Yet if they return to their heart in the land where they were carried captive, and repent, and entreat You in the land of those who carried them captive, saying, 'We have sinned, and have done perversely, we have committed wickedness.' And return to You with all their heart, and with all their soul... Then hear their prayer and their entreaty in heaven your dwelling place, and maintain their cause, and forgive Your people who have sinned against You, even for all their transgressions where they have transgressed against You..." (1Kings 8:46-50) That's something for every Jew living in Diaspora to consider.

Centuries later, God showed Zechariah a vision. "And he

showed me Joshua the high priest standing before the angel of the Lord, and Satan [the Adversary] standing at his right hand to thwart him. And the Lord said to Satan, 'The Lord rebukes you, O Satan; the Lord who has chosen Yerushala'im rebukes you. Is not this a brand plucked out of the fire?'

"And Joshua was clothed with filthy garments, and stood before the angel. And he responded and spoke to those who stood before him, saying, 'Remove the filthy garments from him.' And to him he said, 'Behold, I have caused your iniquity to pass from you, and I will dress you in festive garments.' ...

"[The Lord said]... 'Hear now, O Joshua the high priest, ...behold, I will bring My Servant the Branch/*tzemach*. ...and I will remove the iniquity of that land in one day." (Zech. 3:1-9)

Joshua the high priest represents his people before God, seeking therefore to intercede for Yerushala'im and her children. He is clothed in filthy garments because he represents a people who are guilty and unclean. Satan, the Adversary, is seeking to accuse, and thereby destroy, Yerushala'im and the Jewish people.

"The Branch" is a designation for Messiah. In this vision, represented by Joshua, he is clothed in "filthy garments," recalling the confession of Isaiah that all our righteousnes actions are as "filthy rags". He is bearing the filth of Israel, but in one day God removes that filth and the iniquity of the land. God covers us instead in clean garments to celebrate His feasts before HIm. As we saw earlier, the Midrash equates the hovering Spirit of God with the spirit of King Messiah, and says that repentance will bring him and cleansing from our sins. (Mid. Gen. 2.4)

The Spirit of God hovers over each one of us, watery creatures that we are. But there is also Darkness which hides an abyss that we cannot see. We must choose between the Spirit of God which cleanses and the Darkness which defiles. It doesn't seem difficult to know which is better. The difficulty lies in making that choice and being steadfast in it. For that, we need God's help.

# THE THIRD VERSE

ויאמר אלהים יהי אור ויהי אור

And God said, 'Let there be Light.' And there was Light.

# THE THIRD VERSE

## *vaYomer Elohim* / AND GOD SAID...

When a tree falls, or a baby cries, sound is produced, and that sound has meaning for someone who hears and understands it. That meaning can contain an imperative for the one who understands the sound. "You must run or you will be crushed." Or "You must get out of bed and be a responsible parent." Or "It's time to..."

A groan, a sigh, or a laugh can carry a world of meaning. These are meaningful sounds, but they are not sounds that are "said".

The human body has its own internal communication system — DNA, RNA, hormones, enzymes, proteins, electrochemical neural signals, et al. — which regulates and protects it through the very elaborate nervous, vascular, and endocrine systems. These carry very strong messages, the equivalent of commands, but the messages are not spoken.

A sound that is "said" is part of a language. It is an audible symbol that carries abstract meaning. By convention, that sound refers to something: a physical entity, a relationship, or a concept.

Language is a way of describing things that are tangible and intangible. All words are symbols of something, and not the things themselves, though onomatopoeic words contain the sound they describe. Words point to something other than themselves. Speech involves the use of audible symbols; it relies on ideas and conceptual thinking. Individual words are concepts that are linked together to communicate. The word "tree" has a meaning; "apple tree" has more specific meaning; and "apple tree split by lightning" has even more specific meaning.

The words are not physical things, but, in these cases, they describe physical things. Words can also describe non-physical things, like ideas or relationships. They can even describe things that don't exist.

Saying the words is a way to send their abstract conceptual meaning to those who hear. Not everyone who hears understands. To understand the concepts the words represent is to know what they include and what they exclude.

Sometimes, I enjoy sitting in an airport and waiting for an international flight — unless the flight is delayed. I enjoy hearing people speaking in many different languages, making sounds to each other that carry no linguistic meaning for me, but certainly carry such meaning for them. Parents make these sounds to their little children, and the little children understand. I don't understand, but the little children do.

These children make sounds to their parents and to each other, sounds that carry no linguistic meaning for me, but certainly do for them. They talk, quarrel, and ask questions. The words that they hear or say make them happy, or sad, or angry. To me, the variety of sounds, intonations, emotions, and reactions is amazing. Even without understanding the sounds, I understand a lot of what is being communicated, because much of the communication is not in the words themselves.

Observing, I understand some of the intonations, emotions, and physical reactions. I understand some of the context. The very act of speaking to someone else communicates something in and of itself.

Yet even when people speak the same language, live in the same place, and share the same culture and experiences, much of what the hearer understands is not what the speaker intended to communicate. Since words have a range of meaning, what is understood may be different from what was intended. Miscommunication takes place often. That makes speech all the more amazing: despite unfathomable differences between people, communication does take place through language.

Plato believed everything in this world to be merely an image or copy of some archetypal form or idea that existed in a reality outside this world. One could say, for example, that there is a reality to the concept of "tree," and each tree we encounter in the physical world is merely an imperfect, partial representation of that ideal or universal reality. Accordingly, "tree," or "human," is a category in which many quite different entities can be found, but there is some essential nature shared by all.

Other entities may share any number of the same characteristics and yet be excluded from the category because they lack something essential. One of the challenges of communicating is that different people do not attach the same content or value to particular concepts or sounds.

### Language and God

The text says, "God said..." This means that when only God existed, there was language. No one else existed, but language did. Even when nothing else existed, concepts and thought existed, but they did not exist external to God. When there was only God, there was nothing external to Him. Language is, therefore, intrinsic to the nature of God.

What God said had meaning, even though He was the only one who heard it. What God said had meaning, even though the concepts He spoke into existence had never before been assigned to physical objects. Neither Adam nor Moses nor any human being was there to hear what He said.

God later revealed to a particular human — perhaps Adam or Moses — things which no human had ever witnessed. At some point, someone wrote those things down for others to read and know. God anticipated that, and intended it. In the act of writing, patterns of marks are combined to visually represent sounds, sounds which are combined to invoke meaning, meaning that points to objects, concepts, and relationships.

We can be grateful that the Torah speaks in the language of the children of Adam, since, apparently, there are other kinds of languages which we would not be able to understand. After Jonah repented, "Then the Everpresent spoke to the fish, and it vomited out Jonah upon the dry land." (Jon. 2:11H) God, who created fish, can speak to them in a language they understand.

But what the Rabbis say about the Torah is only partly true. Humanity did not create language. Language is something that exists with God. The Torah speaks in the language of God. It speaks the language of God in the subset He created for the children of Adam.

God implanted language in humanity when He created us

in His own image and likeness. He built it into Adam from the beginning because Adam was designed to understand what God said to him. In God's purpose, that was necessary so that Adam could live in a way that reflected who God is.

The Scriptures present themselves as the revelation of God to humanity. Language and speech come from God. When God speaks, His words have more facets, depths, and power than the way humans ordinarily use words. Encountering His words in life is something much more than simply encountering them in the text. God's words contain much more than the languages of humanity.

Even when I read "God said...," I don't grasp what took place. I understand the individual words, but I don't understand what is being described when the two words are joined together. When the text says "David said...," I understand that and can relate to what took place. When the text says that Abraham, or Moses, or somebody heard the Lord, I understand that also; because it happens on the human side.

But I don't understand what happens with God when He speaks. Do His lips move, or does He simply project His thoughts? How is it that some people hear and some people don't, even if they are in the same place? Throughout the Scriptures, I read that "God said...," or "the Everpresent Lord spoke...," or "the Word of the Everpresent Lord came to...," and I don't really know what physical events happened.

As for what God said, the text tells me that, but the written words are too flat, too two-dimensional — or else I am — to convey the reality of what took place. The impact of the print can be powerful enough to change me, but I still don't witness or experience what took place. Even if I hear the words, even if I visualize them in some way, even if I have an insightful imagination, I know that much of what the words describe still escapes me. The words of God are alive, but I am not alive in the same way or in the same realm. I do not even know how many dimensions they have. The magnitude and power of what they convey is far beyond me. I don't feel them enough or resonate with them.

266

If I were alive with God's word, I would recognize His identity and presence within His voice. I would see it as Abraham did. "The word of the Everpresent came to Abram in a vision, saying, 'Do not fear, Abram; I am your shield, and your reward will be great.'" (Gen. 15:1) Abraham saw/heard the Word of the Everpresent Lord God.

Usually, God's words remain external to me. I do not take them in as Jeremiah did. "Your words were found, and I did eat them..." (Jer. 15:16) I do not encounter Him, at least not in His fullness. I do not melt before Him as Isaiah did: "Then said I, 'Woe is me! for I am undone; because I am a man of unclean lips, and I dwell in the midst of a people of unclean lips; for my eyes have seen the King, the Lord of forces.'" (Is. 6:5) I am too solid, too physical.

The voice (or touch) of a parent communicates to an infant, but not because the infant understands the language or the sounds. The tones and overtones, pitch, volume, and rhythm all communicate, though I don't exactly know what or how they communicate. The voice (or touch) communicates the person and emotions.

An infant knows and feels the presence of a parent. Certainly God wants us to have at least an infantile relationship with Him. But, of course, He wants much more.

After God spoke the Ten Commandments at Sinai, "All the people perceived the voices/*kolot*, the lightning flashes, the sound of the shofar, and the mountain smoking. And the people perceived and trembled, and stood far away." (Ex. 20:18) In commenting on the use of the plural of voices/*kolot*, "R. Yohanan said, 'The voice [of God] went forth and divided into seventy voices, into seventy languages so that all the peoples would hear.'" (Mid. Ex. 5:9)

"R. Yohanan said: 'What is meant by what is written? — *The Everpresent Lord gives the word: those who proclaim the good news are a great army.* (Ps. 68:12H) Every single word that went forth from the mouth of the Omnipotent was divided into seventy languages.' The School of R. Ishmael taught: '*And like a hammer that shatters rock* (Jer. 23:29) — how this hammer divides into many sparks! Even so, every single word that went forth from the mouth of the Holy One, blessed be He, was divided up into seventy languages.'" (Tal. Shabbat 88b)

God's speech, unlike human speech, creates and rules over reality. "The voice of the Everpresent is powerful; the voice of the Everpresent is full of majesty. The voice of the Everpresent breaks the cedars; the Everpresent breaks the cedars of Lebanon." (Ps. 29:4-5ff) In comparison, human speech is almost impotent.

Even at a physical level, human speech, unlike that of God, cannot take place without a physical medium, like vocal chords or air, to carry and transmit the sound vibrations. That's why it takes time for sound to travel distance. Without a physical medium, there is no transmission of the sounds that humans make.

But God could speak in an absolute vacuum, at absolute zero, and His word would go forth and instantaneously reach all of space. Since God, however, is everywhere, it is therefore not clear what we are to understand when the text says, "the word of the Lord came to Samuel..." (1Sam. 15:10), or "the word of the Lord came to Abram in a vision..." (Gen. 15:1).

We will soon look at how "the word of the Lord" was viewed in the Midrash and the Targums. At this point, it is sufficient to note that when God speaks, His word is intended to cause the one who hears it to respond. The one who hears is to become the physical medium through which the sound is transmitted. In effect, the one who hears is to vibrate at the same frequency as what was said.

When God speaks, He has a purpose.

## God's Purposes for His Word
### 1) To Create
The word "beginning" in the phrase "in the beginning" is neither a physical thing nor a description of a physical thing. The reference is to time, a non-physical dimension of existence. It is a concept that rules over the lives of humanity.

We understand time to be one of the dimensions of our

existence. We can't exist without time, even as we can't exist without space. God created time and space by His word.

"The heavens were made by the word of the Everpresent Lord, and all their forces by the breath/*ruakh* of His mouth." (Ps. 33:6) In the account of the creation of heaven and earth, we are told that:

"God **said**, 'Let there be light.'...

"And God **said**, 'Let there be a firmament in the midst of the waters, and let it divide the waters from the waters.' ...

"And God **said**, 'Let the waters under the heaven be gathered together to one place, and let the dry land appear.' ...

"And God **said**, 'Let the earth bring forth grass, herb yielding seed, and fruit tree yielding fruit after its kind, whose seed is in itself, upon the earth.'...

"And God **said**, 'Let there be lights in the firmament of the heaven to divide the day from the night; and let them be for signs, and for seasons, and for days, and years. And let them be for lights in the firmament of the heaven to give light upon the earth.' ...

"And God **said**, 'Let the waters be filled with many kinds of living creatures, and birds that may fly above the earth in the open firmament of heaven.' ...

"And God blessed them, **saying**, 'Be fruitful, and multiply, and fill the waters in the seas, and let the birds multiply in the earth.' ...

"And God **said**, 'Let the earth bring forth all kinds of living creatures, cattle, and creeping things, and beasts of the earth after their kind.' ...

"And God **said**, 'Let us make humanity in our image, after our likeness; and let them have dominion over the fish of the sea, and over the birds of the air, and over the cattle, and over all the earth, and over every creeping thing that creeps upon the earth.' ..." (Gen.1:3,6,9,11,14-15,20,22,24,26)

God chose to speak the universe into existence. He wants us to know that He created all things by sending forth His word. And He defined His Creation by speaking His word.

"And God **called** the light 'Day,' and the darkness he called

'Night'....

"And God **called** the firmament 'Heaven'....

"And God **called** the dry land 'Earth'; and the gathering together of the waters He called 'Seas'..." (Gen.1:5,8,10)

He spoke and it was so. As Rav Yehudah said, "Blessed be the One who created the Heavens with His word, and all their inhabitants with the breath/*ruakh* of His mouth." (Tal. Sanh. 42a)

The Scriptures do not tell us explicitly why God did that, but they do tell us that He did. The role of God's Word in Creation is presented as being similar to that of Wisdom personified in Proverbs 8.

## 2) To Instruct Humanity

From the beginning, God instructs humanity according to His purpose. "And God blessed them, and God said to them, 'Be fruitful, and multiply, and fill the earth, and subdue it; and have dominion over the fish of the sea, and over the birds of the air, and over every living thing that moves upon the earth.'

"And God said, 'Behold, I have given you every plant bearing seed, which is upon the face of all the earth, and every tree, on which is the fruit of a tree yielding seed; to you it will be for food. And to every living creature of the earth, and to every bird of the air, and to every thing that creeps upon the earth, where there is life, I have given every green plant for food.'" (Gen.1:28-30)

God told Adam and Havah what the purpose of their lives was, and how they were to sustain it. But they turned away from God, despising His instructions. They and their descendants have reaped the bitter fruit of that choice. (The fruit grows from the seed, and contains another seed within it.) Yet people as a whole haven't changed; Individuals do, but humanity doesn't.

Some things that God says can be difficult for us to understand, because He doesn't think the way we think. But our major problem is not a failure to understand what God says; it is a failure to do what we have correctly understood.

After the flood, God repeated some simple instructions to those who survived: "...Be fruitful, and become many, and fill the earth." (Gen. 9:1) But it wasn't long before their descendants rejected God's instruction and purpose.

"And they said one to another, '**Come**, let us make bricks... **Come**, let us build us a city and a tower, whose top may reach to heaven; and let us make us a name for ourselves, so that we are not scattered abroad upon the face of the whole earth.'" (Gen. 11:3,4) They were determined to work directly against what God had said. So God said, "**Come** let us go down... So the Lord scattered them from there over the face of all the earth.." (Gen. 11:7,8) Their actions brought the very thing they wanted to avoid. (cf. Prov. 10:24)

Because the nations continually turned away from God, He created Israel to be a light to them, to draw them back. And He gave us a lot more specific instruction so that we could fulfill that role. And He commanded us, "Listen, O Israel..."

But there is more to listening than just hearing and understanding. "When Moses went and told the people all the words and laws of the Everpresent Lord, they responded with one voice, 'Everything the Everpresent Lord has said we will do.'" (Ex. 24:3) Unfortunately, they didn't do what they said, much less what He said, and so God brought the judgment that He had said He would bring.

David knew that "The Torah of the Everpresent Lord is without defect, causing the soul to return. The testimony of the Everpresent Lord is steadfast, making the simple wise. The statutes of the Everpresent Lord are right, rejoicing the heart. The commandment of the Everpresent Lord is pure, enlightening the eyes." (Ps. 19:8-9H)

God is ever present, and what He says is always right. "Your word is a lamp to my feet and a light for my path." (Ps. 119:105) Unfortunately, David didn't always walk in that light.

His son Solomon correctly observed the purpose of God's instruction for everyone: "To know wisdom and instruction; to perceive the words of understanding; to receive the instruction of wisdom, justice, and judgment, and equity." (Prov. 1:2-3) God speaks so that we will know how to live.

God is steadfast and faithful to what He says, "declaring the end from the beginning, and from ancient times what is not yet done. ...Listen to Me, you stubborn of heart, who are far from righteousness.'" (Is. 46:10,12)

### 3) To Nourish and To Heal

We are told that God's Word "gives seed to the sower and bread to the eater." (Is. 55:10-11) That means at least two things: **First**, if planted in good soil, God's Word will produce fruit. That fruit will have seed within it, seed which can likewise be planted. (cf. Gen. 1:11)

So, there is life in God's Word, life which can reproduce according to its kind. As with all plants that grow, that life has the power to break through hard ground — in this case, hard hearts.

God says that Leviathan is "king over all the children of pride ...his heart is hard as a stone; hard like the lower millstone." (Job 41:26,16H) Pride hardens the heart. Pride makes us untouched by the needs or pains of others.

But a heart of stone brings death to its owner. Moses showed Pharaoh the signs from the God of Israel, signs which could have caused him to change. But his heart became hard instead, and he did not listen to the signs. (e.g. Ex. 7:22) The Septuagint text has *esklerunthe ten kardian*, a hardening of the heart. The root is more familiar to us in the medical condition of *arterio -sklerosis*, i.e. hardening of the arteries.

The heart needs to be supple and flexible to perform properly. If I harden my heart, whether to God or to my neighbor, it is at my own peril. That is why God counselled our fathers, and He counsels us: "Therefore, circumcise the foreskin of your heart, and do not be stiffnecked any more." (Dt. 10:16)

His word is able to penetrate and break up that hardness, but I need to choose to let it. "Sow to yourselves in righteousness, reap in mercy. Break up your fallow ground, because it is time to seek the Everpresent Lord, till He comes and rains righteousness upon you." (Hos. 10:12) I understand that the God who created the universe by His word can produce good fruit in my life, if I become His garden.

God promises that one day, "Truth will sprout from the

earth; and righteousness will look down from heaven." (Ps. 85:12H) God's Word is like a seed, and when properly planted and watched over, it will produce good fruit. In this case, it will produce living Truth.

**Second**, God's Word is food for the soul. "Man is not to live by bread alone, but by every Word which goes forth from the mouth of God." (Dt. 8:3) Humanity was not designed to live without a Word from God. Nevertheless, most people do; at least they live without a Word from God on a regular basis.

Lack of physical food has obvious, physical consequences that are visible to everyone. The consequences of a lack of God's Word may not be so visible, but are certainly just as debilitating. God's Word is necessary for living according to His purpose. I can excel in many things and yet still fail in what is most important: God's reason for my existence.

Ordinary bread sustains us for daily physical life. God's Word sustains us for daily meaning and for life everlasting. These are intended to be complementary purposes.

God speaks to people in many different ways. "The heavens declare the glory of God; and the firmament proclaims His handiwork. Day to day utters speech, and night to night expresses knowledge." (Ps. 19:2-3) Anyone can hear from God.

But hearing from God is not sufficient in itself. We need to receive and absorb what we hear, as Jeremiah did. "Your words were found, and I did eat them..." (Jer. 15:16) The body transforms physical food into energy. Even so, the heart can transform God's Word into direction and commitment.

God promises to respond by giving health and healing. "If you will diligently listen to the voice of the Everpresent Lord your God, and will do that which is right in His sight, and will give ear to His commandments, and keep all His statutes, I will put none of these diseases upon you, which I have brought upon the Egyptians; for I am the Everpresent Lord who heals you." (Ex. 15:26)

We can be sick in ways that no human doctor can heal. "The heart is deceitful above all things, and desperately wicked; who can know it?" (Jer. 17:9) We can look good on the outside and yet be rotten inside.

If health is important to us, there is a proven cure. "He sent His word, and healed them, and saved them from their destructions." (Ps. 107:20) God prescribes what we need. "This book of the Torah is not to depart from your mouth; but you are to meditate on it day and night, that you may observe to do according to all that is written on it. For then you will make your way prosperous, and then you will have good success." (Josh. 1:8)

People think of prosperity and success in terms of things; God thinks of prosperity and success in terms of life.

### 4) To Enable Us to Know God

Speech communicates both a specific message and something about the one speaking. When God speaks to humanity, He wants us to understand and respond to what He has said, but He also wants us to know Him.

If God had only wanted the world to function according to His commands, then He wouldn't have created humanity, or He wouldn't have given humanity the ability to choose to disobey. He would always have spoken as He did in the beginning: "Let there be...," and it would be. God doesn't need anyone else to accomplish His will. He can accomplish it Himself. There is something more that He wants when He speaks to humanity.

When a parent speaks to a baby, the baby doesn't initially understand the words, but begins to recognize the voice, and begins to know the one who speaks. The voice communicates a lot more than just the words — love, comfort, concern, displeasure, or something else. When two people know each other well, the words may have more meaning. And sometimes, when people know each other well, they can tell just as much from what isn't being said.

God wants us to know Him. When He says something, He provides us with an opportunity to do more than obey or disobey. He provides us with an opportunity to know Him.

"And Pharaoh said, 'Who is the Lord, that I should obey His voice to let Israel go? I do not know the Lord, nor will I let

Israel go." (Ex. 5:2) Pharaoh found out. He came to know the Everpresent Lord, but not in a way that he expected or wanted.

As we look at the lives of the Fathers, the lives of the kings, or the lives of the prophets, we see that knowing God is an adventure. Moses and the generation he brought out of Egypt came to know God by His powerful works and His word, but also by His timing and His testing.

"From heaven He made you hear His voice, that He might instruct you. And upon earth He showed you His great fire; and you heard His words out of the midst of the fire." (Dt. 4:36)

God taught, but the people didn't learn. They heard the voice of God, but they didn't want to hear it again. That is one reason why the most frequent phrase in the Bible is "And the Everpresent Lord spoke to Moses..." Nothing else is even close. The people didn't want to hear directly from God; they wanted to hear through an intermediary.

They said they would obey, but they didn't want to know God. That, however, is the goal of obedience: to know Him. And it then becomes the source of obedience.

Moses had heard God's voice out of the burning bush. He wasn't interested in being part of God's plan to deliver Israel, but he was always willing to listen. "So the Everpresent Lord spoke to Moses face to face, as a man speaks to a friend..." (Ex. 33:11)

The infinite, almighty Creator of all things spoke with a little creature in a desert wilderness, on a small planet, in a small solar system, in a small galaxy of no apparent significance. He spoke with this little creature face to Face, as a man speaks to a friend. That tells us something important about God, about who He is and what He wants.

That generation didn't want to be friends with Him, and so they died in their sins in that wilderness. Joshua led their children into the land that God had chosen for them. Then that generation also died, "...and there arose another generation after them, who did not know the Everpresent Lord, nor the works which He had done for Israel." (Judg. 2:10)

That's a variation of an echo of what had happened in Egypt:

"And there arose a new king over Egypt, who did not know Joseph." (Ex. 1:8) That lack of knowledge affected Pharaoh's heart. The result was not good.

The time that followed Joshua, the time of the judges, was disastrous because every "man did what was right in his own eyes." (Judg. 21:25) They didn't know God, and so, instead of seeking Him, each person did whatever he or she thought was right. And, since "all the ways of a man are pure in his own eyes" (Prov. 16:2), what they did was very different from what God thought was right.

In the wilderness, God had commanded our fathers — or more precisely, God had told Moses to tell the people: "You are to love the Everpresent Lord your God with all your heart, and with all your soul, and with all your might. And these words, which I command you this day, are to be in your heart; and you are to teach them diligently to your children..." (Dt. 6:5-7)

We are commanded to love God with all that we are, and we are commanded to teach our children to do the same. But we cannot love a vague unknown, no matter how powerful He may be. Nor can we teach our children to do that. We need to know Him to truly love Him.

Our biblical history is full of ups and downs, mostly downs. God called Israel to be a faithful bride, an illustration of the closeness of the relationship He desires. But we have not been that. It was not only during the time of Hosea the prophet that we were not faithful. "Their doings do not lead them to return to their God, because the spirit of harlotry is in the midst of them, and they have not known the Everpresent Lord." (Hos. 5:4) Our eyes seem to be always looking elsewhere for something or someone else. Our ears seem to be always listening to someone or something else.

Yet God promises to change that. He intends to have that intimate relationship for which He created Israel. "And I will betrothe you to Me for ever; I will betrothe you to Me in righteousness, and in judgment, and in grace, and in mercies. I will betrothe you to Me in faithfulness; and you will know the Everpresent." (Hos. 2:421-22H)

The drama is intense, whether one is obedient or not. Job was obedient, and that righteousness made him a target for every kind of evil. It wasn't until the end of his anguish that God restored his life. God didn't bring back what was taken away from Job, but He restored his life.

After God spoke to Him, Job replied: "I have heard of you by the hearing of the ear; but now my eye sees you. Therefore I loathe myself, and repent in dust and ashes." (Job 42:5-6) Job heard the Everpresent Lord, and Job saw Him. Job was confronted with the tremendous difference between himself and God. And he humbled himself.

It's much better to be obedient, even though it does not bring an exemption from trouble. It may even be an invitation to trouble. But it's one thing to hear about God, it's another thing to hear from God. It's one thing to know about God; it's a very different thing to know Him.

God is the author, director, and producer of this drama. And He has definite purposes in His scripting. In His plan for Israel, He promises a new covenant. It is His means of making us what He intends for us to be.

"'I will put My Torah in their inward parts, and write it in their hearts. And I will be their God, and they will be my people. And they will no longer teach — every man his neighbor and every man his brother — saying, *Know the Everpresent Lord*; because they will all know Me, from the least of them to the greatest of them,' says the Everpresent Lord. 'For I will forgive their iniquity, and I will no longer remember their sin.'" (Jer. 31:33-34) We will then know Him as Job did, because we will see Him and hear Him as Job did.

Elijah the prophet did not have a comfortable life, but God spoke to Him often. Perhaps that is why he didn't have a comfortable life. God spoke to Him often, and spoke to him in different ways.

At one of those times, in one of those ways, the Everpresent Lord said to him: "'Go out and stand upon the mountain before the Everpresent Lord.' And, behold, the Everpresent Lord passed by, and a great and strong wind tore the mountains, and broke the rocks in pieces before the Lord; but the Everpresent Lord was not in the wind. And after the wind an earthquake; but the Lord was not in the earthquake. And after the earthquake a fire; but the Everpresent Lord was not in the fire. And after the fire a still small voice.

"And it was that when Elijah heard it, he wrapped his face in his mantle, and went out, and stood in the entrance of the cave. And, behold, there came a voice to him, and said, 'What are you doing here, Elijah?'" (1K. 19:11-13))

The Everpresent initially spoke to him in a way that Elijah knew. And then the Everpresent spoke to him in a different, very quiet way. But Elijah knew His voice.

"What are you doing here, Elijah?" What a question! When God, who already knows the answer, asks a question, the question is designed to provoke self-examination. The question is filled with the answer.

This particular question belongs in a list of God's greatest questions:

"Adam, where are you?"

"Ka'in, where is Abel your brother?"

"Moses, what is that in your hand?"

"What are you doing here, Elijah?"

" ... "

How we hear and understand these questions greatly influences the choices we make, the direction we choose. When God speaks like this, His Word penetrates the heart in a very personal way. Perhaps that is one reason why the Word of the Everpresent is personified in the Targums.

# "HEAR THE WORD OF THE LORD"

God created the earth, and He created Adam to rule over it for Him. But Adam and his wife chose not to listen to God. They chose their own desires instead.

God spoke to Ka'in, but he didn't want to listen. He didn't want to listen to his brother either. His pride was offended by what they said.

We are told that at a very early time, people "began to call upon the Name of the Lord." (Gen. 4:26) But we are never, at any time, told that 'people began to listen to the Lord calling them.' It's normal for people to expect God to listen to them; it's unusual for people to choose to listen to God.

Nevertheless, even in the times of greatest rebellion, God continues to speak to humanity, urging people to listen to Him. When Noah and his family came out of the ark, "God blessed Noah and his sons, and said to them, 'Be fruitful, and multiply, and fill the earth.'" (Gen. 9:1)

One would think — if one didn't know the past or observe the present — that people would have learned something from the destructive judgment of the flood. But people are stubborn. God said to fill the earth; people wanted to stay where they were. They united to put all their efforts into resisting what God had commanded them to do.

The problem was not with their ears, for they had heard. The problem was not with their minds, for they had understood. The problem was with their hearts, for they did not want to obey what they had heard and understood.

God spoke to Joseph through a dream, which he chose to tell his brothers. "And he said to them, 'Please listen to this dream which I have dreamed. For there we were binding sheaves in the middle of the field. And know that my sheaf arose, and also stood upright; and truly your sheaves stood around, and bowed down to my sheaf. Then his brothers said to him, 'Will you surely reign over us? or will you surely rule over us?' And they hated him even more for his dreams, and for his words.'"

# THE THIRD VERSE

(Gen. 37:6-8)

People often say things without thinking about how what they say will affect others. Even when something is true, it's not always wise to say it. It doesn't seem as if Joseph thought it through before he told the dream to his brothers. (Perhaps he should have remembered what happened to Abel.)

His brothers already hated him for being Jacob's favorite. They didn't want to hear what he had to say, especially if it seemed like sef-exaltation. So they plotted to kill him, settling for selling him into slavery. When he pleaded with them to set him free, they closed their ears.

You know the story: God raised up Joseph to be a ruler in Egypt, to save the Egyptians and the surrounding nations by storing grain for the famine that God said would come. When Joseph's brothers came before him to get grain, they didn't recognize him, but he recognized them. He devised a plan, and a trap, to test them, to reveal what was in their hearts.

Apparently, twenty years later, there was a lot of guilt in their hearts. That's good, because they were guilty. "And they said one to another, 'We are truly guilty concerning our brother [Joseph], in that we saw the anguish of his soul, when he besought us, and we would not hear; therefore this distress has come upon us.' And Reuben answered them, saying, 'Didn't I speak to you, saying, *Do not sin against the child*; and you would not hear? Therefore, behold, also his blood is required." (Gen. 42:21)

Years before, they hadn't listened to Joseph, and they hadn't listened to Reuben. But now they were starting to hear God speak to them through their consciences.

And it worked out well for them because Joseph had also been hearing from God. As he said to them later, when he made himself known to them, "But as for you, you intended evil against me; but God intended it unto good, to make it as it is this day, to save many people alive." (Gen. 50:20)

Years before, Joseph had heard what they said about him. And in slavery and prison in Egypt, he had heard what his own heart said about them. But he had also been willing to hear

God's purpose over and above what they and his own heart had said.

God tells us these things in the text not so that we will think how terrible Joseph's brothers were, but so we will learn something about ourselves. And He tells us these things so that we will learn about Him and the importance of listening to Him. God's view of reality can be quite different from what people see and think.

In observing myself, I have found that sometimes I'll ask someone for directions, or for some other helpful information, and then not even listen to the answer. Not listening is a very bad habit. It makes it much harder to get to where I should be going.

But it seems to me that I'm willing to listen, but I don't focus on what is said. But what about people who aren't willing to listen? They may be able to get where they're going, but where they're going may not be where they're supposed to be going.

How does a person become willing to listen? Some people know everything; so it's really not necessary for them to listen to anyone, including God. But what if something they know isn't true?

### "Earth, earth, earth..."

In the days of Jeremiah, which were days of rebellion and rejection, God continued to entreat His people. "O earth, earth, earth, hear the Word of the Lord." (Jer. 22:29) But His entreaty was ignored. At that time, no one listened.

It is unusual for God to repeat a word three times in succession: "Earth, earth, earth..." It is an entreaty, but also a declaration. It is similar in tone to the seraphim calling out: "Holy, holy, holy is the Lord of forces, the whole earth is filled with His glory." (Is. 6:3) The repetition is intended to communicate the somber nature of the message.

God spoke to Moses in the wilderness and wanted him to go back to Egypt. But Moses didn't want to go. He had heard and understood what God was asking of him, but he had his own personal reasons for not wanting to obey. Fortunately for the rest of us, God was, and is, persistent.

He told Moses to go speak to Pharaoh even though Pharaoh wouldn't listen. Moses spoke, and Pharaoh didn't listen. He heard, but he didn't listen. So God sent Moses to Pharaoh again: "And you are to say to him, 'The Lord God of the Hebrews has sent me to you, saying, *Let My people go, that they may serve Me in the wilderness; but, behold, to this point you haven't listened.*'" (Ex. 7:16)

People who are like Pharaoh, people who are accustomed to getting what they want — either because of their power, wealth, charm, or something else — often have difficulty listening. In particular, they often have difficulty in listening to God, because God doesn't obey them. He seems to have His own agenda. People like Pharaoh resent that, because they themselves have a "God complex".

For the Egyptians, Pharaoh was a god incarnate. Likewise, there were times in Roman history, when Caesar, the emperor, was proclaimed to be a god. At those times, it was necessary to offer sacrifices to Caesar.

The Japanese emperors were believed to be descended from the gods. Accordingly, they demanded complete, unlimited obedience. Similar views prevailed in parts of Southeast Asia concerning their kings.

In Europe, there was the similar, but more sophisticated doctrine of the divine right of kings. In this doctrine, the kings weren't actually gods or descended from the gods, but they were appointed directly by God and were therefore not subject to any human authority. They were free to do as they pleased. They didn't have to listen to anyone.

In contrast, the Chinese emperors ruled by the Mandate of Heaven. This belief was similar to the European "divine right of kings," but the Mandate depended upon the emperor's virtue, whereas the "divine right" did not. When the emperor ceased to be virtuous, the Mandate of Heaven was withdrawn. The Mandate was as much an obligation as it was an authorization.

It's not unusual for governments, no matter what their form, to present themselves as the highest authority, demanding complete obedience. It's not unusual for leaders to consider God irrelevant or, at least, secondary to themselves. But God doesn't see it that way.

Daniel listened to God, and learned, among other things, that "He changes the times and the seasons; He removes kings, and sets up kings. He gives wisdom to the wise, and knowledge to those who have understanding." (Dan. 2:21)

When Nebuchadnezzer became proud, God spoke to him through a dream which he did not understand. Daniel had to explain to Nebuchadnezzar what God decreed in the dream: "You will be driven from men, and your dwelling will be with the beasts of the field. And you will be made to eat grass like an ox, and you will be wet with the dew of heaven, and seven seasons will pass over you, until you know that the Most High rules in the kingdom of men, and gives it to whom He pleases." (Dan. 4:22,29)

I probably shouldn't say this, but God Himself has a little bit of a "God complex". He thinks He knows everything, and that everything exists for Him. Even more than that, He thinks He can do whatever He wants and not give account to anyone.

He does, however, listen to anyone who wants to talk to him. In fact, He invites people to talk to Him, anytime; and He carefully considers what they say. He listens to everyone all the time, even when they're talking to someone else or to themselves. But He expects, He commands, people to listen to Him and obey.

We all know that God commanded Israel to listen to Him and obey. As He told Moses, "...Gather the people together, and I will make them hear My words, that they may learn to fear Me all the days that they will live upon the earth, and that they may teach their children." (Dt. 4:10)

And as Moses told Israel: "From heaven He made you hear His voice, that He might instruct you; and upon earth He showed you His great fire; and you heard His words out of the midst of the fire. And because He loved your fathers, therefore He chose with their seed after them, and brought you out, He Himself being present, with His mighty power, out of Egypt."

(Dt. 4:36-37)

God made the people hear His voice, but, unfortunately, they didn't want to hear it any more. If people don't want to hear from God, what should God do?

Moses and God honored their request, and they didn't hear directly from God any more, to this day. So Moses acted as an intermediary between the people and God, declaring God's Word to the people. "And Moses called all Israel, and said to them, 'Hear, O Israel, the statutes and judgments which I speak in your ears this day, that you may learn them, and keep, and do them.'" (Dt. 5:1) And for many centuries, there have been those who claim to be intermediaries between Moses and the people. We can learn from others without putting them in the place of God.

Moses set forth the *Sh'ma* and *v'ahavtah*: "**Hear** therefore, O Israel, and take care to do it; that it may be well with you, and that you may increase mightily, as the Lord God of your fathers has promised you, in the land that flows with milk and honey. **Hear**, O Israel: the Lord our God is one Lord. And you are to love the Lord your God with all your heart, and with all your soul, and with all your might. And these words, which I command you this day, are to be in your heart; and you are to teach them diligently to your children, and talk of them when you sit in your house, and when you walk by the way, and when you lie down, and when you rise up. And you are to bind them for a sign upon your hand, and they are to be as frontlets between your eyes. And you are to write them upon the posts of your house, and on your gates." (Dt. 6:3-9)

It's not a formula, mantra, or magic password; it's a command. God and His Word are to be the atmosphere we breathe, and the road we travel. God and His Word are to be the love of our lives. But how is it possible to love Someone whose voice you don't want to hear? How is it possible to love Someone when you insist on having a mediator between you and Him?

### The Language of Power
Rulers usually stay far from God, because they don't like

Someone else telling them what to do. But God is able to speak the language of power.

Nebuchadnezzar was a powerful man, ruling over an empire that enforced its will and rule upon its neighbors. That empire had its way in the earth, until God put an end to it. Nebuchanezzar himself was powerful and exalted, until God took his mind away and made him eat grass like the beasts of the field.

Years later, God restored Nebuchadnezzar's mind, and even restored him to his throne. It was an amazing demonstration of God's grace, from which Nebuchadnezzar learned something which he decided to share with other powerful people. "Now I Nebuchadnezzar praise and extol and honor the King of heaven, all whose works are truth, and His ways judgment; and He is able to abase those who walk in pride." (Dan. 4:34H)

In the 2500 years since, how many powerful people learned from his experience? and how many not-so-powerful people? How many continue to speak and act as though they own and rule the earth?

But big or small, "The Lord brings the counsel of the nations to nothing; He frustrates the thoughts [makhsh'vot] of the people. The counsel of the Lord stands forever, the thoughts [makhsh'vot] of His heart to all generations." (Ps. 33:10-11)

God continues to teach today much the same things that He has been teaching for a long time. "Yes, from the first I am He; and there is none who can deliver from My hand. I will work, and who will reverse it?" (Is. 43:13) "There is no wisdom, nor understanding, nor counsel against the Lord." (Prov. 21:30)

God is patient, but He sent the flood and destroyed all the earth. God is patient, but He destroyed Sodom and Gomorrah. God is patient, but He destroyed all the tribes of Canaan. God is patient, but He sent us into exile for our sins. God is patient, but He will judge the earth.

We know what the Lord requires of us: to do justice, love mercy, and humble ourselves to walk with God. (Mic. 6:8)That's what God requires, but it's not what He gets. So He continues, in the next verse, to speak in the language of power. "The voice of the Everpresent Lord cries out to the city; and the man of wisdom will see Your Name. 'Hear the rod, and Who has appointed it.'" (Mic. 6:9) I.e., Listen and learn something from the judgment that God has sent.

"The rod" is a way of expressing God's forceful judgment. Job pleaded, "Let Him take His rod away from me, and let not His fear terrify me." (Job 9:34) He was in agony as he compared his condition with that of the wicked: "Their houses are safe from fear, and the rod of God is not upon them." (Job 21:9, cf. Lam. 3:1)

God spoke of His promises to David, His anointed. "If his children forsake My Law, and do not walk in My judgments; if they break My statutes, and do not keep My commandments, then I will punish their transgression with the rod, and their iniquity with strokes." (Ps. 89:31-33H)

Sometimes God uses the nations to bring judgment on Israel, even as He used Israel to bring His judgment on the tribes of Canaan. This was true for each exile, and much more. But God cautions the nations whom He uses. "Woe to Assyria, the rod of My anger, for the staff in their hand is My indignation." (Is. 10:5) Every nation is to be subject to Him.

But they choose not to be. Unfortunately, the Scriptures present the end of this age as a time when world leaders lead a total rebellion against God. They reject His restraints, His King, and His government.

"Why do the nations rage, and the peoples mutter a vain thing? The kings of the earth set themselves, and the rulers take counsel together, against the Lord, and against His Messiah, saying, 'Let us break their bonds asunder, and cast away their cords from us.'" (Ps. 2:1-3)

God is patient, so people think He doesn't see or care. God is patient, so people think He is powerless. People mock God, impressed with themselves and their own bravado. But they will find reality to be different than what they think it is.

"He who sits in the heavens will laugh: the Lord will mock them. Then He will speak to them in His wrath, and terrify them in His fury. 'But I have set My king on My holy mountain of Zion.'" (Ps. 2:4-6)

Does that sound like much of a response? It is. People will be terrified by what God does. From Zion, the heart of Yerushala'im, God's King will pour out His wrath on the raging nations.

"'I will tell of the decree; the Lord has said to me, *You are My son; this day I have begotten you. Ask of Me, and I will give you the nations for your inheritance, and the uttermost parts of the earth for your possession. You will break them with a rod of iron; you will dash them in pieces like a potter's vessel.*" (Ps. 2:7-9)

People should listen closely. God has given the rod of judgment to His son, His Messiah, His King. With that rod, he will shatter the nations as an iron rod shatters a clay pot. The nations belong to him, but they are worse than useless the way they are.

"Now therefore be wise, O you kings; be instructed, you judges of the earth. Serve the Lord with fear, and rejoice with trembling. Kiss in purity, lest He be angry, and you perish from the way. For in a little while His wrath will blaze. Happy are all who put their trust in him." (Ps. 2:10-12)

God's Anointed will rule from Zion to the uttermost parts of the earth. God says these things so that people and nations can choose accordingly. "For the nation and kingdom that will not serve you will perish; yes, those nations will be completely destroyed. ...The sons also of those who afflicted you will come bending to you; and all those who despised you will bow themselves down at the soles of your feet; and they will call you, 'The city of the Lord, the Zion of the Holy One of Israel.'" (Is. 60:12,14)

Is anyone listening? It's possible for kings, rulers, and everyone else to humble themselves and listen. Josiah did. "And like him was there no king before him, that turned to the Lord with all his heart, and with all his soul, and with all his might, according to all the Torah of Moses; neither after him arose there any like him." (2K. 23:25H)

People don't need someone else to enable them to hear what God is saying. Most people don't hear because they don't want to hear. And they don't want to hear because hearing from God limits what they can do, instead of enabling them to do what they want to do.

And so most people don't hear from God because there are other things they want more than they want God. "But you will seek Me and find Me when you search for Me with all your heart." (Jer. 29:13) God does not present Himself as one option among many; He presents Himself as the sole reason for our existence.

The prophets understood that. Their lives were often filled with pain — think of Jeremiah or Hosea — because the people were not willing to hear what God said. God instructed Ezekiel: "But when I speak with you, I will open your mouth, and you will say to them, 'Thus said the Lord God: *He who hears, let him hear; and he who refuses to hear, let him refuse to hear;*' for they are a rebellious house." (Ezek. 3:27)

It's a choice, whether to listen to God or not. We determine the attitude with which we hear the Word of the Everpresent. It's a choice we make with our hearts.

Before Moses was about to die, as the people of Israel were poised to enter the land of Israel, he reminded them of all the miracles the Everpresent had performed on their behalf. But the most necessary miracle was still far from them: "Yet the Lord has not given you a heart to perceive, and eyes to see, and ears to hear, until this day." (Dt. 29:3H)

In saying that, Moses indicated Israel's greatest need: a heart to perceive, eyes to see, and ears to hear. When you ask for that with all your heart, God will respond. "And your ears will hear a word behind you, saying, 'This is the way, walk in it, when you turn to the right hand, and when you turn to the left.'" (Is. 30:21)

# THE WORD OF THE LORD

God sends many things upon the earth: plagues, thunder and hail, fiery serpents, wild beasts, mighty winds, and famines. He sends prophets, judges, kings, armies, and angels. But the most powerful thing that He sends upon the earth is His Word.

He sends His Word to the earth to accomplish His purpose. "For as the rain and the snow come down from the heavens, and do not return there, without watering the earth and making it bring forth and sprout and give seed to the sower, and bread to the eater; so will My word be that goes out of My mouth. It will not return to Me empty, but it will accomplish that which I please, and it will prosper in the thing for which I sent it." (Is. 55:10-11)

Sometimes God sends His Word to the earth to bring about restoration; sometimes He sends it for judgment. Sometimes He sends it to heal and save. "He sent His Word, and healed them, and saved them from their destructions." (Ps. 107:20)

God sends His Word to the earth for many reasons. The specific phrase "the Word of the Lord" appears about 250 times in Tanakh. From the beginning, throughout human history, and until the end of the Age, God sends His Word to the earth.

We are told, for example, that "By the Word of the Lord, the heavens were made, and all the forces of them by the *Ruakh* of His mouth." (Ps. 33:6) God's Word does more than communicate information; it is a creative force. It has the power to create what it communicates. The Word of the Lord is everlasting; it doesn't change or lose its power.

But human languages do change with the passage of time. Words change their meanings, and new words are introduced. Grammar and syntax also change.

This is true of Hebrew, as well as other languages. About 2000 years ago, 2000 years after Abraham, the language that Israel spoke had changed enough so that the Biblical text was no longer easily understood by the average person. In particular, the time of exile in Aramaic-speaking Babylon had a significant linguistic impact.

So Targums, Aramaic paraphrases of the Hebrew text, were produced to make the text accessible to the people. The translators tried to present the meaning of the original text in the common language of their day. Those who read these Targums [*targumim*] understood them to be "the Bible," in much the same way that those who read a myriad of modern translations do.

In these Aramaic paraphrases, the Word of the Everpresent is personified. "'The Word,' in the sense of the creative or directive word or speech of God manifesting His power in the world of matter or mind; a term used especially in the Targum as a substitute for 'the Lord' when an anthropomorphic expression is to be avoided."[1]

The translators of the Targum saw scriptural passages that spoke of God having human appearance or characteristics. They chose to assign these passages to a personified Word of the Lord, the *Memra*. In these passages and others also, they presented the *Memra*, the Word of the Everpresent, as the personification of God.

Here are a few examples to give a sense of what the Targum translators understood and, therefore, communicated to the common people.

**1)** "And the Word of the Lord created man in His likeness, in the likeness of the presence of the Lord He created him, the male and his yoke-fellow He created them." (Gen. 1:27, Jerusalem Targum)

In this paraphrase, the Word of the Everpresent is the Creator, creating humanity as a visible, tangible likeness of God's presence. This implies that part of God's purpose in creating humanity was to fill the earth with His own presence.

**2)** "And I will establish My covenant between MY WORD and between you." (Gen. 17:7, Targum Onkelos)

God promised to establish an ongoing relationship, legally specified in a covenant, between Himself and Abraham and Abraham's descendants. In the rendering of the Targum, God's Word is God's representative in establishing that legal relationship. The *Memra*, the personification of God's

Word, establishes a special closeness with Abraham and his descendants. The *Memra* functions as an intermediary.

**3)** "And Jacob vowed a vow, saying, 'If the WORD OF YHVH will be my support, and will keep me in the way that I go, and will give me bread to eat, and raiment to put on, so that I come again to my father's house in peace; then shall the WORD OF YHVH be my GOD.'" (Targum Onkelos, Genesis 28:20-21)

In this rendering, the Word of the Everpresent upholds and protects Jacob, feeds and clothes him. The *Memra* is the practical way that Jacob encounters God upon the earth. The Word of the Lord IS God, to be trusted, served and praised.

**4)** "And Moses brought the people out of the camp to meet the Word of the Lord..." (Ex.19:17 Targum Onkelos) "And Moses brought the people out of the camp to meet the Shekhinah of the Lord..." (Ex.19:17 Targum Pseudo-Jonathan)

As we have seen, the Shekhinah is understood to be the visible presence of God. In Targum Onkelos, the Word of the Lord is understood to be the same. By meeting a personified Word of God, the people meet God.

"Like the Shekinah (comp. Targ. Num. xxiii. 21), the Memra is accordingly the manifestation of God. 'The Memra brings Israel nigh unto God and sits on His throne receiving the prayers of Israel' (Targ. Yer. to Deut. iv. 7).... So, in the future, shall the Memra be the comforter (Targ. Isa. lxvi. 13): 'My Shekinah I shall put among you, My Memra shall be unto you for a redeeming deity, and you shall be unto My Name a holy people' (Targ. Yer. to Lev. xxii. 12).... 'In the Memra the redemption will be found' (Targ. Zech. xii. 5)."[2]

**5)** "...the Word of the Lord sits upon His throne high and lifted up, and hears our prayer when time we pray before Him and make our petitions." (Dt. 4:7, Targum Pseudo-Jonathan)

The *Memra* is described as being enthroned as God, echoing the words of Is. 6:1: "In the year that king Uzziah died, then I saw the Lord sitting upon a throne, high and lifted up, and His train filled the Temple." Isaiah saw the Lord, and described what he saw. The Targum says that the *Memra*, the Word of the Lord, is enthroned as God, listens to the prayers of Israel and responds.

**6)** "But Israel will be saved by the WORD OF YHVH with an everlasting salvation ... By the WORD OF YHVH all the seed of Israel will be justified and glorified." (Targum Jonathan, Isaiah 45:17, 25)

The *Memra* is the means of providing justification for Israel before God. The Word of the Lord is the means of bringing salvation to Israel.

In sum, the Word of the Lord is presented as a way in which God interacts with His Creation, especially the creature He made in His own likeness and image. The Word of the Lord existed before Creation and is everlasting. The Word of the Lord is not something other than God, but the Word of the Lord comes from God into the world to represent Him and accomplish His purposes.

All of this parallels the way that the Spirit of the Lord is presented.

**Footnotes**
1. http://www.jewishencyclopedia.com/articles/10618-memra
2. Ibid.

# *Yehi Ohr* / "LET THERE BE LIGHT"

In the beginning of Rashi's commentary on Torah. The very first thing he says, quoting Rabbi Yitzhak, is, "It was not necessary to begin the Torah with these things [the story of Creation], but rather from 'This month is for you [the beginning of months]...' (Ex. 12:2), for this is the first commandment that Israel was commanded.'"

He refers to this text: "And the Lord spoke to Moses and Aaron in the land of Egypt, saying, 'This month is the beginning of months for you; it is the first of the months of the year for you.'" (Ex. 12:1-2) Grammatically, there is no command, but simply a statement of fact. But when God states a fact, the fact often contains a command. In this case, the command is clear: i.e. 'You are to recognize this month as the first month of the year.' So it is clear that this statement of fact is a command.

Nevertheless, Rashi, and Rabbi Yitzhak whom he cites, are incorrect in two very important ways.

**1) This was not the first commandment which God gave to Israel.**

**2) Giving commandments to Israel is not the purpose of Torah.**

**Rashi is wrong because 1) This was not the first commandment which God gave to Israel.** Many commandments were given to Israel before our deliverance from Egypt. As God told Isaac centuries earlier: "...I will perform the oath which I swore to Abraham your father; and I will make your seed multiply as the stars of heaven, and I will give to your seed all these lands; and in your seed all the nations of the earth will be blessed; because Abraham obeyed My voice, and kept My charge, My commandments, My statutes, and My laws." (Gen. 26:5)

Long before the exodus, God had given Abraham commandments, which he kept. Long before the exodus, God had given commandments to all of humanity, which they mostly didn't keep. These commandments were already required of all the descendants of Abraham, Isaac, and Jacob. These were required of Israel, though not specifically given to Israel only.

But it was to Abraham, long before Sinai, that God gave the special commandment of circumcision. That commandment was binding upon Israel, as Moses found out. While Moses was on the way to return to Egypt, God threatened to kill him because he had not circumcised his son. (Ex. 4:24-26)

For God had told Abraham "I will establish My covenant between Me and you and your seed after you in their generations for an everlasting covenant, to be a God to you, and to your seed after you. And I will give to you, and to your seed after you, the land where you are a stranger, all the land of Canaan, for an everlasting possession; and I will be their God." (Gen. 17:7-8) Ishmael, Abraham's servants and slaves were all circumcised because they were in Abraham's household (Gen. 17:12-13). Later, Esau was, for the same reason.

But the covenant of circumcision, and of the land, was made with Abraham and the seed which God would choose: Isaac, but not Ishmael, Jacob, but not Esau. Abraham pleaded for God to accept Ishmael as his heir, "But God said, 'Sarah your wife will bear you a son indeed; and you are to call his name Isaac; and I will establish My covenant with him for an everlasting covenant, and with his seed after him.(Gen. 17:19, cf. 26:3-4)

To escape Esau, who wanted to kill him, Jacob fled out of the land. As he slept, God appeared to him in a dream, and said, "I am the Lord God of Abraham your father, and the God of Isaac; the land on which you lie, I will give it to you, and to your seed." (Gen. 28:13, cf. 35:10-12)

With the promises to Abraham come the obligations of Abraham. (cf. Is. 51:1-2) It is the life and calling of Abraham that defines Israel as a people, and sets us apart. In one of the most unusual passages in the Bible, we are told of what God said to Himself: "And Abraham will surely become a great and mighty nation, and all the nations of the earth will be blessed in him. For I have known him that he will command his children and his household after him, and they will keep the way of the Lord, to do justice and judgment; that the Lord may bring upon Abraham that which He has spoken of him." (Gen. 18:18-19)

God established a covenant relationship with Abraham so that he would "command his children and his household after him." God knew that Abraham would command his children to keep the commandments of the Lord. Had there been no commandments, Abraham could not have commanded his children to keep them.

Abraham's faithfulness to command his children "to do justice and judgment" is what would make Israel a great nation. It is also what would enable the nations to be blessed in Abraham. All the commandments, statutes, and laws which Abraham kept, his children, including all Israel, were also commanded to keep. That includes commanding their children and their households to keep the way of the Lord.

And there were commandments given to Israel before Abraham was born. When the Rabbis spoke of the Noachide Laws, they were speaking of commandments which were given to all the descendants of Noaḥ. They saw some of these commandments as having been given to Adam. The commandment "But of the tree of the knowledge of good and evil, you shall not eat of it..." is understood to contain a prohibition of theft, i.e. taking what belongs to someone else. When Adam was commanded this, Israel was, too.

And even before Adam was created, there was a commandment given to Israel. The first commandment given to Israel is the very first commandment given in Torah: "Let there be light."

God had a purpose in Creation. He had the same purpose in creating and calling Israel: "Let there be light." Many centuries after the exodus, God pointed back to Creation in describing His calling for His servant: "Thus said God the Everpresent, He who created the heavens and stretched them out; He who spread forth the earth and that which comes out of it; He who gives breath to the people upon it, and spirit to those who walk in it; 'I the Lord have called you in righteousness, and will hold your hand, and will keep you, and give you for a covenant of the people, for a light to the goyim.'" (Is. 42:5-6)

"...I will also give you for a light to the nations, to be My salvation to the end of the earth." (Is. 49:6) I.e., 'Bring My salvation to the Gentiles to deliver them out of darkness."

It might, however, be more accurate to translate Gen. 1:3 as: "And God said, 'Light exists,' and light exists." Grammatically, as in Ex. 12:2, there is no command, but simply a statement of fact. What God says is what defines reality, and that definition contains many commands. In this case, "Let light be."

Actually, there is a command that appears in Torah even earlier than this. It is contained in the third Hebrew word, *elohim*, i.e. God. By definition, the word contains relationship and authority. All the other commandments depend upon it. That's why the first of the Ten Commandments is, "I am the Lord your God."

**Rashi is also wrong because 2) Giving commandments to Israel is not the purpose of Torah.** The purpose of Torah is to give light. The unfolding of Your words gives light; it gives understanding to the simple." (Ps. 119:130) God gives light to Israel so that we can give light to the Gentiles. "Listen to Me, My people; hear Me, My nation: The law will go out from Me; My justice will become a light to the *goyim*." (Is. 51:4)

The purpose of the Torah is to enable Israel, and the nations, to know God. The story of Creation, the rebellion of Adam and Havah, Ka'in's murder of Abel, the judgment of the flood, the tower of Babel and the beginning of the nations, the history of the patriarchs, etc., etc. are essential for that purpose.

"What is the meaning of the text: 'You are to walk after the Lord your God'? [Dt.13:5] ... to walk after the attributes of the Holy One, blessed be He. As He clothes the naked, for it is written: 'And the Lord God made for Adam and for his wife coats of skin, and clothed them.' Even so, you are to clothe the naked. The Holy One, blessed be He, visited the sick, for it is written: 'And the Lord appeared unto him by the oaks of Mamre.' Even so you are to visit the sick. The Holy One, blessed be He, comforted mourners, for it is written: 'And it came to pass after the death of Abraham, that God blessed Isaac his son.' Even so, you are to comfort mourners. The Holy one, blessed be

He, buried the dead, for it is written: 'And He buried him in the valley. Even so you are to bury the dead.'" (Tal. Sotah 14a)

God clothed Adam, visited Abraham, and comforted Isaac. He did these things before Israel existed, but they are recorded for Israel's benefit and instruction. They are recorded for the benefit and instruction of all the earth.

God created humanity to be like Himself. That's what He wants of Israel. Torah, including what happened in the beginning, shows us who God is and how to be like Him. All of the Scriptures do. "Your Word is a lamp to my feet, and a light to my path." (Ps. 119:105)

### The Light of His Countenance
God's Word is light, because God is light. As David said, "You are my lamp, O Everpresent. The Everpresent turns my darkness into light." (2Sam. 22:29)

Darkness hides things, sometimes dangerous things. Light reveals what is there, and drives back the darkness. As David also said, "The Everpresent is my light and my salvation — whom shall I fear? The Everpresent is the stronghold of my life — of whom shall I be afraid?!" (Ps. 27:1)

God promises Israel that the day is coming when, "The sun will no longer be your light by day; nor will the moon give light to you for brightness; but the Lord will be to you an everlasting light, and your God your glory. Your sun will never set again, and your moon will wane no more; the Everpresent will be your everlasting light, and your days of sorrow will end." (Is. 60:19-20)

The light we have in this world is a representation of who God is. God enables us to see. The closer we come to Him, the more light we have; the more we can see things as they are. That is why we are entreated, "Come, O house of Jacob, let us walk in the light of the Lord." (Is. 2:5)

God commanded Aaron and his descendants to place this blessing upon Israel: "The Lord bless you, and keep you. The Lord make His face shine upon you, and be gracious to you. The Lord lift up His countenance upon you, and give you peace." (Num. 6:24-26)

God's face is radiant. We want and need His face to shine upon us. If His face does not shine upon us, then we are surrounded by darkness. We cannot see the abyss that it hides. We do not hear the warning God gave to Ka'in: "If you do not well, sin lies at the door, and its desire is for you. Yet you are to rule over it." (Gen. 4:7)

It's not always easy to rule over sin instead of letting it rule over us. Some people don't try; they think sin is a pet or a friend, but it's not. They can't see that it is waiting to rule over, and then devour, them.

Some people boast of their sin. They're proud to be pursuing whatever they desire. They don't see that they are following the desires of sin, and that it won't work out well for them.

Some people are grieved at their own sin and that of others. "Many are asking, 'Who can show us any good?' Let the light of Your face shine upon us, O Everpresent." (Ps. 4:6) "For with You is the fountain of life; in Your light we see light." (Ps. 36:9)

Though he didn't always walk in the light, King David knew that "The precepts of the Everpresent Lord are right, giving joy to the heart. The commands of the Everpresent Lord are radiant, giving light to the eyes." (Ps. 19:8H) As another psalmist prayed, "Cause us to return, O God of forces; make Your face shine upon us, and we will be saved." (Ps. 80:8/20H)

God's face shines with an everlasting light. The *ner tamid*, the eternal light, is a representation of the presence of God. "Happy is the people who know the joyful sound; they will walk, O Lord, in the light of Your countenance." (Ps. 89:16H)

Light is the source of all energy. It is the source of all that is in Creation. Light is the source of all warmth, all nourishment, all life. Through photosysnthesis, plants feed directly off light. The (ultraviolet) light of the sun enables our skin to manufacture vitamin D, which plays an important role in the health of bones and the entire body. We get it free through sunlight.

### Moses, Adam, and Messiah

Moses went up the mountain to be in the presence of God.

"And he was there with the Lord forty days and forty nights; he neither ate bread nor drank water. And he wrote upon the tablets the words of the covenant, the ten commandments." (Ex. 34:28) For forty days, Moses didn't eat or drink. He didn't need to, he was in the presence of God. In an unusual kind of photosynthesis, Moses was nourished by the light of God's countenance. Light is energy.

"And it came to pass, when Moses came down from Mount Sinai — and the two tablets of Testimony were in the hand of Moses when he came down from the mount — that Moses did not know that the skin of his face shone while he talked with Him." (Ex. 34:28-29) The light of God's countenance emanated from Moses.

Light carries images; that is what makes sight possible. At this moment, light from the sun is coming through my glass windows. Some light is being absorbed by the objects it hits; other light is bouncing off of those objects. When the light bounces, it carries different frequencies from the object off of which it bounces. When those different frequencies strike my eyes, some light is reflected, some is absorbed.

My brain interprets the complex of light frequencies that my eyes absorb. That interpretation gives me internal images that have color, shape, depth, location, texture, etc., etc.

Light does not reflect off God; light emanates from God. With Moses on the mountain, the light emanating from the face of God carried God's image to Moses. That light and image were absorbed by Moses and also reflected off him.

From the beginning, God's purpose was that humanity reflect His image and likeness. "Six things were taken away from the first Adam, and will be restored through the son of Nahshon, that is, the Messiah. ...his radiance, his [eternal] life..." (Mid. Numbers 13:12, cf. Mid. Gen. 12:6)

According to the Midrash, the light that the first Adam lost in disobedience will be restored by the second Adam, the Messiah, presumably by his obedience. And he will come to Israel as a second Moses. "'The Redeemer will come to Zion, to those in Jacob who repent of their sins,' declares the Everpresent." (Is.

59:20)

"I the Everpresent Lord have called you in righteousness, and will put strength in your hand and will keep you, and give you for a covenant of the people, for a light to the goyim; to open blind eyes, to bring out the one who is bound from the dungeon, and those who sit in darkness out fromwssa the prison house." (Is. 42:6-7)

This Servant of the Lord is given to establish a covenant between God and the people (of Israel). At the same time, he is also given to be a light to the goyim, a healer of the blind, and a deliverer of those imprisoned in darkness. God's light radiates to Israel from him; Israel is to absorb some of that light and reflect the rest to the nations.

In that day, Israel will arise and shine. In the beginning, Darkness was over the surface of the abyss. At the end of the age, Darkness will cover the whole earth. Then God will say to Israel: "Arise, shine; for your light has come, and the glory of the Lord has risen upon you. For, know that the darkness will cover the earth, and thick darkness the people; but the Lord will arise upon you, and His glory will be seen upon you. And the nations will come to your light, and kings to the brightness of your rising....

"The sun will no longer be your light by day; nor will the moon give light to you for brightness; but the Lord will be to you an everlasting light, and your God your glory." (Is. 60:1-3,19) Israel will be transformed, and so the nations will also be transformed.

Years ago, in a different culture, some of us used black lights to help us see. They distorted reality, but we thought we were seeing things as they truly were. That's because we ourselves were filled with darkness, mistaking it for enlightenment. "Nevertheless, there will be no more gloom for those who were in distress. In the past He humbled the land of Zebulun and the land of Naphtali, but in the future He will honor Galilee of the Gentiles, by the way of the sea, along the Jordan. The people walking in darkness have seen a great light; on those living in the land of the shadow of death a light has dawned." (Is. 9:1-2)

Darkness is everywhere, and some people mistake it for light, and advocate it as light. "Woe to those who call evil good, and good evil; who put darkness for light, and light for darkness; who put bitter for sweet, and sweet for bitter!" (Is. 5:20)

But maybe they don't know; maybe it isn't clear. Perhaps. But sometimes, they do know, and it is quite clear. They simply do not want to acknowledge what is clear. They do not want to know what is true. They want others to acknowledge what they want as being true.

Some people are afraid of light. "And when Aaron and all the people of Israel saw Moses, behold, the skin of his face shone; and they were afraid to come closer to him." (Ex. 34:30) Not everyone is comfortable with light. Not everyone is comfortable in the presence of God. In the presence of God, in the light of His countenance, nothing is hidden, and all things are revealed. In the presence of God, things don't appear the way I, or you, think they are, they appear as they truly are, the way He says they are.

## Governed by Light

"God made two great lights [*me'orot*] —the greater light to govern the day and the lesser light to govern the night. He also made the stars. God set them in the expanse of the sky to give light on the earth, to govern the day and the night, and to separate light from darkness. And God saw that it was good." (Gen. 1:16-18)

It's an amazing architectural design. This outside light comes to the earth from the sun, 93 million miles away. Without it, the earth would be dark and cold. We don't pay for this radiant heat and light. Fortunately, it is a free gift, that comes with our well-furnished planet. Without this free outside light, there would be no life on the earth.

God is telling us about Himself. It's a very large analogy, an illustration that shouldn't be missed.

We couldn't afford to pay for any of this. We couldn't pay the heating bill, we couldn't pay the lighting bill. We couldn't even pay the water bill, much less the oxygen bill. We should not assume that it is our due, for it is the Landlord who owns everything and controls all the settings.

He is very patient, but He expects us to abide by the terms of the lease, and has promised that there will be equitable judgment on every human action. Unfortunately, we have trashed the place, fought and abused the other tenants, and convinced ourselves that there is no authority over us, no one who can dictate terms for our occupancy or existence.

Instead of rejoicing in the Light, we have wallowed in the Darkness. Every so often, the Landlord lets us know that we need to change our ways. But we don't listen, and we don't read the Manual. The nature of God's judgment is that He gives people what they have chosen, not what they think they have chosen.

By God's design in the beginning, Light is supposed to rule, whether by day or by night. It is to govern life upon the earth. Unfortunately, when we think of the governments people have created, we don't find them to be sources of light. Though there have been some notable exceptions in human history, the complete story is rather dark.

At an individual level, "There are those who rebel against the light, who do not know its ways or stay in its paths." (Job 24:13) It's a choice an individual makes. The most basic level of sight is to distinguish between light and darkness.

People convince themselves — "Oh, I didn't know." And in a certain sense, they don't know. But God knows, and He has already shown each one what is right. "God does all these things to a man — twice, even three times — to turn back his soul from the pit, that the light of life may shine on him." (Job 33:29-30)

People try to hide in the Darkness. That's like Adam and Havah hiding behind a tree. But David learned: "Even the darkness will not be dark to You; the night will shine like the day, for darkness is as light to You." (Ps. 139:12)

Sometimes God sends darkness to distinguish, to separate, and to redeem. In Egypt, God gave the Egyptians the darkness they had chosen. "No one could see anyone else or leave his place for three days. Yet all the children of Israel had light in the places where they lived." (Ex. 10:23) Darkness was what empowered Egypt, and it was darkness that shut Egypt down.

God created Darkness; He knows how to use it. "The Everpresent Lord has made all things for Himself; even the wicked for the day of evil." (Prov. 16:4) All things exist for, and will accomplish, God's purposes.

Pharaoh sent his armies after Israel, catching up to them at the sea. God had been leading Israel by a pillar of cloud. "And the pillar of the cloud went from before their face, and stood behind them, coming between the camp of the Egyptians and the camp of Israel. And there was the cloud and the darkness [for Egypt] and it gave light to the night [for Israel]. And neither went near the other all night long." (Ex. 14:19-20)

God looks on the heart, and in response to what He sees, He gives people light or He gives them darkness. "Light rises in the darkness for the upright, for the one who is gracious and compassionate and righteous." (Ps. 112:4) We choose a direction, and God responds to what we choose.

"The path of the righteous is like the shining light, shining more and more until the day has fully come. But the way of the wicked is like deep darkness; they do not know what makes them stumble." (Prov. 4:18-19)

David earnestly prayed, "Look upon me and answer me, O Lord my God. Give light to my eyes, or I will sleep in death." (Ps. 13:4H) If the choice is between light and death, then I choose light, even though I know that Light makes great demands upon me.

If there are two possible destinations ahead of me, I want to go to the Light. God asked Job, "Which is the way to the dwelling of light? And darkness, where is its place? so that you can take each to its border, and because you understand the paths to its house. You know, because you were born then, and the number of your days is great." (Job 38:19-21) In the presence of God, Job had nothing to say in his own defence.

Daniel knew how to get to the dwelling of light. "May the Name of God be blessed for ever and ever; for wisdom and might are His. ...He reveals the deep and secret things; He knows what is in the darkness, and the light dwells with Him." (Dan. 2:20,22)

God and Light dwell together; they are inseparable. "Bless the Lord, O my soul. O Lord my God, You are very great. You are clothed with splendor and majesty, wrapped in light as with a garment; stretching out the heavens like a curtain." (Ps. 104:1-2)

God is bioluminescent. Light radiates from who He is. Though that light is energy and power, we can't harness it for our own purposes. It will destroy those who reject the Truth that it reveals. "The Light of Israel will become a fire, his Holy One a flame; and it will burn and consume His thorns and His briers in one day." (Is. 10:17)

Light is energy and life. It's worth seeking. God tells me what to do to fill my life with the goodness of His light. "Isn't this rather the fast that I have chosen? to open the chains of wickedness, to release the bands of the yoke, and to send the oppressed in freedom, and to tear off every yoke? Is it not to share your bread with the hungry, and that you bring to your house the homeless poor? And that you cover the naked when you see him; and that you do not hide from your own flesh?

"Then **your light** will break forth like the dawn, and your health will sprout speedily. And your righteousness will go before you; the glory of the Lord will be gathered to you. Then you will call, and the Lord will answer. You will cry for help, and He will say, 'Here I am.'

"If you take away from the midst of you the yoke, the pointing of the finger, and speaking iniquity; and if you offer your soul to the hungry, and satisfy the afflicted soul; then **your light** will rise in darkness, and your darkness be as noontime." (Is. 58:6-10)

The universe came into existence when God said, "Let light be." God wants something for me and from me: Light. Everything else is detail.

## *Yehi... vaYehi*

## "LET THERE BE... AND THERE WAS"

The traditional English translation of Gen. 1:3 is: "And God said, 'Let there be light.' And there was light." It could also be translated as: "And God said, 'There is light.' And there is light."

Grammatically, God does not issue a command, He states a reality. Reality then conforms to what God has said. It's difficult to understand what He says as a command, because there isn't anyone or anything that He is commanding. He is declaring, and thereby creating, what will be. The expression of His desire is sufficient to cause it to exist.

In this first chapter of the Bible, which describes the calling into existence of the universe we know, the Hebrew word *yehi* appears twenty-three times. That is an amazing number of times for any word to appear in any chapter in the Bible. And this chapter is the story of Creation, the beginning of all that follows.

*Yehi* is what we would call a state-of-being verb. It is a form of the same verb that God used to describe Himself to Moses: *Ehyeh asher ehyeh.* I.e., "I will be what I will be." Or, "I am that I am."

It is as though God wants to make everything clear from the beginning. He is the One who exists; everything else depends upon Him for its existence. Everything else exists because of His desire for it to exist. Everything else exists for whatever the purpose of its Creator is.

Four of the times when *yehi* is used in chapter one, God is making an authoritative declaration. He is stating what will be. Because He is God, what He says, by definition, is authoritative.

"And God said, '*Yehi* light.' ..." Gen. 1:3

"And God said, '*Yehi* a firmament in the midst of the waters, and *yehi* to divide the waters from the waters." Gen. 1:6

"And God said, '*Yehi* lights in the firmament of the heaven..." Gen. 1:14

Descartes said, "Je pense, donc je suis;" in Latin, *Cogito ergo sum,* and in English, "I think, therefore I am." He understood the existence of his thinking to demonstrate the prior existence of his being. If he didn't exist, then he couldn't be thinking. For Descartes, his thinking was not the cause of his existence — for that would be hopelessly circular — but it was a demonstration of the fact that he already existed.

With God, it's different. He thinks, therefore I am. I exist because He thought of me. This thought amazed David. "When I look at Your heavens, the work of Your fingers, the moon and the stars, which You have established; what is a man, that You are mindful of him? And the son of Adam, that You visit him?" (Ps. 8:4-5)

David couldn't understand why an infinite, Almighty God would be concerned with a finite, nearly powerless him. And he couldn't understand how completely God watched him. "Everpresent Lord, You have searched me, and You know. You know my sitting down and my rising up. You understand my thoughts from far off. You observe my journey and my lying down, and You use all my ways. Because there is not a word on my tongue, but behold, O Everpresent, You have known it all. You have shut me in, behind and in front, and laid Your hand upon me. This is knowledge too wonderful for me; it is high, I cannot attain it." (Ps. 139:1-6)

I, too, exist only for God's purposes. And because I think, I think about what those purposes are. I want to accomplish the purposes for which He spoke me into existence. It is, for sure, too multifaceted for me to wholly grasp, but I'm listening rather than choosing to be oblivious.

### *Yehi* / Let there be
Twelve times, *yehi* appears in the recording of the creation of the days of the week. God set in motion the chronology that frames our existence.

"...And *yehi* evening and *yehi* morning, one day." 1:5

"...And *yehi* evening and *yehi* morning, the second day." 1:8

"And *yehi* evening and *yehi* morning, the third day." 1:13

"...And *yehi* evening and *yehi* morning, the fourth day." 1:19

"And *yehi* evening and *yehi* morning, the fifth day." 1:23

"...And *yehi* evening and *yehi* morning, the sixth day." 1:31

For each of the six days of the week, we are told, "and there was evening and there was morning, the second [ or the fourth, or the sixth] day...." Each of these days comes to an end, and then the next day begins.

"And on the seventh day God ended His work which He had made; and He rested on the seventh day from all His work which He had made. And God blessed the seventh day, and sanctified it; because that in it He had rested from all his work which God created and made." (Gen. 2:2-3)

We are told that God completed His work on the seventh day, but we are not told about the completion of the seventh day itself. For every other day, we are told that 'there was evening and morning,' but we are not told that about the seventh day.

Shabbat is a day different from all the others. It represents something more than itself. That is why it is both a commandment and a covenant.

"On Shabbat they used to say, ...A psalm, a song for the time to come, for the day that will be all Shabbat and peaceful rest for everlasting life." (Tal. Tamid 7:4, 33b, referring to Ps. 92.) Shabbat is given to point us to the rest and fulfillment we will have in the Age to Come. That will be a meaningful, fruitful time that will be free of the anxiety, fear, and frustration that characterizes so much of life in this world.

"Remember the day of Ceasing [from work], to keep it holy. Six days you are to labor and do all your work. But the seventh day is Shabbat to the Lord your God. You are not to do any work: you and your son and your daughter, your manservant and your maidservant, and your livestock, and your stranger who is within your gates. Because six days the Lord made the heavens and the earth, the sea, and all that is in them, and rested on the seventh day; therefore the Everpresent blessed the day of Shabbat, and made it holy." (Ex. 20:8-11) "Therefore the descendants of Israel are to guard Shabbat, to observe Shabbat throughout their generations for an everlasting covenant." (Ex. 31:16)

God is the Landlord of every place. How could He take a day off? What if something went wrong? or needed fixing?

'But what could go wrong or need fixing? Surely everything that God creates is perfect.'

I don't know what "perfect" means. "R. Yohanan b. Hanina said: ...In the ninth [hour of the day Adam was created], he was commanded that he was not to eat of the tree. In the tenth, he was unrestrained; in the eleventh, he was brought to judgment; and in the twelfth he was chased out and he departed." (Tal. Sanhedrin 38b)

In the view of R. Yohanan b. Hanina, humanity remained faithful to God for less than two hours. Perhaps that view is a little extreme, because it would mean that Adam and Havah didn't even make it to Shabbat before they were expelled from the Garden of Eden. They would have spent their first Shabbat in shame and exile.

That can't be true. Or, at least, I wouldn't like it be true. It would be very depressing if it were true. But, in any case, they were not faithful very long.

God didn't create Shabbat for Himself. He didn't need to rest. He wasn't tired.

Nor did He create Shabbat as a religious prison. Shabbat, as R. Yonatan b. Yosef said, "is committed to your hands, not you to its hands." (Tal. Yoma 85b)

God did not create humanity because He needed a workforce for some pyramid building project. Meaningful work is something good that God created for us, but He can work more easily without us. That's why He created humanity after He had already created all the rest of the universe. He did not want, or need, our advice.

Why then did He command Israel to work and also to cease from work? What is it that Shabbat provides that He thinks is necessary for our healthy, purposeful existence? What other Law code has such a law?

Shabbat is an opportunity to find out what life is all about. Shabbat is intended to be something we take with us through every other day. It is a time to rest, trusting God, getting to know Him. "[One who has] an inclination fixed on and trusting in You, You will keep in complete peace." (Is. 26:3)

God created Shabbat because He loves us. When we are commanded to love the Lord our God with all our heart, soul, and strength, we are being commanded to return His love. Not because He needs it, but because we need to do it to be healthy. By its nature, love cannot be stagnant.

Though it is not what we have historically experienced, God has always wanted Rest for Israel. "For He is our God; and we are the people of His pasture, and the sheep of His hand. Even today, if you will only listen to His voice, don't harden your hearts, like you did at Meribah, and like you did in the day of Massah in the wilderness; when your fathers tempted Me and tested Me, even though they had seen My deeds. For forty years I loathed that generation, and said, 'They are a people who err in their heart, and they do not know My ways.' Therefore I swore in My wrath that they would not enter into My rest." (Ps. 95:7-11)

So we erred in our hearts and turned away, reaping what we had sown. We didn't receive what we pursued, but we received what was promised: "And among these nations you will find no ease, neither will the sole of your foot have rest; but the Everpresent Lord will give you there a trembling heart, and failing of eyes, and sorrow of mind. And your life will hang in doubt before you; and you will be afraid day and night, and have no assurance of your life. In the morning you will say, 'Would it were evening!' and in the evening you will say, 'Would it were morning!' for the fear of your heart with which you will fear, and for the sight of your eyes which you will see." (Dt. 28:65-67)

What does it take to make someone who is going the wrong way want to turn back? What does it take to make a people, a nation, a world, want to turn back to God? "Even today, if you will only listen to His voice!" There is healing and rest, encouragement and transformation, even though not everything He says will be pleasant to hear.

Anyone who will humble himself or herself and listen, that one is invited to enter into His rest. God made a special, very serious covenant with Israel to keep Shabbat. "Truly My sabbaths you are to keep; for it is a sign between Me and you throughout your generations; that you may know that I am the Lord who sets you apart. ...Therefore the people of Israel are to guard Shabbat, to observe Shabbat throughout their generations, for an everlasting covenant. It is a sign between Me and the people of Israel forever; for in six days the Lord made heaven and earth, and on the seventh day He rested, and was refreshed." (Ex. 31:13-17)

He made that covenant with Israel only, but He invites every single soul to enter in. "Also the sons of the stranger, who join themselves to the Lord, to serve Him, and to love the Name of the Lord, to be His servants, every one who keeps Shabbat and does not profane it, and all who hold fast to My covenant; I will bring even them to My holy mountain, and make them joyful in My house of prayer; their burnt offerings and their sacrifices will be accepted upon My altar; for My house will be called a house of prayer for all peoples." (Is. 56:6-7)

### vaYehi khayn / And it was so

Seven times in the first chapter of the Bible, *yehi* is used to tell us that what God said became physical reality.

"And God said, 'Let there be light.' **And there was** light [*vaYehi ohr*]." (Gen. 1:3)

"And God said, 'Let there be a firmament in the midst of the waters, and let it divide the waters from the waters.' And God made the firmament, and divided the waters which were under the firmament from the waters which were above the firmament' **And it was so** [*vaYehi khayn*]." (Gen. 1:6-7)

"And God said, 'Let the waters under the heaven be gathered together to one place, and let the dry land appear.' **And it was so** [*vaYehi khayn*].'" (Gen. 1:9)

"And God said, 'Let the earth bring forth grass, herb yielding seed, and fruit tree yielding fruit after its kind, whose seed is in itself, upon the earth.' **And it was so** [*vaYehi khayn*]." (Gen. 1:11)

"And God said, 'Let there be lights in the firmament of the

heaven to divide the day from the night; and let them be for signs, and for seasons, and for days, and years; and let them be for lights in the firmament of the heaven to give light upon the earth.' **And it was so** [*vaYehi khayn*]." (Gen. 1:14-15)

"And God said, 'Let the earth bring forth all kinds of living creatures, cattle, and creeping things, and beasts of the earth after their kind.' **And it was so** [*vaYehi khayn*]." (Gen. 1:24)

"And God said, 'Behold, I have given you every herb bearing seed, which is upon the face of all the earth, and every tree, on which is the fruit of a tree yielding seed; to you it shall be for food. And to every beast of the earth, and to every bird of the air, and to every thing that creeps upon the earth, where there is life, I have given every green herb for food.' **And it was so** [*vaYehi khayn*]." (Gen. 1:29-30

What God spoke, His word, then appeared in the world in a tangible physical form. The physical form was different, but completely conformed to the Word of the Lord.

From this, we are to understand that when God says something, it is reality. This goes beyond Creation to tell us about the character and power of God. "I have spoken it, I will also bring it to pass; I have purposed it, I will also do it." (Is. 46:11)

Creation comes into existence because God purposed it, and then spoke it. "Whatever pleases the Everpresent Lord, He has done in the heavens, and on the earth, in the seas, and every deep place [*tehom*]." (Ps. 135:6)

It's not just in the acts of creation that God's will is accomplished, but also in what has happened since. "The Everpresent Commander of forces has sworn, saying, 'Surely as I have intended, so it will be; and as I have purposed, so it will rise up.'" (Is. 14:24)

God declares the end from the beginning, and then He makes it happen. It is His distinction, by which He challenges all pretenders. "And who is like Me proclaiming and declaring it? and arranging it for Me? Since I set forth the eternal people and the things that are coming, and will come, let them tell it to them." (Is. 44:7)

Some people make promises; some people guarantee the outcome of certain events; but they do not have the power to insure that what they proclaim and promise will happen. There are many who enforce their will on others, but no one who can enforce his will upon God. "There are many plans in a man's heart; nevertheless the counsel of the Everpresent Lord will stand." (Prov. 19:21)

God is convinced that His thoughts will prevail. He is convinced that His power will prevail as well. "Declare, and bring them near; let them even take counsel together. Who has declared this from ancient time? Who has told it from that time? Did not I the Lord? And there is no other God besides Me, a just God and a savior. There is none beside Me. Look to Me and be saved, all the ends of the earth; for I am God, and there is no one else." (Is. 45:21-22)

Why does God entreat the entire earth to look to him and be saved? Be saved from what?

### Yom Heshbon

In the Scriptures, life is not presented as being easier for those who seek to be faithful to God. In fact, we could easily get the idea that life is more difficult for those who seek to be faithful. We can look at Abel or Abraham, Jacob, Joseph, or Moses. We can look at the prophets.

"They cry, and the Everpresent hears, and delivers them out of all their disress. The Everpresent is near to the broken hearted, and He saves those who are crushed in spirit. Many are the evils to the righteous; but the Everpresent delivers him out of them all." (Ps. 34:18-20)

That gives rise to some questions: 1) Why do the righteous have so many troubles and afflictions? Certainly God could prevent the troubles from happening, rather than saving the righteous after the troubles happen. 2) If God is near to the broken hearted, then why doesn't He prevent their hearts from being broken? 3) God "saves those of a crushed spirit," but why not just keep their spirits from being crushed?

We have looked at these questions, or their fraternal twins, when we earlier looked at God's declaration that, "I create evil." (Is. 45:7) But there is something more to consider. In its simplest form, there is the logical question: "Then why should I seek to serve God? Why is it better than not seeking to serve Him?"

God, apparently, is not very good at marketing, since so very few people want what He has to offer. Personally, I'm terrible at marketing, so I have no suggestions for God. But I can explain the simple incentive, both positive and negative, that God offers.

If you eat in a restaurant in Israel, you will receive, at the end of your meal, a bill. Much the same thing happens everywhere in the world. When you're finished eating, you have to pay for what you have ordered. In Hebrew, the bill, or account, is called *heshbon*.

God's simple incentive, both positive and negative, is that there will be a day for settling accounts, a *yom heshbon*. For every individual person, there will be a detailed, lifelong account of what is owed. The Scriptures make it clear that "God will bring every deed into judgment, with every secret thing, whether it is good, or whether it is evil." (Eccl. 12:14)

Some people think that reality is obliged to conform to their own ideas and desires. I used to think that way. About 50 years ago, having an interest in Law and a high opinion of myself, I decided that I was going to appeal the Last Judgment. I didn't know much about God's Law, and I really wasn't interested in taking the time to find out or reconsider the way I was living; but apparently I knew what the Judge would decide in my case. I was too foolish to recognize that my own opinion of how clever and righteous I was would be additional evidence against me.

God is patient, but He will do what He has said He will do. "God is not a man, that He should lie; nor the son of Adam, that He should repent. Has He said, and will He not do it? or has He spoken, and will He not fulfill it?" (Num. 23:19) God says, "Let there be..." and there is.

God has said that the day for settling accounts will come. All accounts. All debts will have to be paid, but there will be many who will be unable to pay for the decisions they have made. Contrary to what a lot of "smart" people think, God will not owe anyone anything.

"Behold, I have found only this: God has made humanity upright; but they have sought out many schemes [*hishvonot*]." (Eccl. 7:29) It's like this: God requires self-examination from everyone. Some people are so busy pursuing what they want to pursue that they do not stop for *heshbon hanefesh*, the accounting of the soul.

Not only do they not have the time or the inclination for a realistic accounting of their actions, they think they are all paid up. Others may agree with their self-assessment. In reality, however, they have only engaged in years of fraudulent accounting.

"Am I my brother's guardian?" We will all find out. We'll also all find out the criminal nature of not loving the clearly defined God of Israel with ALL that we are.

Perhaps we can make amends and change our ways. "Whatever your hand finds to do, do it with your strength; for there is no work, nor scheme, nor knowledge, nor wisdom, in Sheol, to which you are going." (Eccl. 9:10) That's good and necessary, but it won't pay for what we already owe.

The basic problem is that "what is crooked [*avat*] cannot be made straight; and that which is missing cannot be numbered." (Eccl. 1:15) *Avat*, the Hebrew word translated here as "crooked," is used to signify using deceitful scales (Am. 8:5), and perverting or subverting justice. (Job 8:3, cf. 34:11-15) Judging myself, and others, by my own standard is the core of the rebellion.

But God is able to change things and people from what they are into something else. He is able to bring down the high, and raise up the low. "And I will bring the blind by a way that they knew not; I will lead them by paths that they have not known. I will turn darkness to light before them, and make crooked things upright. These are the things I will do, and not forsake them." (Is. 42:16)

# EINSTEIN'S DICE

In classical physics, everything is determined by prior causes. It is therefore possible, if we know enough about those prior causes, to predict with certainty what their result, or effect, will be. In classical physics, a "law" is deterministic, describing something that will inevitably happen. It is an organizing principle that always applies.

Werner Heisenberg posited an Uncertainty Principle concerning subatomic particles: human beings cannot simultaneously know both the position and the velocity of any such particle at a particular point in time. Our observation of one affects the nature of the other. No matter how much we know about the past of such a particle, we can only know the probabilities of it having a certain position, state, or velocity in the present.

This means that instead of the universal applicability of strict cause and effect, there are areas where different results are possible. The resultant quantum uncertainty does not come from a lack of knowledge, but from the nature of the physical universe.

The story, apparently true, is told that Einstein, irritated by and opposed to this quantum uncertainty, said to Niels Bohr, "God doesn't play dice." In reply, Bohr said, "Einstein, don't tell God what to do."

Einstein considered it impossible for God, who knows everything, to not know the outcome of anything, whether that be the roll of a pair of dice or the exact state, position, and velocity of every particle at every point in time. This was a discussion of physics, not one of theology. In effect, all that Einstein meant was that he himself could not accept a built-in uncertainty, or randomness, in the universe; everything had to be determined by cause and effect. There could not be probabilities, because that would mean that there were different possibilities or options.

The gist of Bohr's response was that the nature of the

universe is not dependent upon the way that we think it should be. Nor is it dependent upon traditional understanding, expert opinion, or majority consensus. If God has designed the universe so that there are different possibilities and options, that is His prerogative.

From a scriptural point of view, the exchange between Einstein and Bohr, though amusing, is not at all about God. it is about the limits of human nature. Inasmuch as God is everywhere all the time, there is no physical distance between Him and any event. He is always observing everything everywhere at every point in time. His observation is an inseparable part of the nature of existence, all of it and every aspect of it.

Since He inhabits all of time, He has already observed what to us is still future. So, in a sense, God doesn't play dice, because He knows the end from the beginning. He is never in doubt about what will happen.

We, on the other hand, are outside almost every event that takes place. The universe exists independently of us, and we cannot observe any event at the time it happens. The problem is not primarily our limited knowledge, it is our limited nature. We exist in only one place at a particular time; we exist in only one time at a time.

God doesn't play dice, but He has put the dice into our hands. He gives us the possibility of making a variety of choices. We can choose one option, or we can reject it and choose another.

We therefore have to surf the waves of an oncoming, unknown future that is continually crashing down upon the shores of the present. We don't know what will be; but the choices we make have consequences. The choices we make are causes that will have their future effects.

### Volition and Accountability

"And if it is evil in your eyes to serve the Lord, choose for yourselves today whom you will serve; whether the gods which your fathers served that were on the other side of the river, or the gods of the Amorites in whose land you live. But I and my house will serve the Lord." (Josh. 24:15)

People can choose to serve the Lord, or they can choose to serve someone or something else. They can choose by tradition, or by what everyone around them chooses. Or they may simply choose to serve themselves.

There are influences and pressures. Some choices bring pleasure, and some bring pain. Whatever factors there are to consider, I am the one who makes my decisions. Others are responsible for the choices they make and how those choices affect other people, but I am accountable for my decisions.

We do not choose our genetic makeup or our circumstances, but before God, we are defined by what we do with what we have been given. "The righteous, and the wise, and their deeds, are in the hand of God; no man knows whether it is love or hatred; all is before them." (Eccl. 9:1)

By definition, God is the supreme, ultimate authority. He has delegated some of His authority to humanity. He has delegated to each individual the authority to make his or her own decisions. And He will hold each one accountable for how that authority is used or misused.

When Solomon became king of Israel, he confessed his inabilities to the King of kings. He humbled himself and made this request: "Therefore give to Your servant a listening heart to judge Your people, to discern between good and evil. For who is able to judge this weighty people of Yours?" (1K. 3:9)

Solomon was wise to humble himself and ask for a listening heart. In response, God gave him the wisdom he requested. Unfortunately, Solomon's heart didn't always follow the wisdom God gave him; sometimes it followed his own desires instead. He chose to do what he knew was wrong.

Abimelech, king of Gerar, took Sarah into his harem after Abraham had said that she was his sister. "But God came to Abimelech in a dream by night, and said to him, 'Know that you are a dead man because of the woman whom you have taken, because she is married to a husband.'" (Gen. 20:3)

Abimelech hadn't yet touched Sarah, but God considered him guilty unto death. Abimelech chose to obey God's warning. He had chosen to take her, and he chose to return her to her husband.

God does not prevent people from rejecting His will and purpose. Most people do, most of the time. They choose to do what God does not want them to do, and choose to not do what He wants them to do. To not care what God wants, to proclaim one's indepence, is to declare oneself to be the only judge who matters. That will not sound good when one stands before the Judge of all the earth.

Balaam is an interesting case study. Balak, king of Moab, tried to hire Balaam to curse Israel. Balaam wanted the money, but he first sought direction from God. "And God said to Balaam, 'You are not to go with them; you are not to curse the people; for they are blessed.'" (Num. 22:12) So Balaam refused Balak's offer.

Then Balak offered Balaam more honor and wealth. "And Balaam answered and said to the servants of Balak, 'If Balak would give me his house full of silver and gold, I would not go beyond the word of the Lord my God, to do less or more.'" (Num. 22:18) Balaam turned down the offer, but he told the men to stay, hoping that God would change His mind and let him go with them.

God told Balaam that he could go, but was enraged at the stubborn desire of Balaam's heart. So God sent an angel to stand, sword drawn, in Balaam's way. The angel of the Lord told Balaam, "Your way is perverse before me. ...And Balaam said to the angel of the Lord, 'I have sinned... now therefore, if it displeases you, I will go back again.'" (Num. 22:32)

There was a disconnect between Balaam's mind, which knew quite clearly what God wanted, and Balaam's heart, which kept pursuing the money. For a while, he continued his outward obedience, without changing his heart. When he prophesied, he pronounced blessings on Israel.

"Now when Balaam saw that it pleased the Lord to bless Israel, he did not go as at other times, to seek to use sorcery, but he set his face toward the wilderness. And Balaam lifted up his eyes, and said, '...How goodly are your tents, O Jacob, and your dwelling places, O Israel! ...Blessed is the one who blesses you, and cursed is the one who curses you.'

"And Balak's anger burned against Balaam, and he struck his hands together. And Balak said to Balaam, 'I called you to curse my enemies, and, behold, you have blessed them these three times.'" (Num. 24:1-9)

So Balaam is very interesting. He was obedient to the direct commands of the Lord, but his heart never surrendered to God. He continued to try to find a way to do the opposite of what he knew God wanted. He chose a pretence of obedience rather than the real thing.

He chose to ignore every warning that God gave him, and stubbornly persisted in seeking his own desires. In direct opposition to what he knew to be God's purpose, he counselled Balak on how to defeat Israel. (cf. Num. 31:1-16) Eventually it cost him his life.

Balaam was not the only one. "And the Everpresent Lord said, 'Since this people draws near to Me with their mouth, and with their lips they honor Me, but have removed their heart far from Me, and their fear of Me is a commandment taught by men; therefore, know that I will again do an amazing work with this people, amazing and causing wonder. Then the wisdom of their wise men will be destroyed, and the understanding of their prudent men will be hidden." (Is. 29:13-14)

Later in his life, Solomon used the wisdom that God had given him to think about life and its purpose, to think about death and its meaning. He saw what anyone can see: death comes to everyone, regardless of whether they have chosen good or evil. "I said in my heart, concerning the children of Adam, that God is testing them, that they might see that they are but beasts." (Eccl. 3:18)

Life is a test, an imposed time of problem-solving — sometimes problems for which we have not studied and are not prepared. God tested Abraham (e.g. Gen. 22:1), and He tested Israel. (e.g. Ex. 15:25, 16:4) It doesn't seem right. Life should be a joyous adventure, not a test. But whether we like it or not, we are the students, not the teachers. God designs the curriculum, prepares the tests, and judges the results. (e.g.

Eccl. 12:13-14)

"And you are to remember all the way which the Lord your God led you these forty years in the wilderness, to humble you, and to prove you, to know what was in your heart, whether you would keep His commandments or not. ...He led you through that great and terrible wilderness, where there were venomous serpents, and scorpions, and drought, where there was no water. He brought you water out of the rock of flint, and fed you in the wilderness with manna, which your fathers did not know, that He might humble you, and that He might test you, to do you good in the end." (Dt. 8:2, 15-16)

In terms of the purposes our fathers had for themselves, God's testing didn't make much sense. But it made perfect sense in terms of the purposes that God had for them.

Even with the wisdom which God had given him, Solomon couldn't quite figure it out. "I returned, and saw that the race under the sun is not to the swift, nor the battle to the strong, nor yet bread to the wise, nor yet riches to men of understanding, nor yet favor to men of skill; but time and circumstances happens to them all. For man also does not know his time; like the fish that are taken in an evil net, and like the birds that are caught in the trap; so are the children of Adam snared in an evil time, when it falls suddenly upon them." (Eccl. 9:11-12)

What kind of race or battle is this? Life is an obstacle course. The goal is to fight hard to be faithful despite the obstacles. But this life is not the final event. As Moses said, God's purpose in our lives is "that He might humble you, and that He might test you, to do you good in the end." In a sense, this life is a qualifying heat for the main event, the Age to Come.

# CHANGING THE SCRIPT

God created a world, and placed a tangible, living image of Himself in it. (Many novelists do something similar.) The living image was like Him in some ways — having emotions, language, thought, dominion... — and unlike Him in others — limited, changeable, dependent.... That living image, in vital relationship with God, was designed to rule over that world.

The entire universe was designed in such a way that humanity could, and should, know God. There are five major ways in which God makes Himself known to humanity.

1. The created world. (e.g. Ps. 19:2H) He has given us eyes to see and ears to hear. Whether or not our heart is willing depends upon us.

2. All humanity bears God's image and likeness. (e.g. Gen. 1:26-27) If we understood the purposes of our existence, we would better understand the One who gave us those purposes.

3. The whole range of His Word communicates a portrait of who He is, and directs us to the fullness of life that we need. (e.g. Dt. 8:3) He sends His living Word into the world to work in our lives. (e.g. Is. 55:10-11)

4. He established a multifaceted relationship with Israel so that everyone could know Him as Father, Shepherd, King, and much more. In these aspects of the relationship, He demonstrates His love, faithfulness, and holiness. "For thus says the high and lofty One who inhabits eternity, whose name is Holy; I dwell on the high and holy place, yet with him also who is of a contrite and humble spirit, to revive the spirit of the humble, and to revive the heart of the contrite ones." (Is. 57:15)

5. Messiah will be what Adam failed to be: a faithful Son, ruling over the earth in the image and likeness of God, ruling by His Spirit. (Ps. 2; Is. 11 & 9:5-6H)

But throughout human history, most people don't know God, and don't want to know Him. That's unfortunate, because God is the writer, director, and producer of the entire drama of human existence. With a cast of billions, it has everything: love, music, laughter, and joy, cruelty, anguish, and indifference. It takes place on an amazing set, surrounded by fiery stars and dark matter. And the whole drama is an audition for a future, even longer-running production.

Much of what God has written is a tragedy, climaxing in global catastrophe that brings down the high and mighty, and almost everybody else as well. And though very few people know it, God is not happy with the carefully scripted drama He has prepared. Even though the final result will bring Justice to the earth, God would prefer that more people survived the coming catastrophe.

People can change the script in different ways. They can make it worse. God may have written them in for good, but people are free to turn that to bad. A prime example of that was King Saul.

"And Samuel said to Saul, 'You have done foolishly; you have not kept the commandment of the Lord your God, which He commanded you. For now the Lord would have established your kingdom upon Israel forever. But now your kingdom will not stand. The Lord has sought for Himself a man in accordance with His own heart, and the Lord has commanded him to be ruler over His people, because you have not kept what the Lord commanded you.'" (1Sam. 13:13-14)

God would have established Saul's dynasty as kings forever over Israel. That was the plan. But Saul did not do what God commanded him to do. He could have done it, but he chose not to.

On the more positive side, however, God would like people to improvise and change the script for the better. It can be done. An actor brings life to a role in a script. A good actor brings out feeling and power that weren't visible in a simple reading. A good Director is always open to the possibility of improving the script.

We are able to make choices which have good consequences which were not initially visible. Here are some examples of people who did.

## Intercession

God told **Abraham** about the upcoming, total destruction of Sodom and Gomorrah. He had a reason for telling Abraham, and a purpose in having the episode recorded in the Scriptures. God wanted Abraham to intercede, and God wanted us to know that He responded to Abraham's intercession.

Abraham presented his plea on the basis of the righteous in the cities. "Far be it from You to do such a thing as this, to put to death so that as with the righteous, so with the wicked, so that the righteous should be as the wicked. Far be it from You! Will not the Judge of all the earth do right?" (Gen. 18:25)

Abraham was not being disrespectful. He was appealing to God on the basis of God's own revealed character. He was doing exactly what God wanted him to do, even though God had not explicitly expressed it to him. Abraham was responding in obedience to the basic commandment which God had given to humanity in the beginning: Be actively concerned about the well-being of your brother.

"And the Lord said, 'If I find in Sodom fifty righteous inside the city, then I will spare the whole place for their sakes.'" (Gen. 18:26) Abraham was pleading for the entire population, not just the righteous.

Abraham continued: "Maybe there will be five less than fifty... Maybe there will be forty... Maybe there will be thirty... Maybe there will be twenty... Maybe there will be ten..." (Gen.18:28-32)

The people of Sodom were wicked, and they deserved to be destroyed. They had earned it. But Abraham knew God. "'As I live,' says the Everpresent Lord, 'I have no pleasure in the death of the wicked...'" (Ezek. 33:11)

That was true when God said it to Ezekiel, and it was always true of God. Its truth comes from the nature of God: "'as I live,' says the Everpresent Lord." Abraham, seeking to live in the image and likeness of God, also took no pleasure in the death of the wicked.

Because of who God is and what He desires, Abraham interceded for Sodom. But there weren't enough righteous people within the city for it to be spared. "Yet it came to

323

pass, when God destroyed the cities of the plain, that God remembered Abraham, and sent Lot out of the midst of the overthrow, when He overthrew the cities in which Lot lived." (Gen. 19:29) Because of Abraham's intercession, Lot and his two daughters survived.

Moses was faced with a similar situation in the wilderness after the people had bowed down to the golden calf. "And the Lord said to **Moses**, 'I have seen this people, and, behold, it is a stiff-necked people. Now therefore let Me alone, that My anger may burn hot against them, and that I may consume them; and I will make of you a great nation.'

"Then Moses entreated the Lord his God, and said, 'Lord, why does Your anger burn hot against Your people, whom You have brought out of the land of Egypt with great power, and with a strong hand? Should the Egyptians therefore speak, and say? *He brought them out for evil, to slay them in the mountains, and to consume them from the face of the earth.*Turn from Your fierce anger, and relent of this evil against Your people. Remember Abraham, Isaac, and Israel, Your servants, to whom You swore by Your own self, and said to them, *I will multiply your seed as the stars of heaven, and all this land that I have spoken of I will give to your seed, and they will inherit it forever.*'

"And the Lord relented of the evil which He thought to do to His people." (Ex. 32:9-14)

God had determined to destroy Israel, but He told Moses about it. Moses was given the opportunity to do something to prevent the destruction. Because Moses interceded, the people of Israel survived. But not only that, by interceding, Moses chose who he himself would be.

"Deliver those who are being taken to death, and those who are stumbling to be killed. If you say, 'Surely, we did not know this;' doesn't He who weighs the hearts consider it? And He who keeps your soul, He knows. And He will give back to every man according to his deeds." (Prov. 24:11-12)

God weighs every heart. He told Belshazzar, king of Babylon, "You are weighed in the balances, and are found wanting." (Dan. 5:27) Belshazzar lacked what he should have had. The handwriting was on the wall.

### Improvisation

For centuries, God had patiently waited for all the tribes of the land of Canaan to turn away from their abominations. They never did. So when it came time for Israel to enter the land, Israel was commanded: "And when the Lord your God will deliver them before you; you are to strike them, and completely destroy them. You are not to make any covenant with them, nor show mercy to them." (Dt. 7:2)

That command applied to Jericho, the first city to be attacked, and all its inhabitants. Two men were first sent to the city to spy it out. In a city full of people living in and for darkness, they stayed at the house of a prostitute named **Rahab**. Surely she was one of the most unclean people in an unclean city.

Some people in the city saw the spies go into Rahab's house, and reported it to the king. The king sent and told Rahab to bring them out. At the risk of her own life, she hid the men on her roof, and then lied to the king, saying that the men had already left the city.

When those searching for the spies went out of the city to try to pursue them, Rahab went up to the men on her roof, and said to them, "I know that the Lord has given you the land, and that great fear of you has fallen upon us, and that all the inhabitants of the land faint because of you. ... Now therefore, please swear to me by the Lord, since I have shown you kindness, that you will also show kindness to my father's house, and give me a true sign; and that you will keep alive my father, and my mother, and my brothers, and my sisters, and all that they have, and save our lives from death." (Josh. 2:9,12-13)

They promised to do that. When the city was taken, everyone else was put to death. "But Joshua saved Rahab the harlot alive, and her father's household, and all that she had. And she lives in Israel even to this day, because she hid the messengers, whom Joshua sent to spy out Jericho." (Josh. 6:25)

God had decreed that all the inhabitants of Jericho be destroyed, but Rahab changed the script by risking her life to protect the spies. Ra<u>h</u>ab and all the people she had gathered into her house were spared. They chose to seek mercy from the God of Israel, and He honored their choice.

Many centuries later, God was engaged in bringing judgment upon Israel, the people He had brought into the land. For the sins of His people, He decreed death, destruction and exile. But He still offered to change the script for anyone who would change. And He had it written down for our instruction.

"When I say to the righteous, that he will surely live; if he trusts in his own righteousness, and commits iniquity, all his righteousness will not be remembered; but he will die for the iniquity that he has committed. And when I say to the wicked, 'You will surely die,' if he turns away from his sin, and does that which is lawful and right; If the wicked restores the pledge, gives back what he has robbed, follows the statutes of life without committing iniquity, he will surely live, he will not die." (Ezek. 33:13-16, cf. 18:21-24)

The offer is still available. The conditions still apply.

### The Gibeonites

In obedience to God's command, Israel began to destroy city after city. So all the kings of the land joined together to fight against Israel. (cf. Josh. 9:1-2) But the inhabitants of the city of Gibeon and three nearby towns schemed to save their lives.

"They acted with cunning, and went and pretended to be envoys, and took worn-out sacks upon their donkeys, and old, torn, mended wineskins; and worn-out, patched shoes upon their feet, and worn-out garments on themselves, and all the bread of their provision was dry and crumbly. And they went to Joshua to the camp at Gilgal, and said to him and to the men of Israel, 'We come from a far country; and now make a covenant with us." (Josh. 9:4-6)

The leaders of Israel did not "ask counsel at the mouth of the Lord. And Joshua made peace with them, and made a covenant with them to let them live; and the princes of the congregation swore to them." (Josh. 9:14-15) Soon enough, the leaders of Israel found out that they had let themselves be deceived. But they had already made a covenant and sworn an oath by the Lord; and they knew they needed to honor their commitment. (cf. Ps. 15:4)

God had commanded that no covenant was to be made with any of the inhabitants of the land, nor was any mercy to be shown to them. But the Gibeonites changed the script, and saved their own lives. The entire people were spared the destruction that God had decreed for them.

### Nineveh

After some divine persuasion, Jonah finally agreed to obey the command of the Lord: "Go to Nineveh, that great city, and proclaim to it the message that I speak to you." (Jon. 3:2) So Jonah went and proclaimed the message that God gave him: "Another forty days, and Nineveh will be overthrown." (Jon. 3:4) God meant exactly what He said.

"But the people of Nineveh believed in God, and proclaimed a fast, and put on sackcloth, from the greatest of them to the least of them. And word came to the king of Nineveh, and he arose from his throne, and he took off his robe, and covered himself with sackcloth, and sat in ashes. And he caused it to be proclaimed and published through Nineveh by the decree of the king and his nobles, saying: 'Neither man, beast, herd or flock should taste anything! They should not feed, nor drink water! And let man and beast be covered with sackcloth, and cry mightily to God; let them turn everyone from his evil way, and from the violence that is in their hands. Who can tell if God may yet turn and relent, and turn away from His fierce anger, so that we do not perish?" (Jon. 3:5-9)

What an extraordinary event. Sometimes particular individuals turn away from sin and back to God. Sometimes a family turns to the Lord. But in this case of the large city of Nineveh, the entire population repented and turned to God for mercy. All the people and the animals went without food and drink, and were covered in sackcloth. Simply amazing.

"And God saw their doings, that they turned from their evil way; and God relented of the evil which He had said that He would do to them; and He did not do it." (Jon. 3:10)

God had decreed destruction, but He was glad to change the script. He's always willing to change the script. He has said that, and He has put it in writing.

"If at any time I speak concerning a nation, and concerning a kingdom, that I will pluck it up, and that I will pull it down, and that I will destroy it; if that nation, against whom I have so pronounced, turns from its evil, I will relent of the evil that I intended to do to them.

"And, if at any time, I speak concerning a nation, and concerning a kingdom, to build it and to plant it; if it does evil in My sight, by not obeying My voice, then I will relent of the good, with which I said I would benefit them." (Jer. 18:7-10)

That's a promise for any nation on the earth. God had already given similar promises to Israel. As He told King Solomon at the dedication of the Temple: "If I shut up heaven so that there is no rain, or if I command the locusts to devour the land, or if I send pestilence among My people; if My people, who are called by My name, will humble themselves, and pray, and seek My face, and turn from their wicked ways; then I will hear from heaven, and will forgive their sin, and will heal their land." (2Chr. 7:13-14)

What causes a nation to turn from its wicked ways? That's hard to say, because it rarely happens. But it always begins with humility.

Sometimes one single person can make all the difference in the world. Yerushala'im had earned destruction by her sins, but God said to Ezekiel: "I sought from them a man who would build a wall and stand in the breach before Me on behalf of the land, so that I would not destroy it. But I found none. Therefore I have poured out on them My indignation; I have consumed them with the fire of My wrath. I have given back their own way upon their heads,' declares the Lord God." (Ezek. 22:30-31)

God was looking for someone who cared enough to stop the inevitable destruction. Inevitable? No, God was willing to not do it. He didn't want to do it, but there was no one willing to stand and intercede. People, and therefore nations, can choose to change. If they do, then their future will also change.

Look around. God has already decreed destruction upon all the nations of the earth for their arrogance, filth, and violence. It is a time like it was when He spoke to Zerubbabel: "I will shake the heavens and the earth. And I will overthrow the throne of kingdoms, and destroy the strength of the kingdoms of the nations; and I will overthrow the chariots, and those who ride in them; and the horses and their riders will come down, everyone by the sword of his brother." (Haggai 2:20-23)

God invites, encourages, and commands humility and repentance. Will it happen? Probably not.

He doesn't force anyone to believe Him. But, thousands of years before it happened, He said He would regather the people of Israel to the land of Israel, in the last days. The End of this age, will be as He said, from the Beginning, it would be.

Very few people see the need, the urgent need. And usually those who do see the need are looking for someone else to rise up and do something — someone important, some big person. The one who responds is the one who is important.

Some people will respond to the challenge to trust God and live in His image and likeness, to be their brother's guardian. Some people will plead with God for Israel and the nations. Maybe someone you know. Maybe even you. We were, after all, created as theomorphic beings.

CPSIA information can be obtained
at www.ICGtesting.com
Printed in the USA
BVHW091302260421
605879BV00014B/344